MEDIEVAL SICILY

A HISTORY OF SICILY

ANCIENT SICILY
By M. I. FINLEY

MEDIEVAL SICILY: 800–1713
MODERN SICILY: After 1713
By D. MACK SMITH

A
HISTORY OF SICILY

MEDIEVAL SICILY
800–1713

Denis Mack Smith

THE VIKING PRESS
NEW YORK

Copyright © D. Mack Smith 1968
All rights reserved

Published in 1968 by The Viking Press, Inc.
625 Madison Avenue, New York, N.Y. 10022

Library of Congress catalog card number: 68-22872

Printed in Great Britain

To
Catharine Mack Smith

The passage on page xiii from Lampedusa's *The Leopard* is quoted by permission of the publishers, William Collins Sons & Co. Ltd and the Harvill Press.

CONTENTS

Introduction   xiii

PART 1 Arab-Norman Sicily 800–1200
Chapter

1 The Arabs   3
2 The Norman Conquest   13
3 The *Regnum*   24
4 The Disintegration of Norman Sicily   36

PART 2 Hohenstaufen, Angevins and Aragonese
1200–1375

5 *Stupor Mundi*   51
6 The Sicilian Vespers, 1282   65
7 The New Feudalism   76

PART 3 Submission to Spain 1375–1525

8   The End of Independence   87
9   Alfonso and the Economy   94
10 A Province of the Castilian Empire   105

PART 4 Spanish Administration 1500–1650

11 Governors and Governed   115
12 Parliament   124
13 Foreign Policy, Piracy and Defence   133
14 Disorder and Brigandage   146
15 The Baronage   152
16 Church and State   161

PART 5 The Economy 1500–1650

17 Economic Policy and the Revenue   171
18 Changes in Agriculture   181
19 Industry and Urbanisation   188
20 Economic Difficulties after 1600   199

PART 6 The Disintegration of Spanish Sicily
1640–1713

21 The Palermo Revolt of 1647   211
22 The Rebellion of Messina, 1674–8   220
23 The Last Years of Spanish Administration   231

The Bibliography and Index will be found at p. 545, at the end of the second volume.

MAPS

Sicily in the Mediterranean   *page* 2

Contour map of Sicily   170

Sicily: the main towns and villages   *facing page* 240

ILLUSTRATIONS

Plate   *Facing page*

1   Christ crowning King Roger: mosaic, Palermo   32

2   Building the Ark: mosaic, Monreale   33
    Mosaic in the royal palace, Palermo

3   At the court of the Norman Kings: manuscript,   48
    Peter of Eboli

4   San Giovanni degli Eremiti, Palermo   49

5   Fountain and cloister: Benedictine abbey, Monreale   96

6   Palazzo La Zisa, Palermo: the main hall   97
    San Cataldo, Palermo: domes

7   Castello Ursino, Catania   112
    Palazzo Aiutamicristo, Palermo

8   Baronial stronghold: Caccamo   113

9   Town hall and the Pretoria fountain, Palermo   192

10 The Quattro Canti, Palermo   193

11 Portrait by Antonello da Messina, Cefalù   208
    The Triumph of Death: fresco, Palermo

12 The eruption of Mount Etna in 1669: fresco,   209
    Catania

INTRODUCTION

We are old, Chevalley, very old. For over twenty-five centuries we've been bearing the weight of superb and heterogeneous civilisations, all from outside, none made by ourselves, none that we could call our own. We're as white as you are, Chevalley, and as the Queen of England; and yet for two thousand five hundred years we've been a colony. I don't say that in complaint; it's our own fault. But even so we're worn out and exhausted. . . .

This violence of landscape, this cruelty of climate, this continual tension in everything, and even these monuments of the past, magnificent yet incomprehensible because not built by us and yet standing round us like lovely mute ghosts; all those rulers who landed by main force from every direction, who were at once obeyed, soon detested and always misunderstood. Their only expressions were works of art we couldn't understand and taxes which we understood only too well and which they spent elsewhere. All these things have formed our character, which is thus conditioned by events outside our control as well as by a terrifying insularity of mind.

Giuseppe Tomasi di Lampedusa, *The Leopard*
(trans. Archibald Colquhoun)

In these words, Prince Fabrizio in Lampedusa's novel tried to convey to an outsider something of the resigned disillusionment of a Sicilian when faced with yet another invasion of his country. He was speaking under the impact of Garibaldi's victories in 1860 which joined Sicily to a united Italian nation; but for him this was just one of many similar events in a long, sad history. As well as being ruled from Turin and Rome, Sicily had formerly been governed from Madrid, Vienna and Constantinople; she had been occupied at various periods by French, English and Germans; and, earlier still, she had been colonised by Greeks and then by Arabs and Norsemen. Several times she had been severed from Europe and joined to North Africa. But the legacy of these episodes was an abiding consciousness of defeat and the conviction that more wars and conquests would be likely to follow every change in the Mediterranean balance of power. Even in 1860 and afterwards there were many who thought that her union with Italy could not last.

This variegated and eventful history has been to a considerable extent conditioned by geography. Linked to the Levant and Africa as well as Europe, Sicily has sometimes seemed the very centre of the civilised world; yet for the same reason she has always been the envy of any powerful neighbour and a meeting-ground on which outside empires fought out their private quarrels. The Phoenicians came here to set up trading posts, the Vandals and Goths to plunder the wealth accumulated in antiquity. Popes and Emperors came in search of tribute and the wheat produced by this granary of ancient Rome. Here was a battlefield where Habsburgs fought Valois and Bourbons, where Aragon had fought against Anjou, Hohenstaufen against Hauteville and Rome against Carthage.

So long as the main route between east and west passed through the straits of Messina, there was a special economic and strategic value in possessing Sicily. The island was an obvious base from which to attack the Italian mainland, just as it was to be an obvious base for the British fleet in their fight against Napoleon, and for Mussolini in his attempt to cut the Mediterranean in two. Always it was a refuge for pirates and smugglers who needed a secure post on land near this most important of all trade routes. As the shortest distance between Sicily and Africa was less than a hundred miles, it was also a springboard for successive invasions of Tunis and Tripoli. In no great European conflict could Sicily stay neutral, for the same reason that she could never escape the influence of any intellectual and artistic fashions anywhere in the Mediterranean.

One result was to create an exotic fusion or confusion of cultures, and this has given Sicilian history some of its particular fascination. Many successive peoples were to leave traces of themselves in the local architecture, in methods of agriculture, popular customs and speech, and even in the landscape. Nevertheless, as if in payment for these gifts, a once rich country was economically impoverished. The Sicilian countryside used to be famous for its fertility, while Syracuse and Palermo were once among the largest and richest cities in the world; but foreign invaders often came as predators on these riches, as colonialists rather than colonisers; and the sheer destruction brought by one conquest after another not only makes their history difficult to reconstruct, but was something which in the long run the economy of the island could not stand.

These are some of the themes which run through Sicilian history. On the other hand we have a succession of invading peoples imposing themselves on this society, layer upon layer; on the other hand there is the underlying society itself, the subject population. Who were the Sicilians, and how did they react to their successive rulers? Since each regime left far more memorials of itself than of those it ruled, the actions and views of ordinary native citizens are often hard to know. E. A. Freeman, who had still not completed the Greek period in his *History of Sicily* when he died in 1892, stressed that migration and conquest resulted in an almost continuous change in the population, and hence anything like a Sicilian nation never had much chance of existence. Indeed the resident population has always been divided against itself, and it could be argued that this fact has done as much damage as any act of foreign oppression. Sicilian Arabs fought against each other. They also fought against their Lombard fellow citizens in the twelfth century, just as the Catalan and Latin factions fought each other in the fourteenth, and Palermo squabbled incessantly with Messina; and again and again this resulted in one party invoking some outside champion who ended as the *tertius gaudens*.

The ordinary people who made up the population of Sicily may have been always divided, always changing, and at any time difficult to identify and study, but they are as interesting and important as the foreign conquerors who provided most of the drama in the foreground of Sicilian history. The more we learn about them, the more we can explain certain enigmas and apparent gaps in that history. The interior of the island has seldom been controlled by any government, but was almost continuously a law to itself. Only when it exploded to impose this law on the cities of the coast did it come within the purview of ordinary official documentation. The Sicilian Vespers in 1282 is one of dozens of popular revolts which show that, even in the cities, many powerful forces existed of which central governments had little understanding; and the long history of brigandage and the mafia tells the same tale.

Whether one accepts or denies the existence of a Sicilian nation is a matter of words. What is hard to deny is the pervasive presence of what Lampedusa calls "a terrifying insularity of mind". No doubt the origins of such an attitude must be sought in the reaction of a much-conquered and misruled people to one government after another. Its effects, however, are more difficult to ascertain. It could be heroic and even constructive in its manifestations; or it could be thoroughly negative and stultifying. Much of the worst as well as the best in Sicilian history has come from this proud insularity, and the material impoverishment of modern Sicily is not unconnected with it. Since 1860 it has diminished, as roads and railways brought the island closer and closer to Italy and the rest of Europe. The grant of regional autonomy after 1946 has paradoxically accelerated this process, simply because it was less easy thereafter to identify any obvious external scapegoat for economic backwardness. Forced back on their own resources, though with considerable help from the rest of Italy, Sicilians in the twenty years after 1946 were to do more to improve their society than at any time since the Greek tyrants. At last there seemed to be a possibility that long centuries of existence as a dependent protectorate were coming to an end.

PART 1

Arab-Norman Sicily 800–1200

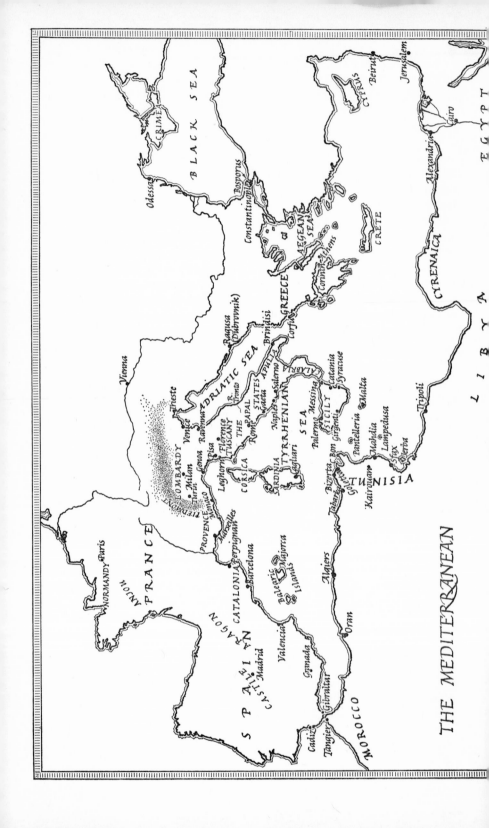

THE MEDITERRANEAN

Chapter 1

THE ARABS

When the Roman Empire disintegrated under the impact of the barbarian invasions, Sicily experienced a century of turbulence, but then finished up securely in the hands of Justinian and the Eastern Emperors at Constantinople. Syracuse, after Ravenna had fallen to the Lombards, became the chief outpost of Byzantium in the west. Perhaps Latin went on being spoken here and there in the island, but for three centuries after 535 Greek remained the official language of government, and the Church adopted Greek rites and an allegiance to the Patriarch of Constantinople.

Byzantium was eventually displaced only when faction fights in the imperial capital and wars in Persia and the Balkans forced her to withdraw much of her army and navy from the central Mediterranean. Her influence was then supplanted by that of Islam. With their fast-moving cavalry the Arabs quickly overran the Greek garrisons and Berber tribesmen of North Africa. By 643, ten years after Muhammad's death, they had reached Tripoli; by 652 an Arab expeditionary force from Syria had landed briefly in Sicily. Before the end of the century they had captured Carthage and were beginning to build shipyards and harbour facilities in Tunisia from which further attacks on Europe could be launched.

A full-scale Moslem invasion of Sicily did not take place until 827, but when it came it posed a frightening challenge to Christian Europe. Control of sea power in the Mediterranean was temporarily lost. Arab raiders were able to reach Rome itself and force the Vicar of Christ to make terms. Tunis was only a day's journey from Sicily, and any strong North African power, following the example of the Vandals and Carthaginians earlier, would be tempted to attack this rich island whenever Christian disunity gave them a chance. They were helped in 827 by a disgruntled general in the Sicilian army who led a mutiny and asked for help from the Aghlabids of Kairouan.

As well as Arabs, the invaders included Berbers from Tunisia, Spanish Moslems, perhaps also Sudanese Negroes. Their initial

3

aim was to capture food and coin, to take slaves and pillage churches. Landing at Mazara, they crossed the island to besiege the island capital, Syracuse: after a long siege, this town was saved, perhaps by malaria in the surrounding swamps; the invaders then fell back on their bridgehead in the south-west. Yet the profits had been considerable. Another force arrived in 830, and the next year Palermo fell to them, the second city in the island. In 835 Pantelleria was taken. The Eastern Empire, having to fight on many fronts, could send little help, while the Western Emperor and the Pope were both more concerned with fighting other Christians than supporting Greek Christianity against Islam. Some Italian Christians even encouraged the invaders, and Christian Neapolitans in 843 helped these Moslems to besiege Messina in return for trading concessions. Once they were in charge of Messina, the Saracen forces could control the straits and prevent Byzantine ships entering the western Mediterranean.

Half the island was thus overrun in twenty years. Enna, the towering hill town dominating the interior, fell in 859 when a Christian traitor led the attackers through a drain into the fortress. Soon afterwards they also took Malta. The Saracens were nearer to their home base than were the Byzantines; they had more experience of this kind of warfare; they were more unified and single-minded. We hear of them using flame-throwing vessels, for possibly they had learnt the secret of 'Greek fire' and could now use the naphtha and sulphur deposits of Sicily. They had the great advantage of possessing land-hungry people who wanted territory to settle. Their tactics were also effective. Any cities which surrendered were allowed to continue the practice of their religion; but, wherever resistance was encountered, the male inhabitants were usually killed, and the women and the more beautiful boys sent to the Khalif or sold into slavery.

In 878 Syracuse was destroyed after fifteen hundred years as the chief town of Sicily. An account by the monk Theodosius described how big engines and subterranean mines breached the walls. Most of the prisoners were killed, though the archbishop was spared once he had shown where the cathedral treasure was hidden; and an enormous booty was taken, perhaps a bigger haul than in any other town captured in all the triumphs

4

of Islam. It was said that no living thing remained in a city which had once rivalled Athens and Alexandria and which far surpassed contemporary Rome in wealth and beauty.

By the end of the ninth century the Byzantines had almost entirely withdrawn from Sicily. Local pockets of Christian opposition still remained but could not be effectively supported from so far away. In 902 the Aghlabid Emir captured the last major fortified outpost at Taormina; he slaughtered the inhabitants and set fire to the town. Other places understandably preferred surrender, and at Rometta in 965 was extinguished the last flicker of organised resistance.

The division of land and spoils led to quarrels among the victors, and already by the 880s there was talk of Arabs fighting against Berbers. It is probable that the latter settled predominantly in the south-west near Agrigentum, now to be called Girgenti, and soon there was some kind of rivalry between this area and Palermo. Probably these Berbers were mostly farmers who had come in search of land, whereas the Arabs were primarily soldiers who preferred to let the Christians stay to work on their behalf. These differences were increased when a further wave of newcomers arrived from Africa to share the fabled riches of Sicily, only to find the plunder already exhausted. An invading African army thus did tremendous damage in the south-west between 938 and 940.

After centuries of Byzantine autocracy and taxation, the existing inhabitants of Sicily seem to have taken not too unkindly to a change. Obviously the conquest must have brought destruction and disorder; possibly some areas became entirely deserted, though the disappearance of Selinunte and other Greek settlements had taken place earlier during the invasion of the Vandals, if not even earlier. Once established, however, the new masters of the country were fairly easy-going. Some towns were left virtually independent with not even a garrison. The new regime may well have seemed less oppressive than were the Christian Lombards or Franks on the mainland, and less religiously intolerant than the iconoclastic Church at Constantinople. Local institutions were often retained, and though many churches became mosques, in general Christians could live by their own laws, with the same legal guarantee of person and property as Moslems.

5

Naturally a subject population suffered some penalties. How far the regulations were enforced is difficult to say, but Christians—and Jews, of whom there were by now a considerable number—were required to wear distinguishing marks on their houses and clothes; they paid more taxes; they could repair churches and synagogues but not build new ones. Though they could practise their religion, they could not ring church bells or carry the cross in procession, nor could the Bible be read within earshot of Moslems. They were forbidden to drink wine in public, and were expected to rise when Moslems entered the room and make way for them in the public road. It was forbidden for Christians to carry arms, or ride horseback, or to saddle their mules. They were not allowed to build houses as large as Moslem houses. Christian women were not to stay in the baths when Moslem women were there.

All this was harsh, but it hardly amounted to religious persecution. Conversion to Islam was not particularly encouraged, especially as the non-converted paid more tax; nor did the local Christian clergy put themselves at the head of a religious resistance movement. Although many Christian monks emigrated to Calabria, this was likely to have been as much because of famine and insecurity caused by internal wars, and in general passably tolerant relations existed between the two religions. If the vast majority of Christians eventually gave up practising their faith, it was due to a natural process of change during two centuries of Moslem colonisation.

Above all an enlightened economic policy helped to reconcile the subject population. Taxation seems to have been lower than under Byzantium, perhaps in part because it was allocated and collected more efficiently. The new rulers removed the tax on draught animals which had hindered agriculture, and instead used a land tax which made it disadvantageous to leave fields unproductive. Islam also had a more sympathetic attitude than Christianity to slaves, and preferred labourers with a positive interest in increased production. Commerce flourished, because Sicily once again had the benefit of a central position in an immense economic commonwealth which stretched from Spain to Syria. So united was North Africa that a chain of watchtowers could flash news from Alexandria to Ceuta in a single day; this huge area was now at the zenith of its prosperity, for

6

the coastal rulers had temporarily succeeded in controlling the camel-riding nomads from the interior, and inland oases were becoming rich with traffic across the desert. Caravan routes led to abundant gold in Senegal and in the Sudan and Niger territories, with the result that the Tunisian currency became the soundest in the Mediterranean; and so free was commerce that drafts on eastern bankers payable in the west were negotiable in the southern Sahara. Sicily, as a colony of North Africa, shared marginally in this affluence at a time when seaborne trade in western Europe was slackening and when Sardinia and Corsica continued to decline economically. She also shared in the civilisation of Kairouan, a great centre of religion and scholarship, of beautiful enamelled pottery, fine textiles and carpets.

Visitors to Palermo, the Arab capital, were impressed to find a population which included Greeks, Lombards, Jews, Slavs, Berbers, Persians, Tartars and Negroes. Theodosius already in the ninth century found it a magnificent town, and he had known Greek Syracuse. Arabs travelled thither from Spain, Syria and Egypt. Persian traders in the tenth century knew Sicily as rich in cereals, cattle and slaves. Ibn Hauqal, a Baghdad merchant, admired the market gardens round Palermo and the fertile arable land throughout the island. There were hundreds of mosques in Palermo, more than he had seen in any town except Cordoba. He criticised the dirtiness of the people and their excessive onion-eating as a practice which dulled the senses and damaged the brain; and yet this Palermo was indisputably becoming one of the great cities of the world, surpassed by Baghdad but by few other towns. Some people have deduced from his account a population of over 300,000, but the more likely figure of 100,000 would still have made it larger than any Christian town except Constantinople.

From Ibn Hauqal and later Moslem writers we learn of an excellent irrigation system and abundant springs and rivers. Some of these rivers were still navigable, many of which later were to disappear altogether because of the destructive agricultural methods of subsequent generations. The Arabs had learnt in the desert the vital importance of irrigation, even if it were only a mule or stream turning a water wheel; they brought certain hydraulic techniques with them from Persia; they must

7

have profited from observing the relics of Roman engineering work in North Africa and the siphon system of irrigation which the Romans had also used in Sicily. Tunisia under their rule became rich agricultural land. In Sicily they planted lemons and bitter oranges. They brought the knowledge of how to cultivate sugar cane and crush it with mills. So far as we know, they introduced the first cotton seeds, the first mulberries and silkworms, the date palm, the sumac tree for tanning and dyeing, papyrus, pistachio nuts and melons, all of which together made a fundamental change in the economy. Probably it was due to them that rice was first cultivated here, and they seem to have brought with them a new variety of wheat.

No doubt there was a fair amount of poetic exaggeration in Arab descriptions of Sicily as a garden paradise: the word 'springs' might sometimes mean 'cisterns' and refer just to the storage tank for a single house. Nevertheless, a degree of real economic advance is incontestable. Reservoirs and water towers from this period continued to exist for many centuries and can still be identified today. Most sources of water obtained Arabic names and were to keep them permanently; so did weights and measurements acquire a terminology which is still heard in the twentieth century—they included measurements for waterflow as well as for ordinary length and bulk. Apart from agriculture, there was a vigorous fishing industry, and perhaps an altogether new and elaborate technique of tunny fishing was now adopted. Ibn Hauqal speaks, surprisingly, of an iron mine. Silver, lead, mercury, sulphur and naphtha, vitriol, antimony and alum were produced. Sicilian rock salt and sea salt became well known abroad, and salammoniac found near Mount Etna was exported to Spain. The art of silk manufacture and weaving was soon to play a substantial part in the economy.

Apart from the disruption and devastation caused by the conquest, there are other conjectural qualifications to be made on the negative side of the balance sheet. The Arabs, accustomed to nomadism, probably encouraged the goats which hindered growth of new trees in the forests. During their conquest and in the process of clearing land for settlement they evidently set fire to crops and woodland. Cargoes of timber were carried overseas because Africa lacked supplies of hardwood, and the ship-building necessary to keep maritime domination of the Mediterranean probably led to cutting down the more accessible areas of the Sicilian forests. Olive growing was largely abandoned at some time between 400 and 900, possibly owing to deliberate vandalism by invading armies; and North Africa took over production of the oil which had once been such a source of wealth.

Michele Amari, the great historian of the Moslems in Sicily, thought that they distributed the land into smallholdings, but probably it would be oversimplification to think that the *latifundia* disappeared and then returned in the twelfth century. A territorial nobility existed and was presumably endowed with large estates; yet Moslem succession law did encourage the subdivision of properties among younger sons. A large number of Arabic names have survived for small places and farms, and often this must have signified a fragmentation of property. The existence of intensive cultivation near the cities, replacing the extensive type of cereal cultivation peculiar to the *latifundia*, also indicated the spread of smallholdings and either secure leaseholds, or actual peasant proprietorship. The diffusion of habitations throughout the countryside must have helped agriculture, and so must the fact that villages were far more numerous now than later in the Middle Ages.

Moslem Sicily was at first a dependency of the Aghlabids, but early in the tenth century a civil war, complicated by the advance of the heretic Shiites, overturned this Tunisian dynasty. In 909 the Fatimid Mahdi became Khalif of Kairouan. To some extent these newcomers represented the reaction of various Berber tribes against Arabisation. As Shiites, they were also a protest against orthodox Islam. Led by their famous General Gawhar, apparently a man of Christian Sicilian origin, the Fatimids moved eastwards and in 969 transferred their capital to Egypt. This left Sicily much more independent. Several revolts took place against the heretic Khalif, and orthodox Sicilian Moslems even joined the Christians in attacking Tripoli. By the 960s the Kalbid family had established themselves as the effective rulers of the island, binding the military nobility by ties of interest and patronage; and from their number came the man who was sometimes referred to as the 'Sultan' of Palermo.

The move of the Khalif to Cairo was followed by the gradual

break-up of the flourishing North African civilisation to which
Sicily belonged. Early in the eleventh century, starving refugees
were fleeing from Africa to Sicily. The Fatimids revenged themselves on the Zirids and other dissident local governors by in-
citing Bedouin tribes to leave upper Egypt and devastate
Cyrenaica and Tripoli. Other nomadic tribes appeared farther
along the Mediterranean coast, having been driven from their
desert homes by political, economic or climatic conditions; and
these newcomers had little respect for the highly evolved
civilisation which they found. By the 1050s the Beni Hilâl and
Beni Solaim were destroying towns and plantations in the
prosperous area between Kairouan and Cape Bon. Sometimes
they were joined by native Berber tribesmen who looked on
farming and city communities as their enemy. Effective
government disappeared, and much of the ancient irrigation
system was now destroyed; moreover the main caravan routes
were cut, so that no longer did gold cross the Sahara to stimulate Mediterranean trade. When the holy city of Kairouan
itself was assaulted, the Zirid ruler moved his capital to the
fortress town of Mahdia. Moslem Sicily was thus isolated, and
Christian Europe at last had a chance to counter-attack.

An early sign of this was in the 1030s when the Kalbid Emir,
confronted with rebellion by rival Saracen families, and open
warfare with the Zirids, made a treaty with Byzantium. Some
local Moslem support was therefore forthcoming when a
Byzantine general, George Maniaces, landed with a large force
near Messina. As well as Russian soldiers of the Varangian
guard, several hundred Normans took part as mercenaries in
this expedition; and among them was Harald Hardrada, hero
of Scandinavian sagas, the same man who later invaded
England. No doubt these Normans observed the richness of the
country and propagated among their friends the idea of further
piratical raids. Maniaces occupied much of eastern Sicily for
several years and did a good deal of damage. He also tried to
restore the fortifications of Syracuse as a bridgehead to Constantinople. But this was the last serious attempt by Byzantium
to recover Sicily, and court intrigues at Constantinople soon
forced Maniaces's recall. The Mediterranean balance of power
had changed to the disadvantage of both Constantinople and
Cairo, and the really aggressive naval forces were now those of

Pisa and Genoa. It was these forces of western Christianity which drove the Moslem pirates from Sardinia and Corsica, and which then took the attack to the shores of Sicily and Africa. Sicily was moving into a new phase of the contest between Islam and Christianity, a contest which was cut across by a secondary conflict between Byzantine Hellenism and Latin Catholicism. When Roger the Norman, taking advantage of this new balance of forces, landed near Messina in 1060, the days of Moslem Sicily were numbered.

The contribution of the Saracens to Sicilian history is difficult to assess. Their occupation lasted over two centuries, and still for a third century and more they continued to occupy high positions at Palermo under Christian rulers. They brought with them their religion and laws, their literature, arts and sciences; and so doing they made Sicily part of a splendid African civilisation at the same time as a meeting point between Arabic, east European and Latin cultures. Like the Greeks before them, they came to settle and not just to rule and exploit. From North Africa, Spain and the Levant they arrived in great numbers, probably in greater numbers than any other conquerors of Sicily before or since. All early population estimates are based on flimsy evidence, but some estimates went so far as to speak of half a million Moslem settlers. They settled more densely in the western and south-eastern provinces, but elsewhere too there must have been a considerable immigration as well as a very substantial conversion of Sicilians to Islam. Their repopulation of the Sicilian countryside was an important fact.

Few tangible remains survive today of this Moslem occupation, though some are still uncovered from time to time. Many Saracen buildings were destroyed during the civil wars or as a result of the Norman conquest, and so were public and private archives; writing materials, just like tufa building stone, perished easily. A little poetry was preserved in Spain and Damascus, but it is hard to discern any single individual of note in Sicilian-Arab culture before the arrival of the Normans. African chroniclers sometimes wrote about Sicily before 1060, and Amari was able in part to reconstruct the period from later sources, but the picture still remains vague. The Moslem legal system left few relics, since subject communities were allowed to keep their own laws. The Aghlabids had been piously orthodox and unfriendly towards cultural innovation, while the Kalbid Emirs lacked the power as well as the organising ability and enlightened interest necessary for productive patronage. Furthermore the Christian chroniclers were ignorant and prejudiced about this period and understated or omitted to note its achievements. Hence the known memorials of the Arabs in Sicily are mainly relics of the later Norman-Arab civilisation; the Normans depended heavily upon Arab craftsmanship and governmental traditions, and this acknowledgement of the past is convincing proof of its quality.

As a language of government, Arabic proved very durable and lasted for over a century after the Norman conquest. There is little evidence to show what particular dialects were spoken, but many linguistic traces can still be observed. In the topography of Sicily, Gibel and Calta are familiar Arabic formations. Among many changes of place name, Enna became Kasryanni and so Castrogiovanni. Lilybaeum was changed to Marsala, the harbour of Allah or of Ali. Still today, after nine centuries, some hundreds of Arabic words and expressions are in currency, and only the arrival after 1060 of another invader speaking a Latin tongue can have prevented Sicily being left with a language close to those of Malta and North Africa. It was the Norman invasion which took Sicilians back permanently into the orbit of Europe.

Chapter 2

THE NORMAN CONQUEST

Early in the eleventh century there were several groups of adventurers from French Normandy earning a profitable living as professional soldiers in southern Italy. Some of them were straightforward mercenaries; others preferred the life of robber chiefs who plundered trade, stole cattle, and inflicted appalling devastation to spread the terror of their name. They hired themselves out as fighters, changing sides at will, or even fighting for both sides at once. Byzantium employed some of them for the expedition of Maniaces in Sicily; sometimes, with papal encouragement, they attacked the Greek Christians of southern Italy; and sometimes they found it more profitable to raid the Papal States.

Among these warriors were half a dozen sons of a certain Tancred de Hauteville, one of whom was Robert Guiscard, fair haired and "taller than the tallest", enormously ambitious and the most dedicated fighter of them all. Guiscard with his youngest brother Roger staked out a territory in Calabria and Apulia. Occasionally these two brothers fought against each other, but usually they were in league; and as they had a real genius for both fighting and administration, by ruthless pillaging they accumulated the fortunes on which a famous dynasty was to be built.

Guiscard was strong enough to capture Pope Leo IX in 1053, and hold him prisoner for nine months. Subsequently this brigand leader offered to restore papal authority at Rome against a factious citizenry. In 1059, another Pope, Nicholas II, authorised these warlike if not very obviously Christian freebooters to govern as much of southern Italy as they could conquer; and Guiscard in return agreed not to recognise the religious authority of Constantinople. The papacy had developed a specious claim to feudal lordship over Sicily, basing this on the multiple fiction that first Constantine and later the Carolingian Kings had owned Sicily and later 'given' it to the Pope. The Normans accepted feudal investiture for Apulia, but when they crossed the straits into Sicily they preferred to do so as conquerors in their own right.

This was a weak moment for the Sicilian Arabs, because different families were trying to establish independent Emirates at Mazara, Girgenti and Syracuse, and little help could now be expected from North Africa. Just as some Christians had invited the Arab invasion of 827, so Ibn at-Tumnah and other Moslems at Syracuse and Catania actively assisted the Christian counter-attack in 1060–1. By agreement with Guiscard, the conquest of Sicily fell mainly to Roger de Hauteville. After defeating the Greeks of Calabria, he first crossed the straits with only some sixty knights, perhaps intending just to spy out the land and practise the technique of transporting horses by sea. Once he had tested Arab resistance, another larger expedition captured Messina. Making occasional forays, setting up a few small garrisons, by 1064 Roger became master of the northeast, and he brought back much booty to divide with his elder brother. Probably he had by now about a thousand cavalry. Two years later their valuable experience of combined operations was going to be used in the Norman conquest of England.

The papacy did not provide Roger with money or men to carry out this first and most successful crusade against Islam; nor did he receive much help from Genoa or Pisa, the two Italian cities which afterwards benefited so much from his conquest; but what the Normans lacked in numbers and outside support they made up in courage, skill, sometimes in discipline, and always in ambition for profit and power. They were helped by the crumbling of the Fatimid Empire, and also by the Seljuk Turks who prevented Byzantium trying to recover its position in Italy. In north-eastern Sicily there was a surviving Christian community which delivered to them the inland hill city of Troina. Roger made Troina his capital and set up a bishopric there, but when the Norman soldiers reverted to their usual buccaneering habits, the same Christians joined the Arabs and for some months blockaded Roger's garrison in the citadel. Evidently they found the Saracen yoke less oppressive, and this may have taught him to treat with more skill and sympathy those who helped him or surrendered without a fight.

During the 1060s the Normans built up their fleet, because it was clear that further advance depended on command of the sea. In 1071 they arrived in front of Palermo. Guiscard, who was in charge of this expedition, was by now able to afford mercenaries and siege engines; after blockading the Arab capital for five months by sea and land, he accepted a surrender by which the inhabitants acknowledged his rule and were allowed their own religion and some autonomy. In other places his soldiers were more ruthless, killing prisoners and selling women and children into slavery: the expectation of acquiring slaves was one of the inducements by which the Normans persuaded other freebooting adventurers to join their army.

After taking Palermo, they began to develop an administration. Guiscard, as Duke of Apulia, received Palermo as his share, but had to return to defend his possessions on the mainland and so left Roger, as Count of Sicily and Calabria, to complete the conquest and set up a government. Roger saw the advantage of being able to offer generous terms so as to be able to employ Moslem civil servants and accountants who understood the existing administrative machinery. There was no massive invading population, so existing farmers had to be courted: many Arabs were therefore allowed to keep their goods and land, sometimes even their castles. Equally important, Moslem soldiers, without abjuring their faith, were from the very beginning an important nucleus of his army and were even used against Norman and other Christian enemies. Roger in 1075 made a treaty of friendship with the Zirid ruler of Tunis, and sent Sicilian grain to Mahdia.

The last stage of the conquest was slow and destructive. Roger had frequently to return to Calabria to support his brother and raise more troops. Other Normans sometimes plundered his estates while he was away fighting, and even his own son rebelled—with typically dramatic severity Roger blinded the other rebels and sent his son away unharmed but disgraced. The help received from Greek Christians in the north-east was, so it seems, not repeated elsewhere, and there is little mention of Christians in other parts of Sicily. Roger did not have the forces for a major pitched battle. One by one the castles in each area were captured, but fortune changed frequently, and perhaps there were more military setbacks than the official chronicler, Fra Malaterra, cared to record. Some villages were demolished, and there was deliberate destruction of cattle and crops. One casual reference in a document about an episcopal endowment refers to a wholesale depopulation:

"there is an enormous ruin of castles, villages and Saracen palaces . . . a vast damage that we now have to repair". This and other details are known mainly from Norman writers for whom Sicily was an outlying province and whose interest stretched no further than Count Roger and his immediate court: the conquest did not produce on either side an epic myth in literature as did the Spanish conquest of the Moors. The bare outline of events tells us that in 1088 Castrogiovanni surrendered, the one key strategic point of the interior, and in 1091 Noto, the last major stronghold of Moslem Sicily, fell.

The arrival of the Normans changed the island fundamentally. Henceforward it was to be mainly Roman in religion, basically Latin in language group, and west European in culture. But the change happened gradually, because the invaders were not strong enough to impose their own way of life, even if they had had much of an organised way of life to impose. For a time, indeed, the influence of Greek Christianity even increased.

It has been much debated how far the old Graeco-Latin elements in society had survived under the Arabs. Whatever may be said about Sicily before the Byzantine conquest in 535, by 800 the towns and the educated classes must have been Greek in religion, and some relics of this were still quite clear in 1060. The Norman chroniclers considered all non-Moslems in the population as Greek, and the title of Latin was reserved for the new ruling class of Normans, French and Lombards. A number of impoverished Greek monasteries still existed in the north-east and at least one in the west, while at Palermo there was a last surviving bishop, Nicodemus, whose cathedral had been turned into a mosque but who still officiated in a lonely suburban church. Of Latin Christianity, however, there was little if any sign.

The Normans had an impact on this society altogether disproportionate to their number. Theirs was not to be a settlement *en masse* like that of the Arabs, but their influence came from a quite unusual adaptability and political skill. Recognising that Sicilians possessed a superior culture and administrative system, they adopted both, and added an efficiency and sense of direction hitherto lacking. The Arab division of land was in part preserved, and business relating to land tenure and finance continued to be transacted by the pre-existent office of the *dîwân* (which was latinised into the *dohana* or *douane*). All through the Norman period, coins went on being struck with Cufic inscriptions, some of them dated by the hegira and using the same style as the Khalifs, including the formula that "Muhammad is the Apostle of God". The Saracen title of Emir was assumed by Palermo's first Norman governor and thereafter by the chief minister of the crown.

Although the conquest was violent and often cruel, it was quickly followed by conciliation. There was surprisingly little friction between the Normans and their new subjects, and Sicily was far more submissive than the mainland provinces. Arabs and Jews had to pay a special tax, and yet Norman charters, following Arab precedent, ensured that "Latins, Greeks, Jews and Saracens shall be judged each according to their own law" and by their own judges. Although six other members of the Hauteville family joined the First Crusade, Roger pointedly did not accompany them, and one English observer who came to visit him with St. Anselm reported Roger's unwillingness to have his troops converted to Christianity. The Moslems had to accept an inferior status; but, at a time when Europe was becoming increasingly intolerant, they were allowed freedom of religion; their culture, like that of the Greeks, continued to receive official encouragement, and Greek and Arabic languages went on being used officially alongside the Norman-French and Latin of the court. Many Moslems must have emigrated, for all round the Mediterranean there can be found family names which show a derivation at some time or other from Sicily. Others must have fled to the hill country of the interior to escape the brutalities of the conquest; and yet great numbers stayed and proved industrious, orderly and obedient. The army, navy and civil service all gained enormously from their co-operation.

It is this mixture of different traditions, Arabic and north-European, Roman and Greek, which makes the Norman period so colourful. By skilfully using these traditions, Count Roger turned himself from a poor landless adventurer into one of the most successful rulers in the world, so that Sicily for one golden century was as prosperous and powerful as it had been under the ancient Greeks. Roger came from northern Europe where feudal relationships were being developed as a social bond and a means of government; but in southern Italy he had already learned to fuse the aristocratic relationships of feudalism with the eastern idea that a ruler was not the first among equals, not elected by the people, but sovereign and even divine. Alongside the northern titles of Justiciar and Seneschal, we therefore have the eastern titles of Catapan, Logothete and Strategos; alongside the Viscount was the Baiulo, the Cadi and the Emir of Emirs.

It was in particular the Byzantine element which distinguished Roger's government. Sicily still included the essentially Greek province of Calabria as it had done under Justinian, and much the same Greek dialect was spoken on both sides of the straits. Roger lived for preference in Calabria, and in so far as his administration had any fixed centre, it was in the Greek city of Mileto in Calabria: there it was that he found many of his best administrators and the Byzantine land registers which were his model. Court ceremonial and protocol were taken from Byzantium; so were many formulae used in his Chancery; but more important was the fact that, whereas the Norman King of England depended on feudal dues and a temporary feudal army, the Norman Count of Sicily could afford permanent mercenaries and one of the strongest fleets of the time.

While restoring Greek traditions of government, Roger simultaneously began a decisive process of Latinisation by introducing an altogether new ruling class. His Greek subjects were not warriors and so were not endowed with fiefs or elevated to the aristocracy. None of the chief landowners, none of the bishops or leading abbots, seem to have been natives of the island; to fill the main positions of responsibility he at first preferred trans-alpine Normans and Frenchmen, and then increasingly Italians or 'Lombards' from the mainland. In return for military service they were given land, and sometimes they preferred to bring with them colonists from their home territories. The study of local dialects has indicated many settlements where a Lombard, French or Ligurian origin can be presumed at some time between 1090 and 1250, and Amari noted that there were dozens of villages with names similar to other place names in Italy. The extent of this immigration can only be guessed, but it would explain how a mainly Arabic-speaking country had by 1200 become largely Latinised in speech.

The new arrivals found very little public law in Sicily, and while they followed existing convention and allowed earlier settlers to retain their own private laws, Norman feudal practices were bound to prevail in the public sector. They introduced the general idea of a *curia*, an assembly of nobles who gave advice and might claim some say in administration. Among the aristocracy, feudal ideas of land tenure were also accepted with little question. While Frenchmen followed Frankish practice and recognised primogeniture, the Lombard immigrants preferred to divide property between all the sons, but every nobleman had to accept that fiefs were not freehold, since land was granted conditionally and in trust by the ruler. It was natural for Roger to give out conquered territory as fiefs. In part this was done in order to endow monasteries and bishoprics, and so to begin that gradual process of colonisation at which both the Basilians and Benedictines proved so effective; but fiefs were also granted to recompense military help, or simply because feudal lords would bear the brunt of local administration and fit their tenants into some kind of legal structure. The process was assisted by a movement from below, as ordinary people, wanting protection against other nobles or even against the government, commended themselves and their property to a feudal lord. Either by commendation or imposition, many peasants were eventually tied to the soil as unfree labour.

Feudalisation nevertheless was not so complete as in northern Europe. For one thing, the Count was in a strong position by right of conquest and able to keep a very large personal demesne; for another, there must in general have been a shortage of labour after the destruction of the conquest and hence an inducement to leave existing landowners undisturbed; which resulted in much land remaining outside the feudal system and free of any obligation to the new nobility. On the mainland, Guiscard and Roger had to concede more to the baronage, but in Sicily Roger ruled as a conqueror and with fewer obligations. Perhaps his experience in Calabria had taught him not to grant away too much; at all events his investitures were less substantial in Sicily than in southern Italy. Many of his grants did not carry the right of hereditary succession. Only two large counties were created: one at Syracuse was kept in the family, but was not particularly large and soon lapsed; subsequently a second was created which stretched from Paternò to Butera and was owned by Roger's brother-in-law who was a north Italian and had special authority over the main Lombard settlements. In 1092 Roger gave the city of Catania to the bishop whose diocese he had created and wished to endow, but the other main towns were kept in the royal demesne: they had been independent of the territorial aristocracy under Byzantine and Moslem governments, and Roger wished to keep them so. As well as the towns, it was particularly important to retain the coastal territories under royal supervision. Some cities were allowed land and privileges in return for service: the Bishop of Patti, for instance, owed twenty sailors, and when Nicosia was founded it had to find 296 sailors for the navy and bring timber to the royal arsenals.

In origin, therefore, and by design, Sicilian feudalism was a reinforcement of the ruler's authority. Roger specifically reserved his regalian prerogatives when granting land. He insisted that ordinary citizens had rights against the barons which he as ruler could sustain, and in almost every case major criminal jurisdiction was kept to himself. As the baronies were his creation, he retained a suzerain's superior right of 'eminent domain'. Fiefs were held in return for loyalty and service, and could be confiscated in case of default. They would lapse to the crown if there were no direct heir, and a royal bailiff would administer them during a vassal's minority.

Roger's attitude to religion shows that political considerations came uppermost in his mind. Sicily was a Moslem country when he arrived, and he did not wish to antagonise his non-Christian subjects unnecessarily. Since the surviving Christians were Greek Orthodox, he endowed Greek monasteries more than Latin: nearly seventy Basilian monastic houses are known to have existed in Norman Sicily, and these remained the main focus of religious life. At first the archbishop of Palermo was also a Greek. No doubt Roger took into account that the Patriarch of Constantinople was more distant and ineffective than the Pope and so would be less intrusive as a religious supervisor; no doubt he also appreciated the caesaro-papist tradition of Byzantium which gave more weight to the secular power; and probably he also saw in this judicious balance of patronage a useful pressure on Rome.

Roger prudently granted some favours at the same time to Latin Christianity, but on his own terms. By 1083 he had appointed a Latin archbishop at Palermo. The Gallican liturgy was introduced. Entirely on his own initiative he decided the area of each diocese and how many dioceses there should be; they were privately endowed out of his own purse, and he himself selected the bishops. For the most part he chose French ecclesiastics, one from Rouen at Mazara, a Provençal Benedictine at Syracuse, a Breton at Catania; though English and Tuscans were also included. Likewise the cathedral chapters were recruited from overseas. This was the time of the great Investiture Contest when, over most of Europe, the Church repudiated any interference by the civil power in choosing bishops; but Sicily was different. Here the Church in a sense remained part of the royal prerogative.

Roger never restored to the Roman Church the large Sicilian patrimony which had been confiscated by Byzantium, yet he was extremely generous to his foundations, and he attached his new dioceses to Rome and not Constantinople. Urban II visited Sicily in person to confirm his work, because the papacy urgently needed Norman help against the Western Empire; and when Urban subsequently went too far and named the Bishop of Troina as papal Legate in the island, Roger imprisoned the Bishop and made the Pope annul his appointment. As a result, in 1098 a papal bull conceded to Roger and his successors the exclusive powers of an Apostolic Legate in Sicily and Calabria as authorised representatives of the Holy See. This was to recognise that Roger had something approaching the ecclesiastical authority of an Eastern Emperor. He could claim that ecclesiastical matters would ultimately come before his court, without any appeal to Rome. In virtue of his quasi-religious office the ruler of Sicily assumed the right to wear a pastoral ring and dalmatic, and to carry a crozier. The union of civil and ecclesiastical power gave him a special strength, just as latterly it made more difficult the development of opposition and of representative institutions.

Roger's life was so dedicated to conquest that he had little time to reorganise economic life. Once he had subdued the country, he seems to have held a general inquest on landowner-ship. This rudimentary census of persons and property was similar to the English Domesday Book, but was based on the existing practice of the *dîwân*. In 1093 he promulgated the result at Mazara where he convened his feudatories and gave them rolls containing a description of the lands and the number of serfs and buildings which each possessed.

By reserving for himself the greater part of all conquered territory, Roger made his own family extremely rich; for almost all the towns and some of the best agricultural land were in his portion, and when he granted land to others he reserved the mines, salt works and generally the forests for his own use. In addition he received feudal dues from his military vassals, labour and services from his agricultural tenants; and of course he enjoyed the produce of his own demesne, and certain general taxes. The chief source of wealth in Sicily was wheat, and con-siderable quantities were exported to North Africa where the tribal raids were causing a great food shortage. Early in the twelfth century the taxation of grain exports may already have provided a good deal of revenue. Sicily had one inestimable advantage here: its climate and soil were suitable for a very hard type of wheat which probably had come with the Arabs from North Africa. This hard wheat gave a poor yield and was not easy to mill, but it had a very high gluten content, and it grew well in a hot climate with little rain. Above all, it was wonderfully durable and ideally suited as a long-term reserve against famine and as a basic ration for ships.

Very little is known about the upland areas, because all the towns of Arab and Norman Sicily except Castrogiovanni were on or near the coast, and little documentary or archaeological evidence exists for the interior. One can assume that the new feudal aristocracy fitted with ease into a world of large wheat-growing *latifondi*; and it is certain that, in some areas of once intensive Arab settlement, orchards and gardens gradually gave way to ranches owned by nobles and monasteries. De-population through war, famine and expatriation would have assisted this process. Little market villages of about a hundred families were not uncommon in 1100, but isolated hamlets and farmsteads eventually became rare again in Sicily, and such a long period of warfare must have encouraged the tendency for the rural population to cluster together in large villages often remote from their work.

So long as there was a shortage of agricultural labour, Roger and his baronage had to attract new cultivators and make existing ones stay by creating favourable conditions on the land. After conquering Malta, Roger offered to build a village for the Christian captives he released there, and to furnish settlers with capital and keep taxes low; yet the offer was not sufficiently attractive to make them stay. Every successful landlord would have to confirm the common rights enjoyed by his tenants over mountain and woodland country. A diploma of 1092, for example, granted to a monastery and its dependants full liberty in certain woods and fields: there they could use the rivers, pick nuts and acorns and take wood for making ploughs and houses or for fuel. Many Arabs had lived as wandering cattle-drovers; rights to rough grazing were therefore the most widespread of these old-established common usages. Frequently there were also rights of hunting, fishing and haymaking, even of quarrying stone, and of growing trees whether on public or private land. These common privileges must have been important in the economy of most Sicilians. They made the condition of agricultural labourers in all probability much easier than later, when the bargaining power of the peasantry against the baronage had been reduced and there was no strong monarch to defend their interests.

Roger's success with the Church, and the absence of any serious resistance to him, show how far he had succeeded in pacifying Sicily and Calabria before he died in 1101. Fortunately for the country he had not shared Guiscard's ambitions in eastern Europe. He was able to give large dowries to his daughters, one of whom married Karloman, the King of Hungary, and another Conrad, the son of the Western Emperor Henry IV. Yet though he was renowned through Christendom for his wealth and power, the Norman state lacked a feeling of permanence. Roger had been a nomadic ruler like his Viking ancestors, and spent his time travelling from one province to another with a mobile administration and treasury. He chose to be buried not in Sicily but at Mileto in Calabria; and it was left for his successors to organise a stable kingdom based on the former Arab capital of Palermo.

Chapter 3

THE *REGNUM*

At Roger's death his third wife became Regent. Adelaide was a north Italian, and her family connections favoured an increased immigration of Lombards, especially in east and south-eastern Sicily. Under her regency the Greek Church was still patronised as much as the Latin. She it was who established Palermo as a capital, for she discovered Sicily to be less turbulent than Calabria and a better source of revenue. Adelaide would have found the Moslem citizens of Palermo, like the Greek clergy, a useful support against any ambitious feudatories. Under Arab rule this had become the biggest town in southern Italy, indeed one of the largest towns in Europe; and now it was to enter the most flourishing period in its whole history.

The moment when the younger Roger II took over government from his mother is not known. Certainly it was before 1113 when she was foolish enough to marry King Baldwin of Jerusalem. Eye-witnesses were dazzled by the splendour of her fleet as she left for the Holy Land, by the gold and silver which plated the prow of her galley, and its carpet of gold thread. No doubt this marriage represented a considerable loss of wealth to Sicily. Baldwin was interested only in her dowry, to pay off his debts and his soldiers. He already had another wife, and after spending the money he easily made the Pope declare this new marriage void. Possibly Roger had encouraged his mother's escapade, hoping to inherit Baldwin's throne. Before long, however, he had changed his County of Sicily into a kingdom on its own.

Roger II not only ruled Sicily and Calabria but in 1127 succeeded to Apulia after the death of the heir of Robert Guiscard; and in 1130 he declared that the whole of southern Italy was now part of a new 'Kingdom of Sicily'. The kingdom stretched up to the Papal States, where its frontier was marked roughly by the river Tronto on the Adriatic and the river Garigliano on the Tyrrhenian Sea. Roger boldly styled himself *Rex Siciliae et Italiae*.

This first King of Sicily was one of the most remarkable rulers

24

of the European Middle Ages. He successfully challenged the Pope, and both the Eastern and Western Emperors. He acquired a North African empire, and even aimed at the imperial throne of Constantinople. We hear of him that he was tall, had a loud voice and an insatiable ambition. He was a great worker: thorough, patient, with a remarkable head for details. The chroniclers, being ecclesiastics and disliking his ideas of religious equality, were not always fair, but it rings true when they called him more feared than loved. They agreed that he was close-fisted, unscrupulous and ruthless, but they could not deny his strong intelligence and his dominant personality. One of them said that he seemed to do more asleep than others awake.

Roger's kingdom moved away from models familiar in northern Europe. His teachers in youth must have been Greeks; he knew both Greek and Arabic, but preferred to use Greek even in diplomatic relations with Moslem rulers. He was reputed to keep a harem, and a special part of the palace was reserved for his women and eunuchs; but where at Constantinople the eunuchs were usually Christian monks, Roger's were Arab and Moslem. An Arab cook supervised the palace kitchens. Much is heard of the King's artistic and intellectual interests, and it may be that these (or the reputation for them) were deliberately cultivated to set him apart from ordinary mortals. For the splendour of his court was not simple vanity or luxuriousness, it was also calculated propaganda for the idea of a semi-divine monarchy. Contemporaries were suitably impressed to find the palace floors lined with multi-coloured carpets, the servants clad in silk, and food served on gold plates.

The chief minister, a veritable Grand Vizier, held the splendid title of Emir of Emirs and Archonte of Archontes. By about 1125 the chief Emir was George of Antioch, who had learnt the art of politics in Syria and through serving the Zirids at Mahdia. George was fluent in Arabic, though himself an orthodox Greek Christian; and it can have been no accident that such a prominent schismatic was at hand when Roger undertook his fight with the Pope, nor that a man trained in the precepts of Justinian helped to change a Count into a King.

Different historians have traced Arab, Byzantine or even Anglo-Norman traditions as the main constituent element of

Roger's administration, but George's contribution was probably decisive. The chief officers of state were Greek, though many of the lower bureaucracy were Moslems. The coinage continued to include Arabic in its trilingual inscriptions, but tended more towards Byzantine models. Some official documents were still in Arabic and dated from the year of Muhammad's flight, but alongside them were Latin documents copying the formulae of the papal Chancery, and Greek documents dated from the creation of the world. The tripartite nature of the administration towards the end of the century is shown in an illustrated manuscript by Peter of Eboli, where Arab, Greek and Latin notaries are clearly indicated. Most of the royal seals, however, were Greek. Above all, the concept of royal authority was deliberately modelled on that of Justinian; and this eastern influence became more and not less noticeable as time went by, until Sicily appeared more exotic in western eyes than even the crusader kingdom of Jerusalem.

Symbolic of this development was the coronation in 1130 which took place with legendary luxuriousness in the one-time mosque which was now the cathedral of Palermo. Roger had called certain of his vassals to Salerno and told them that he wanted to become King; then he summoned to Palermo a general assembly of ecclesiastics, nobles and people who acclaimed his proposal. Sovereignty by right of conquest was in this way confirmed by a kind of election. Thus was formed the *regnum*, generally recognised as 'the Kingdom' *par excellence*, which had some special quality unknown to merely feudal kingdoms. It was richer, more civilised, and knew more order and internal peace. The King of this *regnum* was more than the first among his barons; the illusion was even created that he was a Priest-King whose authority came from God alone, so that rebellion against him would be sacrilege. Court ceremonial prescribed that Roger's subjects, including bishops, should prostrate themselves in reverence before him. His seals show him dressed as an eastern *basileus*. A mosaic at Palermo also depicts him with the imperial cloak and the stole of an Apostolic Legate: he wears the Greek crown and receives it not from Pope or Emperor but directly from Christ himself.

The laws of the kingdom clearly show their eastern provenance. While he followed his father in allowing the various groups of his subjects to be governed by different legal systems, King Roger put out a code of laws which applied to all the heterogeneous populations of the *regnum*, and he chose to base this code on 'Roman' legislation familiar to the Sicilian Greeks. In no other western state was so much concern shown for the majesty of the King's person and his powers as a law-maker. This may have been more theoretical propaganda than practical politics; nevertheless, even in minor details—for example the regulations about marriage and prostitution, about ecclesiastical rights of asylum, about forbidding Jews and pagans to own Christian serfs, about the practice of medicine—often the very words were taken from Justinian's code.

As well as a King, Roger was a feudal overlord, and as such he had a special relationship with the landowning military elite of Normans and Lombards. Unlike his father, Roger did not always lead his forces in person, but the feudatories were not allowed to use this fact to assert their own leadership, and their authority was made less by the existence of a strong professional army alongside the feudal levies. Fiefs were usually held in return for military service, and knight service in Sicily was theoretically ninety days a year instead of the customary forty. There was no need to allow the barons much political power, since there existed an able class of bureaucrats entirely dependent on the King; and likewise the development of feudal justice was checked by provincial justiciars who travelled on circuit and enforced the King's law. By the Roman-law concept of *laesa majestas*, full allegiance was owed to the sovereign and not to any intermediary overlord. Roger destroyed private castles and forbade nobles to fight against each other. He did not shrink from executing some of his companions in arms and confiscating their estates. For it was recognised that a fief was a delegation of public power which could be revoked. To ensure that during his minority no vassals had exploited governmental weakness, the *dîwân* was empowered to call on every baron to show the title deeds which proved his ownership and the services to which this ownership obliged him; and if the originals were corroded or worm eaten, they might have to be copied anew on durable cotton paper.

Parliament was an essentially feudal institution. It developed out of the Teutonic tradition which gave the chief warriors a duty and even a right to advise the King, possibly even a right to elect him in the first place. Roger's *curia*, however, was not a restriction on the King but an emanation of the royal will. Parliamentary approval hardly seems to have been indispensable to him, nor is there any likelihood that the barons in parliament did much except listen and applaud. Probably they were summoned just because this would add greater solemnity to the promulgation of laws and give at least the illusion that government was more than arbitrary power. Parliament signified an occasion rather than an assembly of people; and the King used such an occasion to see that his chief subjects knew the royal will and took his wishes back to where they lived.

A ruler with this degree of power was not likely to have much trouble with the Church. Roger was excommunicated on a number of occasions, but obviously this meant little to him. He took advantage of a divided papacy to obtain approval from an anti-Pope for his kingship, and then captured the legitimate Pope, Innocent II, when a papal army took the field against Norman aggression; so doing he won recognition and a withdrawal of excommunication. In return, Roger accepted papal investiture, though in practice he did not let this feudal relationship signify any diminution of his sovereign rights.

In Calabria and Sicily the regulation of Church affairs was claimed as a royal prerogative in virtue of the hereditary Apostolic Legateship. This privilege was already being challenged by Rome, but if the Pope ever repudiated the agreement of 1098, the monarchy could as easily withdraw the royal endowments which provided almost all the income of the Sicilian Church. In practice Roger went on electing bishops whether they were confirmed by the papacy or not. He laid down the law about selling relics, religious apostasy and the punishment of witchcraft. On one occasion he went much further when he allowed, or presumably instructed, the Basilian archimandrite, Neilos Doxopatrios, to write a vigorous attack on the supremacy of Rome. This book was a considerable work of history as well as of religious polemic; its message was that the Pope was no more than on a level with the other Patriarchs, and that the religious allegiance of Sicily and southern Italy should be to Constantinople.

Once he had established that his Church was a national Church, and that non-Christian faiths were to be tolerated even in this age of the crusades, Roger proved that he was no heretic. He was a great church builder; and St. Bernard, with whom he clashed over politics and by whom he was called *tyrannus Siciliae*, had to admit that he was a generous patron. Moreover, even though the Greek clergy were more learned than the Latins, it was the latter whom he favoured in his endowments. Once he had received papal recognition in 1139, he stopped founding Greek monasteries, and gradually the existing Basilian houses were encouraged to change their allegiance.

Sicily now once again became a power in Europe and the centre of a Mediterranean empire. Almost alone in Christian Europe, Roger showed no interest in the crusading movement but hard-headedly used the Second Crusade as an excuse to garrison Corfu. George of Antioch, with a fleet that perhaps contained as many Saracens as Christians, in 1147 overran Greece itself and, it was said, even appeared defiantly in front of Constantinople. This was an especially profitable expedition, because Athens, Thebes and Corinth were plundered, and many silk workers were kidnapped to reinforce the weaving industry at Palermo.

One solution envisaged by Roger for Sicily's economic and strategic problems was to establish a bridgehead into North Africa. To this end he successfully exploited discord among the Moslems, and after capturing the island of Jerba in 1135, he made it a base from which his ships could prey on communications with Egypt. In 1146, George took the city of Tripoli with much destruction and slaughter; then in 1148 Mahdia fell, and this was followed by Susa and Sfax, until Roger controlled all the coast to Cape Bon and inland to Kairouan. There was a large element of risk in this policy, for it meant giving up his father's project for peaceful trade. No doubt, however, it was a calculated risk, and it gave political recognition to the fact that in some years many African cities relied on Sicily for imports of food. Roger encouraged the emigration of Sicilians to Tripoli. He even called himself 'King of Africa'. Many of the local Moslems were easily reconciled to his government, for he allowed existing laws and magistrates to continue, and simply demanded payment of a head tax.

Inside Sicily itself an efficient government tapped the potential sources of wealth in a way which no subsequent ruler could quite emulate. An abundant currency was again supported by African gold, and the ducat now made its first appearance in history. A merchant marine grew up on royal subsidies, while the navy kept command of the seas and levied a tithe on ships passing through the Mediterranean. Cotton growing seems to have diminished, perhaps because of the emigration of Arab farmers, but the silk industry received an impetus from skilled immigrant Greek labour and the requirements of court ceremonial. A fine silk mantle still exists at Vienna with an inscription embroidered in Arabic to say that it was woven in the royal factory at Palermo in 1133–4: this workshop was in the palace itself and contained goldsmiths and jewellers as well as silk-workers. The mining of iron, salt and sulphur was carried on, and coral fishing was already a Sicilian industry. Fishing contributed a good deal to the royal revenue: the salted tunny fish of Sicily was, along with ships' biscuit made from Sicilian wheat, a regular food of sailors throughout the Mediterranean; and special regulations listed the points on the coast between which tunny could be fished when the shoals arrived in May, the number of boats and fishermen to be used, and how much was due to the King.

Apart from the cultivation of wheat, there are references in twelfth-century writers to oranges and lemons, melons and almonds. We know of market gardens around Palermo and of machines used for irrigation. The Arab geographer, Al' Idrisi, though given to exaggeration, spoke of dozens of places where fruit trees abounded. Henna and indigo were grown for colouring. The Sicilian forests still had an important economic function both as fuel and for building: Sicilian timber was used by Innocent II to repair the roof of St. John Lateran and also was indispensable for the royal fleet.

Perhaps no other King in Europe had such a large revenue as Roger, and his income from Palermo reputedly exceeded what his Norman cousins collected from all England. Royal authority was usually strong enough to insist that taxes were paid, and some of his methods of taxation would have been impracticable elsewhere. There was a substantial revenue from numerous public baths, a survival from the past which was unknown in feudal Europe. The King engaged in commerce on his own account. His income from agriculture must also have been considerable; and as local government had not yet been taken over by the feudal aristocracy, Roger retained the profits of justice. As he was able to insist that laws were respected, private citizens were not so prone as they later became to taking the law into their own hands. Commerce profited from this fact as it also gained from the relative peacefulness of these years. On the mainland, in Roger's struggle with the Pope and against rebellion in Apulia, villages were burnt down by both sides, crops were burnt, vines and olives destroyed; but visiting foreigners noted that no other prince had so peaceful and flourishing a realm as the island of Sicily, "so that there is as much security in the King's forests as elsewhere would be found in populous towns".

Al' Idrisi in the 1150s called Palermo, with some hyperbole, "the greatest and finest metropolis in the world, and its beauties are infinite. . . . All around it there are plentiful channels of water and every kind of fruit. Its buildings dazzle the eye, its defences are impregnable". Palermo was an opulent and busy town, far richer and larger than the Rome which the Normans a few years before had largely destroyed by fire. At the other end of the island, Messina, from being a small village, became under the King's peace an important centre of trade. Messina possessed one of the largest, deepest and most easily defended harbours in the Mediterranean, and there was abundant timber near by for the repair of ships. The narrow straits of Messina lay on the main route between western Europe and the East, and after the capture of Jerusalem in 1099 the town flourished as an assembly point and a supply base for provision of food and horses to the crusaders. Especially for French and Spanish ships it was a halfway point to the Levant. A considerable Jewish community lived there, and a number of north-Italian towns were already setting up offices and wharves.

The Sicily of Roger and his two successors was above all a great meeting place of cultures. Byzantine vestments were embroidered with Arabic lettering and worn by Anglo-Norman potentates. Latin basilica-type buildings were crowned with Greek cupolas and covered inside with gorgeous mosaics, while

Arab workmen devised decorations for Christian churches out of esoteric themes from Persian mythology. Books were still being written at Palermo in both Greek and Arabic. French and Latin were languages used at court, and western feudal customs prevailed with the baronial class; but the arts and sciences, like court ceremonial and administrative techniques, seemed part of an altogether different world, and apparently Roger preferred the conversation of learned Saracens to that of Christian monks. No doubt he brought little to Sicilian art and learning except a tolerance and a delight in other traditions and a discriminating patronage; for Norman civilisation was not particularly original, and already before the Norman conquest Christian buildings had sometimes used Islamic forms. But it needed an altogether unusual King to have the taste and the money for works of art on this scale.

As the cultured Arab classes emigrated, and as the Greeks were gradually swamped in the passage of time, it became clear that these cultural traditions had mixed but never completely fused. To some extent, indeed, they depended on people who were not native to the island. By the 1150s, signs were already visible that the religious tolerance which permitted this mixture of styles was wearing thin. Norman-Arab art was an artificial creation of enlightened despotism, not a true interpenetration which was viable on its own. Arab poets had not been influenced by Latin, but continued to embroider on traditional themes brought from Africa and Spain. Learned Byzantines likewise used forms and subjects imported unchanged from Constantinople. The lack of any true synthesis rendered this culture vulnerable and transient, so that gradually the influence of France and Rome predominated in art as in religion and language. Roger introduced the Cistercians, Augustinians, Templars and Hospitalers, and with them came transalpine architectural ideas. Northern barons and ecclesiastics were accustomed to building feudal castles as the symbol and guarantee of their power, and the Bishops of Girgenti were soon using stone for this purpose taken from the old Greek temples. Feudalism thus became dominant in architecture as it was in politics and social relationship.

Norman-Arab art and architecture did, however, exist as a vivid cultural phenomenon for most of the twelfth century.

ΡΟΓΕΡΙΟC ΡΗΞ ·ĪC· X

Christ crowning King Roger: mosaic in the Martorana, Palermo

Building the Ark: mosaic in the cathedral, Monreale

Anderson

Mosaic in Roger's Room, Palazzo Reale, Palermo

Anderson

Woodwork and mosaic, coins and vestments, sculpture and lettering, show how a heterogeneous mixture of styles could become almost a style of its own. The Byzantine mosaics of eastern Europe were mostly destroyed in subsequent Turkish invasions, so that those which survived in Sicily are among the finest examples of the art of twelfth-century Byzantium. St. John of the Hermits, built by Roger in the 1130s, with its five red cupolas, almost seems as much a mosque as a church; and it was in keeping with such a syncretistic background that 'hermits' may have been a corruption of Hermes, son of Zeus and mysterious god of Greek science and alchemy. From the same period dates the church later known as the Martorana, which the Emir George built for a convent of Greek nuns and endowed with a valuable library. Its ground plan was that of a Greek cross, and round the bottom of the dome in Arabic lettering ran the words of a Greek Christian hymn: either this must have been merely a fashion in decoration, or else Christians must have known Arabic.

The great cathedral of Cefalù was built by Roger as an Augustinian church attached to the new Latin bishopric, which he founded during his quarrel with Pope Innocent; it was consecrated by a friendly anti-Pope and staffed with Frenchmen. The most familiar of all Sicilian mosaics is the Christ Pantokrator above the altar. Unlike many other Sicilian churches, this was a Romanesque basilica with a transept, as was customary in the Latin west. The two towers flanking the façade show the influence of northern, or at least Apulian, architecture.

Roger's finest architectural monument is the palace chapel in Palermo. This, too, was built in the 1130s, so says an inscription for a water clock set in the church wall. A western nave is here completed with Arabic pointed arches and Byzantine cupola, while the whole of the interior is covered by mosaic and coloured marble. The mosaics have been considerably restored or even replaced, since later Kings preferred glittering walls to the patina of old surfaces; but, unlike many other monuments, this one was always kept in repair and it was spared even though the palace was often sacked. The mosaics must have been designed by Greek craftsmen, and they used Greek as well as Latin iconography; opposite St. Peter, the

Bishop of Rome, was St. James, Bishop of Jerusalem, and some people have seen this as a visual illustration of the thesis of Doxopatrios that the Pope was no higher than the eastern Patriarchs. Among the wood carvings of the honeycomb ceiling there are winged genii, veiled houris, turbanned chess players, ladies on elephants and warriors on camels—some of them traceable to Indian and Persian legend. Perhaps the clergy, once the gilt wore off, never noticed this ceiling in the dim light, and hence it survived.

The court of Roger was also a centre of science. The King had a special interest in astronomy and astrology, and his water clock was made by an Arab craftsman. According to an English monk who visited the Norman court, he employed a diver to investigate the straits of Messina and the treacherous currents which had created the legend of Scylla and Charybdis. He took pains to regulate medical teaching and compelled doctors to undergo an examination by experts in the presence of a royal official. During the reign of Roger and his son William, Latin translations were made from Plato, Euclid and Ptolemy, and these might have had a big impact on western intellectual life if only they had become widely known in Europe. It was here that Ptolemy's *Almagest* was first translated. Al' Idrisi's work on geography was the most significant production of Sicilian-Arabic literature. No doubt there was some flattery in the suggestion that for fifteen years the King took a detailed share in helping to compile this work, but his keen interest is undeniable; the experience of travellers was consulted wherever possible, and experts were summoned from afar to give testimony. This 'Book of King Roger' became famous in Moslem Africa, little though it was known in Europe.

In literature and scholarship the Arabs in Sicily produced nothing else quite as impressive. There were some writings on science, medicine, jurisprudence and Koranic studies; and a list dated about 1150 gives the names of over a hundred poets from Sicilian-Arab families, though many of them no longer resident in Sicily. Ibn Hamdîs, the best known of these poets, was born in Syracuse of noble family about 1056, and later lived in Spain and Africa. His poems show a nostalgia for the 'paradise of delights' and the voluptuous pleasures of Sicilian wine and gardens in flower, as they also reflect his hatred for

34

the barbarians who had come to displace his own people.

Little of this poetry has survived. Neither do we know much about the French *jongleurs* who came to Roger's court with tales of Roland and the paladins of Charlemagne. The Carolingian legends were at some point transposed into a Sicilian setting, and the popularity of the Breton cycle also suggests that this was no merely superficial culture. Gervase of Tilbury knew that King Arthur had not died but was resting from his wounds on the slopes of Mount Etna, where a stable boy of the Bishop of Catania one day stumbled upon his secret hiding place. These Breton tales later disappeared, though Morgan le Fay remained as *Fata Morgana*, a mirage in the straits of Messina. After eight centuries, however, the paladins are familiar heroes in popular Sicilian legend. Norman-French did not survive as a spoken or written language so well as in contemporary England, but French and Arab poetry together must have acted as a stimulus to the dramatic new vernacular Sicilian literature which began to appear late in the twelfth century.

Chapter 4

THE DISINTEGRATION OF
NORMAN SICILY

The test of Roger's success came under William I (1154–66)—
who succeeded to the throne because three elder brothers had
died. It is not easy to penetrate through the strong hostility to
William shown by the contemporary historian, Falcandus; but
though William was a brave fighter, he must have lacked the
application of other Norman kings and their strength of
character. Whereas Roger signed almost all the acts which
came out of the royal chancery, his son was a soldier rather than
a statesman; he preferred to put off decisions and rule through
ministers, while living apart in the oriental splendour of his
pleasure palaces outside Palermo. He kept even more of a
Moslem entourage than his father. There were tales of favourites
and lavish banquets and excessive sexual indulgence, though
much of this criticism may have come from malice or envy.
Because Falcandus and most of the barons were against him,
he has always been labelled 'William the Bad'.

He came to the throne at a difficult time. A certain restlessness during the last years of Roger's reign indicated the growth
of both feudal opposition and racial tension. Philip the Eunuch,
the naval commander, had already been burnt to death for
suspected treason, and probably this represented a tactical
success for an aspiring Latin element in the administration.
Sicily remained prosperous, but the Western and Eastern
Emperors and the papacy were ready to exploit baronial
opposition at home, at the same time as the Sicilian foothold in
North Africa was collapsing before the advance of the Almo-
hads from the mountains of Morocco. In 1156 there was a
defeat at Sfax; then Tripoli fell and in 1160 Mahdia. The
resources of this small island could not simultaneously withstand a strong challenge in Africa along with treason at home
and war with both the Pope and Byzantium. Yet defeat
damaged an important economic connection and brought
another naval power within striking distance of Sicilian coastal
shipping.

In 1156, by the concordat of Benevento with the English Pope Adrian IV, William neutralised one possible opponent. Though less of a church-builder than either his father or his son, and though tolerant of Islam, in this concordat he realistically accepted the growing power of a reformed papacy. He agreed that bishops should be elected by the clergy, and merely kept his right of veto. Adrian confirmed the Apostolic Legateship but for the island of Sicily alone. He renounced any right to send other Legates or to receive appeals from Sicilian bishops, and in return the King recognised the Pope as feudal overlord of his mainland territories.

The barons were becoming a more difficult problem; economically and socially strong, they also aspired to win political power. They grumbled that law and administration under Roger had been in the hands of low-born professionals, and so had the army and navy, just as they also resented that Roger had countered opposition by banishment and confiscation of property. Since female succession was allowed, he had protected his feudal interests by insisting that sisters and daughters of his feudatories could not marry without his consent; and some nobles now complained that royal rights over wardship and marriage had sometimes been used to reduce their children to celibacy; or else that, since marriage came so late, there was no hope of an heir and their estates would lapse to the crown. Roger had also prevented the building of castles without his consent, and this not only made rebellion difficult, but undermined the barons' authority over their tenants.

Many of these barons were violent and ambitious men. They were, as the Hautevilles had themselves originally been, brigands by upbringing and temperament. Those with estates on the mainland were especially restless against authoritarian government from Palermo. After 1154, the more ambitious of them therefore took advantage of a less popular and less efficient King to shift the internal balance of power. They also stirred up a movement of racial intolerance against the Saracens—it was evidently not a religious movement, because the bishops seem to have sided with the King and his Moslem functionaries. Some of the towns, too, thinking themselves injured by Roger's centralised and paternalistic rule, were ready to profit from any

37

governmental weakness and demand charters and civic freedom.

William's chief minister, inherited from Roger, was Maio of Bari, one of the palace professionals who caused such offence to the feudal aristocracy. We know about him mainly from the slanted criticism which came from his opponents; yet it is possible that Maio was one of the great figures of Norman Sicily. The barons called him an upstart son of an oil merchant, a would-be usurper of the throne, a seducer of young girls and even of the King's wife; whereas he seems to have been a cultured and sensible politician, a patron of poetry and the arts, someone who believed in Roger's ideas of strong kingship and saw that aristocratic pretensions were already helping to ruin Sicily's position in the Mediterranean and North Africa. As Emir of Emirs, his was the responsibility for continuing to use Arab financial experts and refusing to reduce the power of the central bureacracy.

Against this man there was a baronial rising in 1155 coupled with a riot in Palermo perhaps instigated by the barons, but the King put it down with exemplary punishment. Aristocratic opposition continued to exist in Calabria and the Lombard settlements of Sicily; and five years later one of the barons, Matthew Bonellus, organised a more successful revolt. Maio was stabbed and his corpse torn to bits by a Palermo mob. The murderer and his faction, as soon as they discovered that the King was powerless to retaliate, proceeded to capture William himself and declare his young son King. The palace was sacked, prisons were opened, the Treasury pillaged and money thrown to the populace. Some of the registers were also burnt which carried details of who owned which fiefs and what services were owed for them. Many other priceless testimonials of the greatness of Norman Sicily must have been destroyed on this occasion. One principal target of the rebels was indicated by the fact that the Moslems had their shops pillaged, while many of the palace eunuchs were slaughtered, and the women of the harem shared out. Officials, tax collectors and merchants all suffered, and there was a general seizing of land from Arab proprietors. In particular it seems to have been the Lombard settlers who used the occasion to exterminate rural Moslem settlements, and much of eastern Sicily was now cleared of

Arabs and other North African settlers. Neither age nor sex was spared. Probably it was after these events that Al' Idrisi and most of the remaining Arab intellectuals left Sicily.

Discord soon broke out among the rebels, and there seems to have been quite strong popular support for William I. Aided by the bishops, by his Moslem soldiers and some elements of the Palermo citizenry, William soon effected bloody revenge. Butera, Piazza and other Lombard settlements were sacked and destroyed. Bonellus was blinded and hamstrung; his goods and his castle were forfeited. The reign of the eunuchs was restored, and the Moslems took vengeance on those who had despoiled them; for racial and class hatreds had by now destroyed the tolerant equilibrium of Roger's reign.

When William I died in 1166, one partisan observer said that only the Moslem women wept. In his last years the great feudal families had been again excluded from political power, and an attempt was made to reconstitute the feudal and tax registers of the *dîwân* which had been a basic constituent of royal authority and wealth. The Greek section of the royal chancery ceased to function. Saracens controlled the Treasury, yet one ominous sign was that non-Christians were forbidden to carry arms. The barons had killed the last great minister of Norman Sicily, but the administrative class of bureaucrats still included many other southern Italians as well as individual Greeks, French and Englishmen. Norman England and Norman Sicily remained very close: Odo of Bayeux, William the Conqueror's brother, was eventually buried in Palermo cathedral, and Thomas Brown, later of the English Exchequer, was for many years a familiar figure in Palermo, as were John of Lincoln, Richard of Hereford and Herbert of Middlesex; Richard Palmer, friend of St. Thomas Becket, became Bishop of Syracuse; Walter of the Mill—Walter 'Offamilio'—and his brother Bartholomew both became Archbishop of Palermo. These newcomers reinforced the existing Latin–French element, so much so that knowledge of French became an essential qualification for public life. In time they proved to be a strong support for the Norman-French baronage against the professional lay bureaucrats.

Latin monasteries, moreover, were overtaking Greek as the main vehicle of culture, despite the fact that some important translations from Arabic and Greek were still made. The Emir Eugenius, as well as being a politician, was a noted physicist and mathematician and translated Ptolemy's *Optics*; the Grand Admiral of the Kingdom, Aristippus, made the first medieval translations of Plato; but at last literature was no longer mainly Arabic or Greek. Aristippus was a Latin, and so almost certainly was Falcandus, one of the most eminent historians and stylists of the western Middle Ages. Once again in Sicilian history, Greece was giving way to Rome; and from being largely scientific at the court of Roger, intellectual life was becoming classical and humanist.

William II succeeded his father at the age of thirteen, and the regency of his mother, Margaret of Navarre, saw a succession of factions in power. First she ruled through her favourite, Peter, the Saracen eunuch, who was a slave freed by her husband. Peter was backed by the army, but he had to rule in uneasy coalition with the Englishman Bishop Palmer, who in a sense represented feudal Sicily, and with Matthew of Salerno another layman lawyer who had been trained by Maio. Many barons took advantage of the Queen, and returned from exile to regain their estates and rebuild their castles. Peter soon fled to Morocco to escape the conflict which was building up between the Regent and the landowning aristocracy.

Like Adelaide in 1101, Margaret in 1166 then turned for help to her relatives. Many knights were imported from her homeland in Spain, others from France, and nine new counts were created. Her cousin, the young Stephen of Le Perche, became chief minister in 1167, and a future Archdeacon of Bath, Peter of Blois, became William's tutor. Stephen was forceful and efficient; as such he was not liked. To the annoyance of native nobility and officialdom he imposed French feudal customs and gave fiefs and jobs to many strangers. The fact that he was apparently not open to bribes made him yet more unpopular; even worse, he imprisoned the most notoriously corrupt of the chancery officers, and had the governor of Palermo castle whipped publicly for working a profitable prostitution racket. Peter of Blois plaintively wrote home about Sicily's cruel and perfidious inhabitants. He longed for the more tranquil world of England, for its soft sweet air, for French wine and good English food; whereas Sicily gave him malaria, its food disagreed with him and its earthquakes and volcanoes marked it out obviously as the entrance to Hell. Proof of this view came in 1169 when a tremendous earthquake destroyed Catania and a tidal wave swept over the walls of Messina.

When rumour spread that Stephen was taking money away to France, a riot was easily stirred up at Messina, accompanied by horrible cruelties. This was a last rising by the Greeks of north-eastern Sicily before they merged into the rest of the population, but Moslems and Catholics were also among the rebels, and some of the feudal aristocracy took a chance to assert themselves against government by French and Spanish newcomers. Soon it was a general insurrection. Stephen fled to Jerusalem in 1168, and Peter to France, while the Englishman, Walter Offamilio, seized power and used the Palermo mob to make the canons of Palermo elect him archbishop.

For twenty years Walter remained at the centre of power along with his brother Bartholomew and a third Englishman, Bishop Palmer. This was a comparatively tranquil period for Sicily. William came of age in 1172, but did not openly dare to challenge the Archbishop. 'William the Good' received his title since the barons and the chroniclers approved of him; and because of their uncritical approval, his personality is difficult to grasp. He had the reputation of being just, lenient, without avarice, and not disrespectful to what were becoming recognised as the fundamental laws of the kingdom. The times were reasonably prosperous; and the King, while not notably pious, was extravagant in building churches. The feudatories were content that their tax liability was confined to the recognised feudal occasions, for instance when they succeeded to their estates, or if the King had a son, or his daughter was married. Nevertheless a further effort was made to refurbish the feudal documents kept in the *dohana de secretis*. A more specialised office also appeared, the *dohana baronum*, which listed the baronial fiefs and their obligations to the crown. No doubt this was largely the work of Matthew the lawyer. It would have helped the government to discover any usurpation of the royal demesne or the illicit possession of fiefs which should have lapsed to the King. These registers above all, and the bureaucratic traditions which made them possible, kept Norman Sicily rich and strong.

William II lived like an oriental sovereign. Visitors noticed that he patronised Arab poets, that his concubines were Moslems, and he kept a bodyguard of Negro slaves. The number of Moslems in government decreased during the course of his reign, but they still dominated the finance department. At a time when western Christianity was becoming increasingly intolerant, there were still mosques in Palermo; despite the racial riots of the early 1160s, many Moslems lived there and kept their own judges and schools. Even the Christian women at Palermo were said to have assumed the secluded habits and the dress of Arab women—six centuries later, visitors noted this same fact—and the King himself did not scorn to wear Moorish costume. Evidently he was somewhat indifferent in religion: the Spanish Arab, Ibn Jubair, heard that, during the great earthquake, William told everyone in his palace to pray to whichever god they fancied. Though the riots of 1161 showed that Moslems could no longer feel secure, though many were emigrating, it is possible that Girgenti, Syracuse and Catania (until the earthquake) were still largely non-Christian, and Christian abbots used to let their serfs swear on the Koran.

Nevertheless the Christianisation of the country was proceeding, and the Cluniacs and Cistercians were accumulating large endowments for this purpose. William's greatest act of patronage was to build the immense Benedictine abbey of Monreale. Probably the King intended to create a rival institution to the archbishopric of Palermo, held by Walter, since the Abbot of Monreale was made Sicily's second archbishop even though his see was based only five miles from Palermo. Walter had to allow his own diocese to be diminished and to surrender many sources of revenue to endow an abbey which the King intended as a mausoleum for the royal family. The resources of the kingdom were heavily strained to this end. The Abbot became the largest landowner after the King himself; he and his church were to be free of taxes, liberally provided with castles and villages, and even with a whole town in distant Apulia. His estates included mills and a factory for processing sugar cane. He had a tunny fishery and the right to fish with five boats in Palermo harbour. The monks and their servants could demand free hospitality throughout the kingdom, and freedom from toll in the straits of Messina; they were also to have free pasturage for their animals and those of their tenants whenever the flocks were moving between summer and winter pasturage. Finally the Abbot was appointed sole justiciar for all the abbey's extensive territories, with powers of criminal and civil jurisdiction.

In the buildings at Monreale, eastern and western styles met. The nave was essentially Latin, and the arcaded cloister fitted western monastic habits; but the ornamental marble fountain and columns of the cloister were Moorish, and two hundred different carved capitals on these columns seem to show the varied influences of Tuscan, Apulian, Byzantine, Arab and Provençal craftsmen. Inside the abbey were nearly seventy thousand square feet of coloured mosaic bringing the Bible story to a public who could not read: these mosaics belong to the iconographical tradition of the Greek liturgy, and probably only a specialist workshop imported from Greece could have carried out this enormous task so quickly and with so consistent a style; yet the mosaic inscriptions were now in Latin, and there was the earliest representation of the western saint St. Thomas Becket who was canonised only in 1173. This is the largest and most important ensemble of mosaic which has survived from twelfth-century Europe.

The building of this huge abbey, as well as the Arabic-type palaces called the Cuba and the Zisa with their artificial lakes, to say nothing of a new cathedral in Palermo, indicates the considerable wealth of Sicily and the concentration of this wealth in the King's hands. Probably this was the most affluent period in the century. But William was living on capital. At a time when the maritime cities of mainland Italy were accumulating new fortunes, Sicilian commerce did not progress: indeed it received a blow with the loss of Tunisia and Tripoli. There were already signs of political opposition from the commercial centres, Messina and Palermo. Sicilian towns were governed by a royal bailiff whose accounts were checked by the *dîwân*, and although they may sometimes have found this an advantage, they resented the lack of municipal self-government, and indeed it left them helpless against the feudal magnates whenever there was a weak King or a royal minority.

William the Good may have done more to spend than to increase his revenues, but the accumulated resources of the past

43

had not yet been destroyed in civil war. Hugo Falcandus, that enigmatic servant of the crown, wrote with much more enthusiasm than Peter of Blois in praise of a fruitful countryside teeming with melons, pomegranates, sugar cane, date palms and every kind of produce. He recalled the splendid buildings of Palermo, the evergreen trees and abundant springs. He described how water wheels still filled the cisterns from which aqueducts irrigated fields of fruit and vegetables. Likewise Ibn Jubair, who passed through Sicily after being wrecked off Messina in 1184, told how King William came in person to help the stranded passengers with money. Messina seemed inhospitable to Ibn Jubair, but its markets were rich, and a stranger like himself could go about safely by day and night. Large ships could come right up to the quayside. Palermo, too, impressed this visitor with its spacious alleys, its houses of coloured stone, its mosques and splendid palaces, and he noted that the surrounding countryside was cultivated and fertile.

William died in 1189, aged only thirty-six. A picture of his deathbed shows a doctor and an astrologer with turbans and Arab dress. He had no children, and this was fatal in a society which depended on a strong leader and an uncontested succession. The official heir was his aunt Constance, posthumous daughter of Roger II, a lady whom William had married to the Hohenstaufen King Henry of Germany, who later became the Emperor Henry VI, and who was little more than half her age. William had been in need of German help, for he had undertaken a number of ambitious wars—in which, incidentally, Sicilian interests were minimal and which cost far more lives and money than his great-grandfather had spent in conquering Sicily. He was ambitious to become Eastern Emperor, but his wars in Greece were wasted effort; furthermore two hundred ships under his Greek admiral were defeated by Saladin. In order to receive diplomatic support, he had therefore arranged this ill-considered marriage which in effect resulted in handing over his kingdom to a German who would use its wealth to support extraneous interests and embroil it in the perennial contest between papacy and empire. Another result was internal division, for Henry's succession, coming through the female line, was contested by many of the Norman-French who recognised the different precepts of the Salic law, and this

44

meant civil war. Under the Hauteville dynasty the King's person was the one link between all the different elements in society, and with the contested succession after 1189 all sem- blance of a commonweal disappeared.

The barons had at first been persuaded or forced to swear allegiance to Constance, but some of them in 1189 rallied round William's illegitimate nephew. Tancred's accession was in part an act of force, but some Sicilians evidently preferred a local man and a Norman; some, too, may have thought that election should take precedence over hereditary right. Tancred was 'chosen' King by an assembly of prelates, nobles and people in Palermo; and even his opponents agreed that there was a popular element in his favour. One contributory influence was that Palermo risked losing its central position in government if a German King succeeded. Another was that Tancred appealed to the civic bourgeoisie by granting charters to the towns. The papacy supported him, simply because all Popes dreaded any encirclement of the Papal States by a union of southern Italy and Germany. Probably Byzantium backed him: at least his son married the Eastern Emperor's daughter, and Tancred himself spoke Greek and was, like his forebears, an enthusiast for Greek culture. More material was the fact that Tancred was the candidate of the Chancellor Matthew against Arch- bishop Walter and those barons who from the beginning had advocated the marriage of Henry and Constance. Some feudatories must have backed the German candidate just for the reason that a remote sovereign might allow them greater in- dependence; they were glad to see a contest for the throne because that would weaken the monarchy; it would give them a chance to rebuild their castles and annex portions of the royal demesne.

A disturbing factor at this moment was another popular rising against the Moslems. The Arab elements in Sicily, much more than the Greek, defied assimilation and were a restless and sometimes dangerous faction. Other Sicilians envied them for their territorial possessions, or were jealous of their jobs in the bureaucracy; and some were offended at their strange religious beliefs and dress. At any moment of political or economic crisis these anomalous citizens were likely to be made a scapegoat and the object of private vendettas and covetousness. A civil war against the Moslems therefore broke out after 1189, and many were forced into the mountains. There took place another substantial migration to Africa, and this must have included most of the remaining Arab merchants and artisans of Palermo. Further agricultural areas were depopulated. The rich garden suburbs which had astonished Ibn Jubair ten years before were deserted. Those who could not afford to emigrate must often have joined the bandits of the hill country, who became such an expensive incubus on Sicilian society. Though some of the refugees eventually returned and even obtained jobs under Tancred, confidence between the races never recovered.

Another problem was created for Tancred when Richard Cœur-de-Lion of England arrived in 1190, together with the King of France and an army of crusaders. Richard brusquely demanded payment of a legacy made to him by William II, and protested that his sister Joanna, William's widow, was held prisoner in Sicily and her dowry unlawfully retained. The English stayed for six months until these matters could be settled. They were unaccustomed to the high standards of living at Messina, and thought themselves overcharged by the citizens. In their eyes most of the Messinese seemed to be either Greeks or Saracens; and when the crusaders began accosting the local women—"more with the intention of annoying the husbands than of seducing the wives"—any English soldiers caught unarmed were liable to be assassinated. Once Richard himself, after behaving with his usual truculence, only just escaped with his life. In revenge he occupied Messina, sacking the town and burning the Sicilian fleet in the harbour. For a month the English and French flags flew over the town. Tancred was obliged to buy peace, for he wanted English help against his German rival; while Richard, suitably mollified, gave King Arthur's sword Excalibur to Tancred and set out on his crusade.

These enforced concessions showed how reduced was Norman authority in the *regnum*. The King of Sicily could no longer speak on equal terms with England and France. To ensure Church support he had to renounce more privileges of the Apostolic Legateship, and generous grants had to be made to the religious orders and the towns. His coronation was itself another concession to the elective principle and hence marked another stage in the acquisition of power by the baronage.

Meanwhile Henry VI coveted the wealth of Sicily as a means of extending his ambitions into southern Europe and the Mediterranean. This had long been in the mind of the Western Emperors, and the marriage with Constance provided a pretext, as an alliance with the naval powers of Genoa and Pisa provided the means. In 1191 Henry left Germany for Rome in order to be crowned Emperor, and three years later he marched southward to win his wife's inheritance. By this time, Richard of England was a prisoner in Germany and unable to assist Tancred; indeed the English had to pay a huge ransom which helped to finance Henry's campaign. Tancred by 1193 had managed to establish himself with fair success, and had even partially restored the Moslem bureaucracy; but in 1194 he died. His son, who was crowned at Palermo as William III, was only a boy, and for the third time in the century a Queen dowager was left to guard the Hauteville traditions. What was left of the Sicilian fleet, perhaps outnumbered by the Pisan and Genoese ships, made no attempt to stop Henry at the straits, and Messina welcomed the Germans with enthusiasm; so did the Christians in Catania, as a means of getting rid of their Moslem garrison. Most of the nobility hurried to submit. Many Sicilians obviously approved of this invasion as an opportunity to further some sectional interest. As for the Germans, they were astonished at the riches and splendour of the island, and at the way Sicilians strangely prostrated themselves before the Emperor with their foreheads to the ground. At Palermo the eunuchs of the palace presented Henry with the keys of the Treasury, and on Christmas Day, 1194, he crowned himself King of Sicily.

In the eyes of her new sovereign, Sicily was an appendage of Germany, the most remote corner of a large empire. The documents of Tancred's reign seem to have been wantonly destroyed as illegal and hence unnecessary. What with mere loot and the dowry of Queen Constance, the accumulated assets of generations were taken away, and there was mention of a hundred and fifty mules laden with treasure crossing the Alps. This is how King Roger's jewelled vestments ended up in a Vienna museum. Possibly there was some exaggeration in the charge that Henry was particularly rapacious and brutal in his accession to power. In part this accusation simply shows feudal

47

resentment against a strong King, against someone who, despite their initial support, depreciated the local nobility and did not call upon them for counsel; against someone, indeed, who brought them to book for their encroachment on royal prerogatives and called upon them to submit evidence of their claims to privilege. In part the undoubted antagonism to him may have been due to the strangeness of his northern speech and manners. Instead of trying to placate his subjects, Henry certainly gave the impression that he had come solely to collect the spoils of war. He used his soldiers to collect tribute; his German generals were given Sicilian fiefs, and the knights of the Teutonic Order obtained confiscated Cistercian land; while in order to obtain the help of the Genoese fleet, Syracuse was promised to Genoa as almost an independent state. Most tyrannous of all, Tancred's family, who surrendered under promise of safe conduct, were straightway imprisoned, and the unfortunate William III died obscurely, in all probability murdered.

The country which had so meekly accepted Henry's arrival soon broke out in rebellion against him, but the Emperor easily put this down with the troops he had recruited for a crusade. According to the Italian chroniclers, his victims were emasculated, burnt alive or boiled in oil; and his cruelty did not spare clergy, women, or many people who could not possibly have been associated with the rising. One of the Hauteville family was said to have had a red hot crown nailed to his living head. In the middle of this repression, in 1197, the Emperor himself died, at the age of thirty-two, probably from malaria caught while hunting in the marshes. His body was taken to Archbishop Walter's new cathedral at Palermo, from which he had sacrilegiously cast out Tancred's remains.

Doctor and astrologer at the bedside of William II.
Below, Greek, Saracen and Latin notaries at the royal court.
Both from a 13th-century manuscript of Peter of Eboli.

Photographs Bodleian Library

The cupolas of San Giovanni degli Eremiti, Palermo: 12th century

PART 2

Hohenstaufen, Angevins and Aragonese
1200–1375

Chapter 5

STUPOR MUNDI

Frederick II, the next King of Sicily, was on his father's side a Hohenstaufen from Swabia, but through his mother a Norman and the grandson of the great King Roger I. His boyhood was spent in the exotic world of the royal palace in Palermo, and there at the age of three he became King. Private individuals usurped the functions of law and public administration during his minority, all the more so when Queen Constance died in 1198 after appointing Pope Innocent III guardian to her son; and though Innocent was one of the greatest Popes, there was little he could do to defend the interests of his ward. A succession of German barons, enriched by grants from the deceased Henry, defied the papal troops and took possession of Palermo and the young King.

Quite as dangerous, and a threat both to Church and State, were those Arabic-speaking Moslems who still survived in the interior and south-west of Sicily. In 1197, much as in 1161 and 1189, race riots broke out, during the anarchy which followed Henry's death, and the persecuted minority was quick to react. The disappearance of the court eunuchs meant that many remaining Saracen farmers and villeins had new Christian landlords who were less considerate and more exacting; moreover the tithes for Innocent's crusades provoked much resentment among this alien population. Some had altogether lost their means of livelihood in 1189–90; tens of thousands must have left for North Africa, and others now took advantage of this state of civil war to travel round in bands stealing food and trying to recover their property. As their rebellion gathered strength, castles and villages were captured. The rebels seized Girgenti because they needed a port in order to maintain communications with Africa: its cathedral became a barracks and its bishop was their prisoner for a year. The Abbot of Monreale also lost control over a wide extent of his huge domain, and Moslem freebooters despoiled a leper hospital even in the outskirts of Palermo itself. Like subsequent bandits in Sicilian history they were exploited by politicians, in this case by German barons who flourished on chaos and rebellion.

When Frederick took over the government in 1208, one of his first problems was to defeat these bandits, for the whole authority of the state was in jeopardy, and such was the terror caused by the Moslems and their Christian accomplices that farmers were refusing to move outside the villages and cultivate the fields. Moreover there was strong pressure on him by the Church. Ecclesiastics had lent a good deal of money to the state in the time of Pope Innocent, and now they demanded his help when their Moslem villeins absconded and Church lands and revenues were seized. Frederick had to leave Sicily in 1212 and did not come back until he returned as Emperor in 1220, but then he opened a full-scale war in order to control the no-man's-land of the interior. This area was sometimes referred to as the 'March of the Saracens', and here the Moslem leader, Morabit, acted as an independent sovereign. Frederick now called on the Sicilian barons for military service in a succession of campaigns; and by systematically burning the harvests, gradually he starved his opponents to death or into submission.

The barons, too, and other overmighty subjects, had to be brought to order in this restoration of state authority. Gervase of Tilbury, who had been living in Sicily, feared the deceitful and warlike inhabitants of this rich but sinister country: like others after him, he found them "cunning in doing harm, silent under abuse". Many nobles and ecclesiastics had been illegally encroaching on regalian rights, and the Pope had given Sicilian baronies to his friends. The Pisans had established a pirate nest at Syracuse, though subsequently this was wrested from Pisa by the Genoese who set up an independent county in southeastern Sicily and also seized Malta. The royal demesne, on which the Normans had largely relied for their revenue, was gradually being whittled away.

On Frederick's return from Germany in 1220 this trend was at once reversed. He ordered the destruction of all private castles built since 1189, arguing that fortification was a royal prerogative even in baronial territory; and he added that no older castles should be restored without a permit. The Norman laws about feudalism were precisely re-stated. Vassals had to present their charters for verification or rejection, and any grant obtained since 1189 could be voided. The royal demesne had to be restored; royal justiciars took back rights of justice which had been usurped; and barons were once again restricted in alienating or sub-letting their fiefs, since they had merely a right of use, whereas the King kept his title of eminent domain. Heirs could not inherit an estate without paying a succession fee and recognising these regalian rights, nor should widows or daughters marry without royal consent.

Nowhere else in his empire was Frederick so imperious and authoritarian, for whereas in Germany he was a feudal sovereign, in Sicily he lived up to his titles of Augustus and Caesar. Here even his coins were named *Augustales* and their design was copied from those of ancient Rome. When he summoned a parliament in 1221, the country felt a directing authority reminiscent of King Roger; dice and other games of chance were forbidden; citizens had to return home before the third evening bell; Jews had to wear a specified dress; prostitutes had to live outside the city walls and not attend public baths along with honest women. Here was a totalitarian desire to regulate even private behaviour, and these were laws which Frederick meant to be observed. He even tried to prohibit marriage with foreigners.

Traditions of Roman law were very much alive in Sicily; and though justice by ordeal had its place, though feudatories still kept their social and military importance, nevertheless the King employed professional jurists and politicians who were in the tradition of George of Antioch, Maio and Matthew of Salerno. He created a state university at Naples for the training of lawyers and administrators, and forbade both students and professors to attend foreign schools where he could not control the curriculum. One of these jurists, Peter della Vigna, as logothete and protonotary of Sicily, was the main author of the *Liber Augustalis*, the legal code of 1231 which subsumed previous Norman laws and gave them an extra dimension as a charter of Hohenstaufen absolutism. Whereas Roger I had allowed Lombards, Greeks, Arabs and Franks to be judged each by their own laws, Frederick wanted a more unified system. The *Liber Augustalis* was promulgated in an elegant Latin which in itself was a sign of new times, though a Greek translation was put out for the Greek-speaking communities which still survived in the *regnum*.

In their comprehensiveness and detail, and above all in their concept of royal authority, Frederick's laws illustrate the singularity of Sicily in western Europe. The *regnum* was held by the Emperor from God himself. Clerics were not to interfere in secular matters. Criminal justice was reserved to the sovereign despite any apparent concession to the contrary, and though prelates and barons could exercise minor jurisdiction with permission, appeals should lie to the King's court. The island was divided administratively at the river Salso, eastern Sicily being joined with Calabria on the mainland: a justiciar was attached to each section, and he also controlled direct taxation and the army. Justiciars would hold office for one year, and had to be laymen and strangers to their province; they were charged to ensure that trials were based on proper evidence. Only people serving the King and his court could wear swords, and no royal official should accept a gift from people under his jurisdiction. Anyone could be punished who blasphemed the name of God and the Holy Virgin, or who habitually frequented taverns, or prepared love potions. Adulterous women were to have their noses cut off, and husbands were to be publicly whipped if indulgent to their wives' adultery. Torture should not be used except on people of low birth or on those *bravi* whom the barons hired to terrorise the countryside. No one should practise medicine without government licence and a university degree. Jews and Moslems were under royal protection: the Jews were allowed to give loans at up to 10 per cent, but for other people usury was a crime.

Once the jurists had prepared this code of laws, Frederick summoned a general *colloquium* at Melfi in 1231, where his chief subjects in proper feudal style could hear and confirm his proposals. This kind of parliament was becoming a fairly regular organ of government. Leading ecclesiastics, barons and other prominent citizens were appointed to meet twice a year in each province to investigate everything from accusations of heresy to complaints against government officials; while other and more general assemblies met occasionally to lend their extra weight to the imposition of taxes and the promulgation of laws. To attend these parliaments was an obligation rather than a privilege. By the 1230s it was becoming the practice for several burgesses of the main cities to be summoned alongside the chief

54

feudatories, and though at first these citizens were nominated by the royal bailiffs, at the end of the century they were often being elected in a kind of public assembly.

Self-government by the cities, however, was not allowed, for urban communities could not be permitted to escape the net of imperial authority. Sicily was still a fairly rich country where one might have expected a vigorous town life, but in fact she never knew anything like the independent communes which existed in northern Italy; and although this may reflect a simple lack of civic enterprise, it also derived from the fact that the Norman monarchy was too authoritarian and too strong to need to encourage the cities against the baronage. Since there was no tradition of civic freedom, there had been no need to bribe them into submission with charters of freedom. Communal autonomy would have diminished the royal prerogative. Just occasionally, for example at Cefalù where the local bishop had jurisdiction, citizens won some share in choosing their bailiff or *baiulo*; but at Messina the governor, with his Greek name of *strategoto*, was nominated by the crown, and so was the castellan of Palermo. Each city was dominated by a royal castle, and Frederick built other fortresses at strategic points inland. These were not residential castles, but military. Apparently French engineers and stonemasons were imported to build them, and the castle of Ursino in Catania and of Maniaces in Syracuse harbour remained to show some elements of this northern style of military architecture.

More than any other Sicilian town, Messina had experienced some degree of independence. Messina possessed interests which differed from those of agricultural Sicily, and her contacts with the outside world made her more restive. The Messinese had rebelled against William II in 1168. They rebelled against Tancred in 1194; and, in return for supporting the German invasion, Henry then allowed them to have a free port with preferential customs duties. Genoese, Lombards, Pisans, Florentines and Catalans took advantage of this to open or re-open warehouses there, and Queen Constance chose it as her seat of government in 1197–8. At this nodal point of communication, and under the stimulus of having to resist rival armies in successive periods of anarchy, Messina developed a fairly strong civic consciousness and a class of merchants who could sometimes act in concert and carry political weight. Occasionally they invented privileges and obtained forged documents to prove them. They claimed the right to mine iron, to take timber anywhere for their ships, to fish anywhere, to choose their own magistrates, and not to recognise the jurisdiction of any court outside their own walls.

Frederick revoked many of the supposed privileges of Messina as inconsistent with his notion of an overriding state. This action was ill-received, and so was his taxation, especially of the silk trade. Even more obnoxious, his strict government made tax avoidance harder than before, and non-payment sometimes led to distraint on personal property. Hence another revolt at Messina in 1232. Frederick brought over an army from the mainland, and the ringleaders were hanged or burnt. Catania and Syracuse had also been restless, but apparently forestalled his anger by surrendering; and when Centuripe tried to resist him, it was utterly destroyed and its surviving population moved to a new city magniloquently called Augusta. Believing as he did in his own God-given authority, he thought that rebellion was sinful and justified the harshest penalties.

Frederick tied the cities to the state, even though this may have seemed to sacrifice economics to politics. Sicilian history had taught him that prosperity came from a strong kingship, and up to a point he was right: only later events were to show that economic development was arrested in Sicily just when the free maritime communities elsewhere in Italy were becoming adventurous and rich. Frederick's subjection of the towns helped to ensure that there was never any class of merchants or civic officials independent and vigorous enough to offset the landowning aristocracy; and this lack of challenge to the aristocracy was to be a fundamental factor in the political, cultural and economic decline of Sicily. Whenever strong government failed, it was the nobles and not the local cities which filled the vacuum of power. It was therefore foreign towns—Pisa, Genoa, Venice, Amalfi, Lucca—which dominated Sicilian commerce. Foreign merchants showed in the first place that there were profits to be made in Sicily, and in the second place ensured that those profits would leave the country without fertilising local enterprise.

The Emperor no doubt intended to be helpful towards trade

and agriculture, though one suspects that he encouraged them mainly to obtain increased taxation for his imperial policy; but this taxation then counteracted any possibility of economic growth. Since the income from customs duties and crown lands did not suffice to pay for his unusually expensive form of government, one result was that the feudal *collecta*, instead of being an emergency tax on feudatories, became a general tax on property; and it was sometimes collected more than once in the same year. To co-ordinate expenditure with available resources was not easy. Frederick was aiming at the general good, for the proceeds of taxation helped to maintain law and order, and this was an inestimable benefit to the economy. Equally well-intentioned was his attempt to tidy up the diverse systems of weights and measures: even neighbouring villages had utterly incompatible systems of measurement, owing to their multifarious racial and historical origins, and this had been a great obstacle to trade. Frederick also tried to limit usury, that great burden on Sicilian agriculture; and he set up state shipyards and revived the feudal obligation to provide timber and sailors. Another of his regulations prescribed that fairs should be held each year to stimulate internal commerce.

The Sicilian economy must have partially run down in the years 1190–1220, and Frederick's legislation was an attempt to introduce some order into chaos. Nevertheless it was optimistic to believe that such laws could be enforced, as it was optimistic to think that the profits of trade could simply be diverted to the state. All mines and minerals in Sicily were claimed as a regalian monopoly, and, except by royal license, only the crown agents were allowed to sell iron, steel, pitch, hemp, silk and wheat. The dyeing industry was another exclusive prerogative. The salt pans of Sicily were famous and were a main factor in the growth of Trapani, but instead of salt being freely exportable, it now became a crown monopoly, and as a result sold at what was said to be six times its former price. Some of Frederick's regulations and monopolies may not have been particularly harmful, and certainly government revenues must have been increased; but he could not compel people into prosperity, and increased taxation was not automatically an index of economic health.

Agriculture received plenty of direction from Frederick's

attentive and curious mind. The King himself was the chief landowner. He exported a good deal of his own wheat to North Africa, and the port authorities had to give his ships priority in loading. Even when fighting abroad, he wrote to his stewards about sowing and about his vines, and to ensure that feathers were collected to make mattresses. He gave out uncultivated land with the peremptory obligation to clear it and sow wheat, and he ordained that peasants should not have their animals or agricultural implements taken for debt. On receipt of complaints he insisted that his forest wardens should not curtail established rights of wood-cutting, and stray animals were not to be impounded even though their owners could be held liable for damage. Shepherds had special rights when moving their flocks, but animals could graze on other people's property only if their hooves were on the public highway. When the countryside was ravaged by locusts, Frederick set up an emergency committee and ordered people to collect a certain weight of insects or pay a fine. Many of these regulations must have been taken over from previous practice, and their very repetition suggests that they must have been hard to enforce.

One of the industries encouraged was that of silk. Sicily and Calabria had been the first places in Italy to produce silk, and in 1191 the King of England while in Sicily acquired a silken marquee in which several hundred people could dine. This luxury trade was fostered by the Emperor. So was the processing of sugar. Sugar cane had been extensively grown in irrigated fields, and Frederick imported experts to train apprentices in an art which may have flagged with the exodus of Arab artisans. He was the last Sicilian sovereign for many centuries who possessed the authority, the resources, and the technological curiosity and knowledge to develop the methods of irrigation from which prosperity had once derived. Archaeological studies have revealed a dam which possibly he built to make an artificial lake a few miles from Augusta, and this must have been a considerable achievement in early thirteenth-century Europe.

Frederick's inexorable and often cruel adventurousness is shown in the way he shifted whole populations. He re-peopled Malta, and brought Lombards and Greeks to settle in underpopulated areas of Sicily. He obliterated some villages as a punishment, just as he built new ones—Terranova was his foundation, on the old Greek site of Gela. Most ruthless of all, he transplanted many thousands of Moslems to the mainland, and set them up in a military colony at Lucera, near Foggia, which became the headquarters of his professional army. After the defeat of the Moslem rebellion in 1225, these unruly but by now impoverished subjects had for a time given no trouble. Many were shepherds, and to some of them Frederick leased out large flocks of his own sheep; but we know that they were persecuted, and perhaps this explains another Moslem revolt in Sicily which erupted in 1243. Quite apart from race and religion, they were bound to suffer from the perennial hostility between shepherds and farmers, mountaineers and valley dwellers, nomads and tillers of the soil. Frederick tried to protect law-abiding Moslem citizens from injury or offence, but he could not tolerate refusal of the surviving Islamic communities to be absorbed. They desperately resisted the King's armies for three more years after 1243, but ultimately they depended on the plainsmen for their food and so most of them were again compelled to submit. Where possible the survivors were transplanted *en masse* to join Frederick's janissary corps in Lucera. Others no doubt continued to live a troglodyte existence in the inaccessible interior.

This series of campaigns must have done considerable harm to Sicily: it left society more homogeneous, but only by destroying a class of small traders and an element in agriculture which was impossible to replace. Wheat production perhaps never fully recovered from this blow. It is more than likely that most of the industrial artisans had been Moslems, and perhaps most of the industrial entrepreneurs too; if so, their departure would by itself explain a decline in the silk and sugar trades. But this civil war had other deleterious effects. The burning of crops was always the most effective method against such elusive outlaws and could easily become a most destructive forest fire. Between 1160 and 1246, emigration and slaughter of these Moslems left wide areas waste and empty: it has been estimated that half the village settlements which existed in the early Middle Ages were to disappear subsequently, and many of them must have disappeared for this one reason. Of fifty hamlets owned by the abbey of Monreale in an area of Moslem settlement, only a dozen survive today, and nearly all those have different names which suggest a later re-foundation. The evidence of tomb-stones and family names has been used to confirm that, by the late thirteenth century, expulsion or absorption had entirely overwhelmed a people who had recently constituted the bulk of the population.

Frederick turned against the Sicilian Arabs because they were rebels, not because of their religion. His action did not prevent the Moslem states of North Africa continuing to treat him with cordiality. The Pope's propagandists complained that he had Saracen pages and a *seraglio*, and that he employed oriental dancers to entertain his guests. Moslems accompanied his retinue even when he visited the Holy Land; and the core of his army remained the Moslem expeditionary force garrisoned at Lucera in Apulia, where his trumpeters were Negro slaves and the muezzin openly called the faithful to prayer. Frederick when he died was wrapped in a garment with embroidered Cufic charac-ters woven no doubt in the palace factory at Palermo.

No wonder that Popes referred to him as a baptised Sultan. He was altogether of too secular and rationalist a disposition to appeal to them. He was also their most dangerous political enemy, since his empire encircled the Papal States. He was therefore repeatedly excommunicated and verbally deposed. Yet Frederick did not serve the Church too badly. He reduced the residual authority of Islam and Byzantium in southern Italy. He went on a successful crusade and became King of Jerusalem. He set up the Tribunal of the Inquisition in Palermo against the Waldensians, the Paterines, the 'circumcised ones' and many other specified brands of heretic. Heresy offended him, chiefly because it represented disobedience, and because in some of its contemporarily fashionable forms it threatened to disturb social order. Frederick did not claim to depose Popes, and he interfered less than Roger in Church government. Nevertheless he resisted the claims of the papacy to intervene in temporal affairs, as he absolutely rejected their contention that Sicily was by rights a papal fief. Unlike his predecessors, he did not endow new monasteries and bishoprics, but pre-ferred to build castles; and he effectively forbade the Church to accumulate more land in mortmain, for unlike lay feudatories the Church did not die, and this mortmain would diminish the royal rights of eminent domain. Despite the Church council of 1215, moreover, he insisted that ecclesiastics were not exempt from taxes but must pay the *collecta* just like laymen.

It was his boyhood education in Sicily which no doubt gave the Emperor his inquisitive mind and made him want to hear more than the Christian answers. He knew the works of Maimonides, the great rabbi who had died at Cairo in 1204; and the Sultan of Egypt deliberately chose Arab scientists and poets to act as ambassadors to Sicily. Frederick preferred to discuss religious and intellectual questions with Jewish and Moslem philosophers since he thought them particularly knowledgeable. He once shocked the orthodox by sending out a list of enquiries to discover how non-Christians looked upon immortality and the soul. Such horror did his strange beliefs and habits inspire among pious Christians that he was even accused of keeping an army of magicians who practised the horrible cults of Astaroth and Beelzebub. The friars spread— and perhaps invented—tales about him bringing up children in isolated silence to see if they would speak Hebrew, and dissecting living men to observe the physiology of digestion. Even his regular use of baths scandalised many westerners as too strange for comprehension. Yet Frederick's sharp differentiation from contemporary fashions of behaviour illustrates the special environment of Norman Palermo, where society was naturally cosmopolitan, where religious intolerance had not yet become an inveterate obsession, and where numerous public bath houses still provided a welcome service for the community and a good revenue for the state.

In his personal patronage the Emperor inclined more to science than to art. He gave little stimulating impulse to architecture or to monumental and decorative sculpture, but he had a great desire for knowledge. Rare books and scientific instruments were the gifts he most welcomed, and a silver planetarium from the Sultan of Damascus was his most prized possession of all. He was interested in technical problems like draining marshes and making machines of war, but also in abstract problems of physics. When on crusade, he tried to discover from Arab experts why objects partially immersed in water appeared bent. He particularly liked the company of astronomers and mathematicians, and his court therefore became, with Oxford and Paris, one of the centres of mathematics in Latin Europe.

Michael Scot, Frederick's court physician and astrologer, was placed by Dante in hell among the wizards. This Scotsman was a philosopher, zoologist and noted translator from Arabic and Greek, and also an enthusiast for Aristotle and Averroes. After him, the next most important intellectual at court was Theodore, a Greek from Egypt, who prepared medicines and horoscopes for the Emperor. Theodore was a secretary who was also translator, ambassador and scientist, and his translations like those of Scot were not without influence on the Italian Renaissance.

Frederick was particularly interested in animals. He introduced new breeds of horse to cross with domestic strains. At Malta he reared camels and falcons, at Lucera leopards. His zoo included lions, panthers, monkeys, a giraffe, and an elephant given him by the Sultan of Egypt. Sometimes the zoo went with him on his travels, to the embarrassment of his hosts. He was said to mark fish in order to study their movements. He was fascinated by birds and particularly those used in his favourite sport of hunting. He spent thirty years studying falcons, bringing experts at great cost from the east, and importing different varieties from as far away as Ireland, Bulgaria and India: he then helped to compile a treatise in Latin on their various species, their anatomical structure, their mode of nesting, and on ways of catching and training them. The book suggests that he studied the phases of bird flight and the positions which the feathers took when in motion. Believing in direct observation, he was able to correct Aristotle and Pliny by the evidence of his own eyes.

These varied interests confirm that Frederick's education had been much more in Sicily than Germany. Likewise he turned naturally to a 'national' literature and a poetic Sicilian language. The spoken dialect was not dissimilar to the dialect of today—one of the first written examples we possess is a list of magic practices associated with taking a wife, including a recipe for a potion of sugared wine and bear's bile. Frederick's original language may well have been this dialect, since he was in Sicily from the age of two to thirteen; but the language of court was rather Norman-French, and the King must also have known Latin, Provençal, German and perhaps some Arabic and

Greek. From the Provençals he learnt the art of writing poetry, which therefore became fashionable with his courtiers, and the new Sicilian language of court poetry had some of its roots in southern France.

The literature of Provence had a widespread influence in Italy at this decisive moment when a new and truly Italian language and literature were being forged; and the court at Palermo was one point of entry. Many Frenchmen had come to live permanently in Sicily, bringing with them the literary traditions of their homeland. Through the Queens of both William I and William II there had been links with Provence, and many troubadours with their courtly love poetry came to Messina in the army of Richard Cœur-de-Lion. In 1209 the young Frederick married Constance of Provence, who arrived in Palermo with a train of five hundred cavaliers. These influences helped to make his court a creative centre of literature. Among the lawyers who accompanied him on his travels was Giacomo of Lentini, author of a Provençal-type lyric which is the first poem in true Sicilian that has survived, and we know that there were many other writers in this same class of professional administrators. Dante and Petrarch admitted the preeminence of Sicilian vernacular poetry and of this first Italian literary language. To some extent it was the deliberate creation of a royal patron, who not only wrote poetry for his own pleasure but deliberately tried to make the *regnum* a single community with an individual culture and literature of its own.

Frederick died in 1250. His last days were spent in one of his Apulian castles surrounded by his Moslem retinue, and his body was then taken to Palermo for burial. He had been in some ways the most remarkable ruler in medieval Europe, yet his achievement in Sicily was personal, something very much imposed by himself, neither moulded by enduring forces nor genuinely accepted by his subjects. Few of his positive achievements long survived his death. He had made many enemies, and Sicily was to suffer accordingly. The jurists who were the backbone of his administration did not form an enduring class, and as he needed the support of a feudal army he had not challenged the social foundation of aristocratic power. The feudatories were overawed while he lived, but were able to undo his handiwork afterwards.

Frederick said that he loved Sicily above all his other possessions; but in fact his Kingdom of Sicily saw its physical centre of gravity shifting to the mainland, and he came to prefer residence in the royal hunting castles of Apulia. Few, perhaps surprisingly few, of his ministers were natives of the island. Palermo had been a useful capital so long as Sicily was mainly involved with Africa and the East; but Henry and Frederick brought with them a European policy, sometimes a German policy, in which the island of Sicily was cast in a very subordinate role. Her wealth, therefore, or what was left after pillaging by Baldwin of Jerusalem, Richard of England and Henry of Swabia, was further expended on projects in which any Sicilian concern was minimal.

This was a quite fundamental change. So long as Sicily belonged to the world of North Africa and the Levant she had been rich; but when forcibly attached to western Europe she lost many economic advantages, and her geographic position instead of being a boon became a handicap. The straits of Messina, narrow though they were, could be a serious impediment to trade with the mainland, and the Mediterranean instead of a highway became a frontier. After 1194, Sicily was one small peripheral region in a succession of large empires. She had to support Frederick's campaigns in Germany and undergo a conflict with the papacy which from her point of view was as unnecessary as it was damaging. Compared to this, the fact that Frederick ceased to visit Palermo was a minor blow, yet that too marked the end of an age. The silk workers and jewellers of the palace factory seem to have been taken to Apulia along with the other expelled Moslems and probably most of the administrative staff. The mosaic workshop of Palermo was little used after 1225 except for repairs, because in the absence of the King there was no employment. The city had no new buildings in the thirteenth century to compare with those of the twelfth. Palermo was left a dead city. After 1250 the 'Sicilian' poets were not truly natives of the island, and Tuscany took over from Sicily as the most creative centre of Italian literature. Rival European dynasties were now to fight out their quarrels on Sicilian soil and at Sicilian expense.

Chapter 6

THE SICILIAN VESPERS, 1282

The year 1250 began a long period of decline for Sicily, decline in power, prosperity and security. Frederick's achievements may have been a mixed blessing, but without him central authority was defective and the economy deteriorated. Money was no longer invested either in productive enterprise or works of art, so much as in civil warfare which settled nothing. The community spirit was lacking which might have constructed a city-state civilisation as in northern Italy, for although the Sicilian cities tried to assert themselves in the immediate years after 1250, they were torn by internal factions. Government weakness encouraged people to ignore the law and resort to private justice; and so, at the very moment when feudalism showed signs of declining elsewhere, Sicily experienced the defeat of both royal authority and civic autonomy at the hands of an unruly baronage. According to some calculations (on admittedly thin evidence), the population fell by half during the next two centuries of misrule and anarchy. Agriculture suffered inevitably, because of civil wars, depopulation and the precedence taken by private over public welfare.

The Emperor's death was followed by fifteen years of civil discord and family vendettas in which rival contestants fought for what was left of Norman Sicily. Ten of Frederick's children and grandchildren died in prison or by violence. At first his son Conrad attempted to establish himself against the forces of disorder. Frederick's old marshal, Pietro Ruffo, also tried to carve out an autonomous *signoria* based on Messina, but the mercantile elements in this town successfully rebelled in 1255 and declared themselves to be an autonomous commune. In the prevailing anarchy many towns tried to annex their surrounding territory, which they needed in order to control supplies of food. Messina thus subdued and almost destroyed Taormina, while Palermo extended its authority to Cefalù. Meantime many a feudal castle was rebuilt as a base for armed bands who plundered the countryside and obstructed commerce.

An interesting attempt was now made by some cities to set

up a kind of federal republic, and they invited a papal representative to act as their leader; but when Conrad died, many of the barons, disliking mercantile autonomy quite as much as they disliked royal centralisation, backed Frederick's other son Manfred and imprisoned the papal vicar. The Popes were none the less determined to assert their feudal supremacy, and for several years tried to sell the crown of Sicily to Richard of Cornwall, brother of the English King. Richard was tempted, but the price was too high. Another offer was later made to the same King's eight-year-old son, Edmund of Lancaster; it was accepted, and a papal Legate formally invested this English prince with the kingdom. Edmund for ten years called himself 'King of Sicily by the grace of God', and even sent the Bishop of Hereford to collect taxes from his new subjects in order to make up the purchase money; but the prospect of having to conquer a recalcitrant people was daunting, and the barons in England by threatening civil war forced the Pope to think again.

France not only possessed far greater resources than England, but some of its people nurtured strong Mediterranean ambitions. In 1261 a Frenchman became Pope and deposed Edmund for not having paid the agreed price; instead he chose Charles of Anjou, brother of the French King, St. Louis. As a younger brother, Charles was here being given an unexpected chance to acquire a kingdom. The interests of Naples and Sicily concerned him as little as they did the Pope. He therefore agreed to take over the English debt to the papacy, to pay a large annual tribute and to send a white palfrey in sign of feudal subjection to Rome. He promised he would no longer claim the rights of Apostolic Legateship, but would free the Sicilian clergy from the royal tribunals and from payment of taxes. Backed by this agreement, Charles set out from France in 1265 to conquer Manfred, and in the following year was crowned King of Sicily at Rome.

Manfred, the Hohenstaufen champion, had already been crowned much more authentically at Palermo in 1258, and he was not a papal appointee but claimed to rule by hereditary right as well as baronial election. Although Sicilians had not been enthusiastic for Conrad and his German entourage, his half-brother commanded support as someone born and bred in south Italy. Like his father, Manfred was to become a legend in folk memory, as the blond, tragic hero who stood for Sicilian independence against the Pope and the French despoilers of Sicilian wealth. Manfred inherited some of Frederick's scientific and cultural interests. Like his father, and for the same reasons, his enemies called him 'the Sultan of Lucera'. But he, too, preferred to live on the mainland, and the island of Sicily had little to gain from his war against Charles of Anjou.

Charles's main advantage was that the Pope proclaimed a holy war on his behalf, and the money raised in Europe for a crusade was thus used to support a French conquest of Sicily. Not only was the treasure and plate of the papal chapel liberally pledged, but crusaders were released from their vows so that they could fight against other Christians. In 1266, Manfred was defeated and killed, leaving his nephew, the fourteen-year-old Conradin, as the last hope of the Hohenstaufen. Two years later there was an even more decisive battle: the Angevins almost lost the day, but Conradin's army scattered too quickly in search of plunder. The unfortunate boy was taken prisoner and publicly beheaded. The Pope's campaign to exterminate the 'viper's brood' had almost succeeded.

Charles of Anjou by sheer ability made himself the greatest potentate in Europe. The Florentine chronicler, Villani, gives a memorable description of him. He was a good fighter. As a ruler he was severe but magnanimous, faithful to his promises, firm in adversity, a man of few words and little sense of humour. Charles was accustomed to say that sleep was time lost. He was rigorous in justice, generous to his soldiers, and notoriously ambitious to acquire land, power and money. Villani adds that the minstrels did not weep at his death.

Like every invader of Sicily, Charles found some local support. Resentful of government and of taxation, some Sicilians were always ready to invoke foreign help against their rulers, until a new master tried to recoup himself for the expenses of his invasion and so began the cycle of vengeance and rebellion all over again. Almost invariably the population was divided against itself, and individual cities or families were likely to use any change of dynasty to assert their private interest. In this case Messina and Syracuse, the same towns that had once rebelled against Frederick, now helped the French to subdue the island.

Charles's army was largely made up of adventurers whose first aim was land and plunder, and, as participants in a punitive papal crusade, they were under little obligation to respect persons, property or tradition. Charles merely sent his subordinates to conquer Sicily. He ignored the custom whereby Kings of Sicily were elected at Palermo by barons and people. As a usurper, he had first to weaken that sense of the state which the Normans had assiduously cultivated. He represented religious intolerance in a country which had flourished through toleration, and his enemies were therefore treated as impious heretics who could be mutilated with all the sanctions of religion. The invading generals were more cruel than cruelty itself, said one chronicler; and when the town of Augusta remained loyal to the Hohenstaufen, the French, aided by the Messinese, razed it to the ground and slaughtered the survivors. It took some years of civil war before Charles could claim to command the main strategic centres of Calabria and Sicily, and these years left an enduring mark. Many animosities were stored up for the future; rival villages used the occasion to settle old scores, and barons set up as minor potentates outside the law.

Probably the French behaved no more arbitrarily than the Normans and Germans before them, but there were now additional vested interests in existence, and offence was the more difficult to avoid. In order to pay his knights, Charles confiscated many large estates; this enabled him to give fiefs to hundreds of Frenchmen, and at the same time many humbler immigrants were imported to re-people some of the areas laid waste. Those of the old aristocracy who kept their baronies often did so only through bribery, sometimes having to pay two or three times over. Existing fiefs were examined in the now traditional manner to discover any defects in title, for which purpose a great ransacking of parchments was carried out. French barons were appointed to control the cities, and most of the higher royal officers and justiciars were Frenchmen, or else were Italians from the mainland who were equally unpopular.

Angevin feudalism, as a result, took on something of the aspect of a military garrison occupying a resentful province.

New *corvées* were introduced from the alien traditions of France. Hunting or grazing in the royal forests could be severely punished even where sanctioned by custom; while the King's animals could feed anywhere, even on private property and on growing crops. There were complaints that men of birth and title were forced to wait at table and turn the spit in the King's kitchen, and that heiresses were either forbidden to marry or married off to fortune-hunting Frenchmen.

Equally unforgiveable in the eyes of the island aristocracy was that Charles centralised public life on Naples. To him, as to Frederick, the mainland provinces were more pleasant to live in and therefore received more of his patronage. They were richer, more populous, less cut off from the mainstream of social life and politics. There and not in Sicily he found his professional administrators. There he found the strategic base for his foreign policy. The islanders by comparison were difficult people and nurtured a fierce sense of independence. Sicily was hard to conquer and still harder to administer efficiently, while the straits were a big psychological and logistical barrier when seen from the north. Charles therefore lavished his attention on Naples. He visited the island only once, in transit from Tunis, and no parliament met there during his reign.

It is not easy to assess the criticisms of Charles's government, especially as so many of the relevant archives were later destroyed. Subsequent Italian historians were harsh on him as a Frenchman; contemporaries because he was efficient and exacting without being genial. In particular, those who had done well out of the interregnum resented his attempt to reconstitute the royal demesne at baronial expense. He was more favourably disposed towards the cities than Frederick had been —he sometimes allowed them to elect their own judges and tax collectors—though this would have been another reason for the barons to dislike him. Sicilian commerce almost certainly profited from his re-establishment of closer links with Naples; and Charles did something to refurbish royal taxation, basing himself on Frederick's and Manfred's financial registers. Employing many of the experienced Hohenstaufen administrators, Charles obtained more accurate information on baronial lands than any subsequent ruler for centuries, and this would have been a sure cause of unpopularity.

Sicily was going to rebel against Charles as it had never rebelled against Frederick, and it was his taxation and lack of concern for local feelings which chiefly generated the outburst of 1282. Charles had promised to rule by the good laws of William II—which meant, if it meant anything, that he would be less extortionate and less totalitarian than Frederick. In practice, however, he resorted to forced loans and frequently imposed the *collecta* without ever asking for parliamentary advice and consent. Compulsory hospitality was exacted for his retainers, ship money for his navy, fortification money for the upkeep of forty royal castles. He was said to have regularly minted bad coins at Messina, taking the profits for himself and caring little about the damage to trade. He was precluded by his submission to the papacy from adequately taxing the clergy; yet he and the Pope had borrowed heavily to finance his conquest of Sicily, and the cost of this had to fall on someone. He also had an ambitious foreign policy for which Sicily had to help pay. Perhaps he and his Tuscan bankers, deceived by what they knew of ancient history and the fertile plains round Naples and Palermo, shared the illusion that the south was inexhaustibly rich; but in fact these fabled riches depended on good government, social harmony and the constant attentions of an abundant labour force interested in agricultural productivity. Such conditions no longer existed. Sicily simply could not carry the weight of Charles's extensive ambitions, and the result was the most notable rebellion in Sicilian history.

The opposition to Charles centred on the King of Aragon. By amalgamating with Catalonia, Aragon had recently obtained in Barcelona one of the great ports of the Mediterranean, and the bankers and merchants of this town were already established in southern Italy: Sicily, as an agricultural-pastoral country, was to them an obvious source of food and an outlet for the growing textile industry of north-eastern Spain. In 1262, Peter of Aragon married Manfred's daughter Constance, the last heir of the Hohenstaufen, and this gave him a claim to Sicily. He also found that the younger sons of the Spanish feudal aristocracy could sometimes be tempted by the prospect of obtaining principalities in this distant island. In addition there was a straight commercial rivalry, for the Catalans were competitors of the Tuscan bankers and textile merchants who had underwritten Charles of Anjou. Unlike Tuscany, however, Catalonia had a fleet, and history had shown that control of Sicily depended on sea power.

To the Hohenstaufen party in Italy, Peter of Aragon was the leading representative of the anti-papal ghibelline tradition. Another exponent of this tradition was John of Procida who, after being professor of medicine and attending Frederick II in his last illness, became Chancellor of the *regnum* under Manfred; and when his possessions were confiscated by the Angevins, John went to live at the court of Aragon. Others took refuge in Tunis. Stories were told of how John subsequently visited Sicily in disguise to prepare a revolution; and of how he brought together the anti-papal forces of Europe, even persuading the Eastern Emperor to help finance a Sicilian revolt. Some such conspiracy undoubtedly did exist, though the stories contained strange discrepancies and have never been fully authenticated; yet John was an Italian from the mainland, the servant of Aragonese rather than Sicilian interests, and in fact the population of Palermo rebelled ahead of time and defeated the Angevins on their own.

Since about 1500 this rebellion has been called the 'Sicilian Vespers'. Probably the term was a misnomer and there was no connection with any evening hour, but the name has remained as a permanent symbol of the desire for Sicilian independence. On Easter Monday, at the end of March, 1282, people were gathered outside the walls of Palermo on this public holiday. French soldiers were searching people for arms. One soldier apparently was suspected of taking liberties with a woman, something which in this society was a greater offence than political persecution. In a moment of impetuous anger he was killed; and this touched off what may possibly have been an organised political revolt, but which has a much closer resemblance to one of those improvised explosions of popular vendetta and social revolution familiar in later Sicilian history. The most violent feelings of xenophobia were involved even if they lacked constructive aim. Every stranger whose accent betrayed him was slaughtered, and several thousand Frenchmen were said to have been killed in a few hours. Monasteries were broken open and monks killed, old men and infants butchered, and even Sicilian women thought to be pregnant by

Frenchmen were ripped open. Christian burial was often refused. This was not a feudal revolt but a popular revolution,
and just for that reason its immediate success was astonishing;
but, for the same reason, it was particularly barbarous. Only
subsequent political developments made it possible for a
horrible massacre to be magnified into the most glorious event
in Sicilian history.

Some of the leading citizens of Palermo at once called a
'parliament' and the city was declared an independent republic: this suggests that they may have envied the growth of
municipal autonomy elsewhere in Italy. After a few days
Corleone followed suit, and then made a treaty with Palermo.
Armed bands were despatched to organise the rising on a
broader front, and, inspired no doubt by varied motives, the
revolution spread. 'Captains of the people' were elected or self-
elected in other villages of western Sicily, which then sent
ambassadors to Palermo. At some time in mid-April these
representatives met: they seem to have decided that each city
should remain independent, but all would bind themselves to
mutual support, much as some of them had done in 1255. Once
again their confederation was to be under the feudal sovereignty
of the Pope. There were even documents headed "in the first
year of the Dominion of Holy Church". Pope Martin, however,
as a good Frenchman, excommunicated the rebels and ordered
them to return to their allegiance.

Within a few weeks, despite the Pope, Sicily had been cleared
of Frenchmen. As success came, the initial frenzy calmed down,
and a provincial governor who had ruled with benevolence
was allowed a safe conduct back to France. Messina had at first
sent ships to help the Angevins put down the revolt, because the
merchant aristocracy of this commercial town had been strongly
favoured by the Angevins, and Palermo was their natural
enemy; but soon they too were faced by popular rebellion and
forced to change their mind. The French garrison at Messina
was expelled and some of Charles's ships were burnt. The
whole of Sicily was now united.

Those who remained of the old Hohenstaufen baronage,
however much they may have wanted to turn out the new
French aristocracy, must have been astonished by this popular
revolution. It is possible that they had helped to instigate the

revolt while taking care to remain in the background, though probably their fear of municipal independence and a peasants' revolt would have restrained them from connivance. At all events, once the revolution had happened, they needed to take the lead in order to stop it developing in undesirable directions. It is unlikely that they would have approved of the negotiations with the Pope or of the republican tendencies shown by the main towns; on the other hand, some of them had been in touch with Peter of Aragon, and they might now all the more have felt the need of Spanish help to reassert their own authority.

Ultimately the political views of the baronage were almost bound to prevail. The influence of custom, the advantages of property, their experience of politics and administration, not to speak of their private armies, all told in their favour. The help of these professional fighters was indispensable if Sicily were to withstand an Angevin counter-attack, and they alone could canalise the destructive forces of rebellion towards constructive government. The revolution of 1282, therefore, despite its origins, marked another stage in the victory of a feudal aristocracy over the centralised monarchy typified by Frederick and Charles. Subsequently the Vespers was made out to be the very archetype of a patriotic rebellion, but it was also something quite different: it was first an *émeute* and a *jacquerie*; then it seemed to be a republican movement for municipal autonomy; and finally it was a feudal revolt against the strong state, or even the struggle of one feudal class against another, of the Hohenstaufen landowners against the French. Quite apart from this, it was also part of a war in which Catalans and Neapolitans such as John of Procida were using the Sicilian baronage for a much wider scheme of power politics against Anjou.

Quite when and how Aragonese influence became dominant is uncertain. Some people had an interest in maintaining that John of Procida and Aragon had been the chief actors all along: the Angevins needed to ascribe their defeat to more than a civilian mob, and it suited the Aragonese to take credit for everything. But the revolt broke out long before Peter could have been in a position to help, and its first leaders invoked papal sovereignty not Aragonese. Peter's ships did not leave

73

Spain for several months after the Vespers; and even then they spent further weeks in the Balearics, and subsequently sailed not to Sicily but North Africa. Only when he had made closer touch with the Sicilian barons and heard that Charles's ships had been destroyed did Peter try to intervene. A group of Sicilian notables met in another parliament at Palermo and formally requested his help. After an initial affectation of diffidence he accepted, and landed at Trapani on 30 August, five months after the original outbreak. On 4 September he was acclaimed King at Palermo, and in the now traditional formula undertook to safeguard the liberties of Sicily as established by the good King William a century before.

The Pope and Charles of Anjou desperately promised reforms in the hope of retrieving their fortunes. Feudatories were promised the right of judgement by their peers, the right to marry whom they wished, and to bequeath their fiefs freely to brothers and nephews. An undertaking was given that the barons would be taxed less and their wishes more carefully consulted in parliament. But these reforms were a confession of failure, and they came too late. By now the Palermo massacre had effectively weakened the papacy and ruined Charles's hopes of a Mediterranean empire. The *Regnum Siciliae* was effectively severed at the straits of Messina; and one incidental consequence was that Calabria, which for centuries had been closely identified with the island of Sicily, and which even made some effort in 1282 to join the revolution, became attached to the Kingdom of Naples. These 'two Sicilies' were not only divided at the straits, but their rivalry was quickly developing into a central fact of Mediterranean history.

Sicily gained in one direction but lost in another by this split from Naples. She had already been deprived of the stimulating connection with Greece and Africa which had almost seemed a condition of her past greatness, and now her links with Italy were partially severed just when Italian history was entering the golden age of Dante and Giotto. She was cut off from the university of Naples and the professional jurists who had been the backbone of the Hohenstaufen monarchy. Messina lost many of her natural economic connections. For a century Sicily now remained under the ban of Rome, her leaders excommunicated and her churches under interdict; and for four

74

centuries she was attached not to the Italian but to the Iberian peninsula.

Sicilians submitted without difficulty to rule from Spain, for the capacity to initiate a war of independence was not matched by an ability to agree among themselves on any form of home rule. This proves that the rebellion of 1282 cannot have been against foreign domination as such. Perhaps some of them hoped that a distant king in Aragon would leave them more to themselves than the meddling and in many ways anti-feudal governments of Frederick II and Charles.

Chapter 7

THE NEW FEUDALISM

King Peter of Sicily and Aragon needed all the local assistance he could obtain. The Sicilian nobility gladly helped him abolish the republican organisation of the cities under their elected captains; but since, unlike Charles, he could strictly claim no right of conquest, and since Aragon was so remote, he was dependent on the local feudal army and so had to be conciliatory to the more powerful of his new subjects. Palermo was restored to its old position of primacy at the expense of Messina, which had been favoured by the Angevins. Sicilian parliaments also began to be held again as they had never been by Charles, and at one of them Peter agreed that the island should continue as a separate kingdom and not be merged with Aragon. He even undertook that after his death the two crowns should be held by different members of his family; and this concession to local autonomy must have been designed to please the leaders of opinion in Palermo.

Nevertheless, many of those who in 1282 had rebelled for more independence and less arbitrary government were soon disillusioned. The *collecta* was imposed frequently, just as under Charles. Feudal privileges were sometimes ignored. A new Spanish feudal aristocracy began to receive land in return for military service, and naturally it was these men who were closest to the King. Hence some of the Sicilian barons were soon intriguing again but this time with the Angevins. One of their leaders was Alaimo da Lentini: he had in his time deserted Manfred for Charles, and then betrayed Charles in order to join Peter; but now, having obtained even larger estates from Peter, he secretly got in touch again with Charles—which did not stop him denouncing a rival baron to Peter for doing just the same. The motives which inspired the victorious baronage in 1282 were certainly much more complicated than just those of local patriotism.

One aim of the Spanish was commercial gain. Successive Kings continued to trade in cereals on their own account, and tax-free exports from Sicily went to other Catalans as payment for the royal debts, so that large quantities of wheat were soon arriving in Barcelona on special terms. Raw Sicilian silk was sent to be worked by Catalan weavers, woollen cloth being imported from Spain in return—payment in Spanish money was sometimes specified. The lion's share in Sicilian trade was thus transferred from the Florentines to the Catalan merchants who had helped to finance Peter's expedition; and fifty years later there were three Catalan consuls and fifteen vice-consuls in Sicily looking after this commerce. Often the Sicilian government was ordered to pay pensions to individual Spaniards. In North Africa, too, profitable rights pertaining to the crown of Sicily were quietly transferred to that of Aragon.

The occupation of Sicily was intended by Peter as a step towards conquering southern Italy: the Catalan and Sicilian fleets were fused into one unit for this purpose and became the chief means by which Sicily thenceforward remained a dependency of Spain. On the other hand, Charles of Anjou was determined not only to hold Naples but to regain Sicily. Charles and Peter on one occasion agreed to decide the matter by single combat in neutral territory under the English flag; but the two contestants both arrived for the duel at different times so that each could claim that his opponent had failed to appear. The Pope in any case wanted hostilities renewed, with the result that Sicily had to continue fighting a war from which she had nothing to gain either way.

After Peter's death, despite his promise, his son James insisted on remaining King of both Sicily and Aragon, and Sicilians found themselves obliged to go on providing grain, soldiers and ships to the common fund. Indeed, far from allowing Sicilian autonomy, the interests of Aragon eventually convinced James that he should make peace with the Pope and surrender this distant and unimportant island to the Angevins. That meant undoing the work of the Vespers and breaking the 'contract' of 1282 between crown and barons. Return to Angevin rule might have been no bad thing for most Sicilians, but, as it threatened the property and even the lives of some of the chief landowners, the King's plan met stiff opposition.

James had appointed a younger brother, Frederick, as his Viceroy at Palermo. This Frederick had been brought to Sicily as a child and had grown up a Sicilian. Perhaps he also had ambitions of his own which were threatened by James's proposed surrender of the island. At the end of 1295 he therefore took a revolutionary step by summoning a 'parliament' to debate his brother's decision, and this parliament decided that the Viceroy should himself become King of an independent Sicily. Rather than return to Neapolitan rule, the barons thus defied excommunication and took the extreme step of dethroning their legitimate sovereign. More remarkable still, they succeeded without bloodshed or tumult. Even some Spanish feudatories now living in Sicily supported this move, and showed that despite language and origin they were already becoming identified with the indigenous baronage.

The coronation of the usurper, Frederick III, took place in 1296. His forty-year reign has sometimes been extravagantly described as a noble period of warfare against Angevin Naples, during which the heroic Sicilian baronage became a symbol of patriotic independence; but, in fact, selfish interests predominated in this war, and nothing was achieved by it except destruction. The Neapolitan provinces probably had two or three times as numerous a population as Sicily, so the scales were heavily weighted. In addition the Pope proclaimed another religious 'crusade' against the fanatically pious Frederick. For his part, Frederick was backed by the anti-papal ghibelline party in Italy; the Hohenstaufen eagles still appeared on his banner, and it was his professed intention to revive the Norman-Hohenstaufen kingdom and revenge Manfred and Conradin. James eventually landed in Sicily and declared war on his own brother. Some of the leading Sicilian barons, even some who in 1296 had backed Frederick, in 1298 deserted the cause of Sicilian independence and joined the overwhelming coalition of Aragon, Naples and the papacy.

Frederick was lucky to make a compromise peace in 1302 which allowed him to retain his kingdom on condition that after his lifetime it would lapse to the Angevins: he accepted papal feudal supremacy and gave special facilities for exporting Sicilian wheat to Rome; he promised to style himself merely King of *Trinacria*, thus reviving an ancient name for the island. Perhaps this agreement was never more than a trick to gain time, for Frederick went on calling himself King of Sicily; and perhaps he relied on the treaty being in a sense illegal, since a remarkable royal declaration of 1296 had gone so far as to invalidate any act of foreign policy which lacked parliamentary consent. Nevertheless, by making peace, Frederick for a time freed Sicilians from the depredations of foreign bands. The most redoubtable of these bands, the 'Catalan company', now moved away to the Levant, where in 1311 they conquered Athens and attached it temporarily to the Sicilian crown.

War recommenced in 1312 and lasted on and off until 1372. Military maps drawn for the years 1316, 1326 and 1336 would show half a dozen large coastal areas more or less in Angevin possession, but these invasions had only limited success against guerrilla groups which continually retreated into the mountains. The war went both ways, and sometimes Frederick's armies were fighting on the mainland. But the bare details of the war are unilluminating. Enthusiasm flagged as the to and fro became more pointless. The barons were reluctant to fulfil their obligations of knight service, and Frederick had little enough money to hire soldiers. Certain Sicilian feudatories, out of personal interest or vendetta, joined the Angevins and helped foreign armies to sack neighbouring Sicilian towns; for the baronage was little concerned with Sicilian independence for its own sake. At Messina, too, the mercantile classes showed some readiness to restore the Angevin connection, which to them meant the defeat of Palermo, as it also meant food supplies and trade with Calabria and Naples. As for the common people, one may guess that their chief sentiment was a desire to end the war either way and in the meantime to avoid commitment: an invading army of either side would be welcome if it brought shiploads of wheat, but otherwise the sensible attitude was to wait and see and to hope always for peace.

A decline in Sicilian strength and cohesion was accompanied, and not accidentally, by growing pretensions of the baronage who were emerging as the chief victors in the revolutions of 1282 and 1295–6. James at his accession had to undertake at their behest not to use the emergency *collecta* tax too frequently: he promised freedom from arbitrary arrest, and royal officials were to respect rights of property. James also promised not to enforce the forest laws too severely. Above all, in his law *Si aliquem*, he allowed childless barons to bequeath fiefs to collateral branches of their family; and this made it much less likely that feudal estates would ever devolve to the crown.

Frederick III in 1296 likewise had to grant a charter of liberties, for he was a usurper and largely dependent on the barons. He promised to summon a parliament on All Saints' Day every year. He would not leave the island or declare war or make peace "without the full knowledge and consent of Sicilians". There would be no taxes except those prescribed by law or agreed by parliament. He promised that the Justiciars would be Sicilians and be changed each year, while Palermo and Messina could have special magistrates of their own. Other ordinances allowed barons to wear swords and daggers but forbade other people to do so. At his coronation Frederick created a number of counts and three hundred new knights, so broadening the basis of feudalism and of his own supporters.

The feudal character of society had become much more marked since Count Roger in the eleventh century granted baronies to his soldiers. Feudal tenures by now had come to cover a large extent of the island as successive Kings built up a following by grants of land to friends and servants. Many other royal prerogatives, including castles, forests, tunny fisheries, salt pans, tithes and the farming of taxes, had been given out as feudal concessions, and gradually these grants were being thought of as providing revenue and power for the baron rather than military service to the King. Feudalism, instead of reinforcing central authority, as under Roger, was thus coming to represent a principle of disorganisation and a diminution of royal rights.

Frederick's reign marked an important stage in this change, for war naturally increased the power of the military hierarchy and gave every facility for the barons to encroach on royal lands and jurisdiction. The King forbade them to interfere in town government, as he forbade them to keep liveried retainers or to put arbitrary taxes on farmers; and, as a counterpoise, he also made a genuine attempt to encourage municipal self-government. But in practice the nobles came to have a predominant influence even inside the main towns of the royal demesne—as the Ventimiglia did at Trapani and the Palizzi at Messina. A third attempt by the merchants of Messina to set up an autonomous commune like the city states of northern Italy was put down in bloodshed.

Land kept its value in wartime better than commerce, and land meant power. Francesco Ventimiglia soon possessed nineteen large fiefs in various parts of Sicily, the Palizzi family eleven and the Chiaramonte eight. Some newly settled Spanish families were among the richest landowners: the Moncada were given Malta as a county, and the Peralta owned four fiefs and the office of Grand Admiral. Frederick's law *Volentes* in 1296 allowed the almost unrestricted alienation of feudal estates. Whereas the Normans had regarded a fief as a temporary concession by the King and held in trust, now some of the barons claimed to hold their land free of any but the most theoretical obligations either to the King or their tenants.

If the new feudalism of the fourteenth century was a burden on society, this was largely because any sense of obligation was lacking. If only, like the King-makers of 1296, the feudatories had continued to see their own advantage in pressing for an annual parliament, this at least might have allowed the common interest to be discussed and would have associated private individuals more actively with promoting the general welfare; but nothing more was heard of annual parliaments, for the barons now had easier means of making private interest prevail. Though they were uneducated and illiterate, administration fell increasingly into their hands. Frederick had to agree that only nobles could be Justiciars. The counties of Modica and Geraci gradually became states within the state, sometimes even coining their own money. Criminal jurisdiction—the right of *merum et mistum imperium*—had been generally confined to members of the royal family, but after 1297 it was regularly granted to the senior counts and in time became inheritable: its sinister outward sign was the gallows raised outside any village where the baron's word was law. All this was made inevitable and even desirable by the war against Naples, since private coining could be called beneficial when the royal mint was ineffective, and baronial justice was welcome if the alternative was no justice at all.

Frederick III was generous and amiable by temperament. He possessed a cultivated mind and apparently wrote poetry in Catalan. Though he was a poor administrator and diplomatist, the chroniclers wrote of him with some enthusiasm, and he became Dante's favourite because he defied the political intrusions of five Popes. When he died in 1337, Sicily was still independent, but only just; public authority still counted for something, but was declining, and the country must have been poorer than when he had first arrived from Spain.

The archives are too fragmentary to yield any clear indications about the economy. The Vespers and the Angevin war had diminished trade with Naples but opened what must soon have been a more profitable traffic with Catalonia. The main trade route to the East still ran through the straits of Messina, and commerce continued with Africa. There continued to be some very rich Sicilians, and luxury of dress was common enough to be legislated against in 1309. Yet the public sector was becoming poorer, tax revenue fell, and internal commerce must have become very hard when the King's writ ceased to run.

Documentary information is meagre about the Black Death, which Genoese galleys brought to Sicily from the Levant in 1347, though we know that in other parts of Europe this bubonic plague sometimes killed one person in three. Perhaps the administrative chaos was such that government offices simply closed down and documentation ceased. The plague lasted a good six months on this first visit, and there is one reference to Catania and Trapani being evacuated as people fled into the hills. Almost certainly it killed the Regent John, one of the few effective governors of the century, and its recurrence perhaps killed King Louis in 1355. The haunting fresco at Palermo of the Triumph of Death must have reflected this dreadful scourge on one of its frequent recurrences. Yet the incidence of the plague is still conjectural. Almost certainly the population was already declining by 1347, though population estimates after the plague can vary from a third of a million to four times as much, and the uncertainty means that one index of economic and social change is denied to us.

The years after 1350 witnessed a general dissolution of society. Envy of the newly enriched nobility from Spain led to friction between 'Latin' and 'Catalan' factions, and both these factions were themselves divided. The chief division was between the Chiaramonte and Ventimiglia families, both of which had acquired large estates from the dispossessed French barons after 1282. The Chiaramonte then obtained the County of Modica out of the lands confiscated by Frederick in 1296 from the partisans of James. The Ventimiglia received the almost equally extensive County of Geraci. The two families once intermarried, but this marriage, being barren, ended in nullity proceedings, and hence touched off a vendetta by raising many deeply felt questions of honour. Honour, in turn, automatically activated ties of kinship and blood brotherhood, and this soon created a civil war. The Chiaramonte, put out of countenance and unable to restore their respect by a suitable revenge, went to Naples and offered their services to the Angevins; then they returned with German and Neapolitan troops and utterly devastated the coastal territories along southern Sicily. The Ventimiglia, claiming to be the champions of Frederick and Sicilian independence, similarly extended their own power in the north by deliberately starving whole areas into submission.

Peace was eventually reached by simple exhaustion. The young Frederick IV was captured alternately by Latins and Catalans. He had to pawn the crown jewels. He hardly dared visit Palermo, where Manfredi Chiaramonte lived in a mansion more luxurious than the empty royal palace. But he was brave enough to make overtures for peace, and even the barons must have mostly realised by now that there was little more to be gained from civil war. In 1372 Naples agreed to accept Sicilian independence, but only if Frederick called himself King of *Trinacria* and paid an annual tribute. Likewise the papacy, which realised that decades of excommunication and interdict had done untold harm to the Church as well as to churchmen, agreed to peace, though Frederick had to acknowledge the feudal overlordship of Rome and help to finance another war which the Pope was waging in northern Italy.

The cost of ninety years of warfare is impossible to guess. Such revenue as could be collected must have been spent on fighting. Royal prerogatives were liberally sold to build ships, and city finances would have been largely allocated to fortification; yet ships and fortresses could be destroyed faster than they could be built. Often the enemy landed large forces to burn forests and farmsteads, to cut down trees and vines; for their best hope was to exhaust the island, to stop commerce, ruin the tunny fisheries and bring agriculture to a halt. The Angevin forces had thus uprooted many of the orange groves round

Palermo in 1325. "We live only for the war", said one chronicler in 1330; and Villani spoke of each side acting "like savage beasts", deliberately destroying harvests, killing herds and trying to starve out their opponents. There was mention of "innumerable victims" dying of famine.

Armed adventurers from as far away as England made a good living in this world of civil strife. Rarely were there pitched battles, so it was not the soldiers who chiefly suffered: armies learnt to feed off the country. Peasant families fled from the coastal territories, to the great loss of agriculture; some emigrated to Calabria and Sardinia and increased the depopulation which Moslem evictions and the Black Death had already caused; others took to military life in brigand gangs; and probably some villages disappeared altogether. Under these stresses, irrigation works easily fell into decay. The valleys of Sicily, much more than the moister areas of northern Europe, needed constant attention to stop them disintegrating into dust bowls and malarial swamps, and we now hear of large areas empty of all labour, uncultivated and fever-ridden.

It is possible, however, that the chroniclers exaggerated the human tragedy. So long as merchants and bankers still existed, so long as foreign ships still came, so long as rich men used gold ornaments and their ladies wore hairstyles like towers and battlements, clearly the wars cannot have been too universally disastrous. The contending armies were small, and perhaps deserted land could be fairly quickly brought back into cultivation.

PART 3
Submission to Spain 1375–1525

Chapter 8

THE END OF INDEPENDENCE

When Frederick IV died in 1377, he left a young daughter Maria in the care of Artale d'Alagona, leader of the Catalans. Who should marry this girl became an immediate question. Milan and Naples both had designs on Sicily, while the Pope thought of Maria for one of his nephews; and the King of Aragon, after reviving his title to Sicily, seized the duchy of Athens which for sixty years had nominally recognised Sicilian sovereignty. Meanwhile d'Alagona and the leading barons decided to divide the island into four main spheres of influence. D'Alagona would administer most of the east from his castle at Catania. Guglielmo Peralta would govern the south from Sciacca. Manfredi Chiaramonte was best placed of all, at Palermo, and also owned the 'state' of Modica in the south-east. Francesco Ventimiglia, Count of Geraci, had most of the north coast. The four 'vicars' imposed their own taxes and annexed the demesne lands almost at will, yet their mutual jealousies made this experiment short lived. D'Alagona decided to marry Maria to Giangaleazzo Visconti of Milan, hoping to exploit the expansionist policy of that ruthless and ambitious man; but Raimondo Moncada, envious at his exclusion from the vicariate, abducted Maria from Catania castle, whence she was taken to Barcelona and married in 1390 to Martin, the young grandson of the King of Aragon.

Martin and the Aragonese now planned another conquest of Sicily, and the barons realised that their sovereign powers might be overturned by another strong King and more foreign place-hunters. Hurriedly they met in a self-convened parliament at Castronovo in 1391; but personal rivalries, to say nothing of the conflict between old and new landed families, middling and great nobles, Latins and Catalans, made agreement impossible. Ventimiglia, Peralta and d'Alagona each began negotiating privately with the Aragonese for what they could get in return for their support.

Meanwhile Martin collected an army by promising Sicilian fiefs and pensions to impoverished malcontents in Spain, and offering to pardon any criminals except heretics who would join what might prove a rewarding adventure. Barcelona and Valencia, not very enthusiastically, invested in the expedition for a share in the profits, and so did the Kings of Aragon and Castile, while Genoa and Pisa were persuaded to help in return for promises of Sicilian wheat. Other potentially hostile powers were preoccupied—France by war with England, Rome by a papal schism, and Naples by a civil war between two Angevin claimants. Sicilian interests were hardly considered except in so far as Sicily would of course have to pay for this invasion of her territory. She could hardly resist, for her navy had vanished. A fleet could not exist without central authority and well-organised taxes, both of which had long since disappeared.

In 1392 the Spanish landed under their general, Bernardo Cabrera, who had sold off his estates in Catalonia to equip soldiers at his own expense. Two of the four vicars joined him. A third, Andrea Chiaramonte, was besieged in Palermo for a month, and the invaders destroyed many houses and orchards in their blockade of the capital. When Palermo surrendered, Chiaramonte was decapitated and his vast estates were bestowed on Cabrera. Martin's concession of land to foreign adventurers was not much liked by existing feudatories, but gradually they submitted, for in the first place he was obviously winning, and secondly he showed himself ready to confirm the usurpation of crown lands and revenues which they had made in the kingless years. Those who resisted or fled into exile found that their estates were used as a bribe for further defections. The chief cities were glad to yield to any likely victor if only he would confirm their privileges, especially since royal authority was preferable to the local tyrannies of a disorderly baronage.

After many decades of anarchy, Martin could not easily re-establish law or recover abandoned royal prerogatives. Registers had been lost or destroyed, and earlier traditions of government had been forgotten. Nevertheless, support from some of the towns allowed him to employ professional troops which freed him from complete reliance on baronial military service. He also tried to draw up a new feudal register like every strong King before him, prescribing that the main criminal offences must come before his courts alone and that there should always be a right of appeal to him from baronial justice. He made some attempt to recover castles and reassert crown rights over forests and fisheries. As all coastal territory "within bow-shot of the sea" had once been recognised as the King's, he forbade the barons to build port-works and grain storages or to tax grain exports except with permission. Martin also abrogated the treaty provisions of 1372 and entitled himself *Rex Siciliae*. He took advantage of a papal schism to repudiate the Pope's overlordship and to claim the Apostolic Legateship once again, with the right to appoint bishops and regulate the Sicilian Church.

These decisions were often more on parchment than effective in practice, for even a strong King could not reverse the recent tendencies in Sicilian feudalism. The attitude of Aragonese kings towards the baronage was different from what had been customary in Norman and Hohenstaufen Sicily; and the barons were permitted to keep a strong hold on public life, on the towns, on taxes, even on the ports and the export of wheat. In practice Martin allowed Cabrera full rights of criminal juris-diction in Modica, and the Moncada family likewise on the estates confiscated from d'Alagona. Royal Justiciars on their biennial tour of the country found that in some areas they were without authority. In another respect, too, Martin's power was limited, for Sicilian independence of Naples was possible only because of an increasing dependence on Aragon: this second Spanish invasion brought a substantial new wave of land-owners from Spain who before long were to become the leading families of Sicily and fill most bishoprics and government offices.

The King summoned parliaments to meet at Catania in 1397 and Syracuse in 1398. The long Angevin wars had resulted in frequent parliaments being held until 1350, but this institution had then fallen into disuse during the period of baronial anarchy. Martin's assemblies showed that once again there existed a central authority and even a limited kind of public opinion. It was a tradition of Aragon as well as of Sicily that, especially in times of national emergency, the leading citizens should be summoned to hear the King's will, to confirm his accession and render him aid; and if the monarch's predica-ment was serious enough this might also confer on the representatives a qualified right of initiative and discussion. The plea was made in parliament for fewer Catalans to be appointed to government jobs, and the King was asked to apply not Catalan but Sicilian laws. He was also asked to 'live of his own'. So as not to need emergency taxes he was requested not to allow more land to be alienated from the crown, and it was declared that powers of criminal justice should belong to the King alone. At the same time the bold suggestion was made that members of parliament should be represented on the royal council and even given some executive powers if the King were absent; it was also hoped that there would be no secret advisers outside this council.

For a brief moment, parliament seemed to be approximating to a pattern made familiar in England; but Martin rejected this last proposal, and the parliamentarians were in practice too divided and irresponsible to acquire much authority unless he wanted it. He was following Spanish custom when he allowed parliaments to present petitions, and in fact this often added a strength to his government; but parliaments had no force on their own. Petitions could easily be rejected, or they could be accepted and then simply ignored in practice. Legislation was not to become parliamentary. On the contrary, new Spanish procedures and terminology were introduced which allowed laws to be simply proclaimed by 'pragmatic sanction' or royal decree.

At a time when other countries in Europe were growing in cohesion, Sicily was losing her political personality as an independent state. Martin I remained strongly under the influence of his father, and the latter, who was now King of Aragon, watched over every detail of the Sicilian administration. It was the King of Aragon who financed the troops in Sicily, who appointed to jobs and fiefs, and decided about demesne lands and ecclesiastical policy; for the Aragonese regarded Sicily as their advance-guard in the Mediterranean. Martin thus remained an *infante* of Aragon even more than a King of Sicily, and it was as a Spanish general that in 1409 he led an expedition at Sicilian expense to put down a rising in Sardinia. The barons of Sicily found nothing to protest at in this: one of their major interests was war and the profits of war, and they gladly fought for Spain on this colonial mission.

Some Sicilians made a profit from transporting supplies, while others supplied grain, sulphur, saltpetre and even ostrich feathers for helmets.

It was in Sardinia that Martin died, donating Sicily to his father like any other item of personal property. Neither election by the barons nor even papal appointment mattered any longer, and so the crowns of Aragon and Sicily were again united. No new Vespers took place to show that this was unwelcome, nor was there much sign of even minor discontent, for a sufficient number of the ruling class was now either Spanish by origin or bound by material interest to this Spanish dynasty. During the one year in which Martin II reigned, Sicily was therefore governed directly from Spain.

Neither of the two Martins left legitimate heirs, and in 1410 the throne simply became vacant under the contested regency of Queen Bianca. There was some support for the idea of Sicily becoming separate again under Count de Luna, an illegitimate grandson of Martin II; but Count Cabrera of Modica, Grand Justiciar and the strongest of the barons, had rival ambitions for himself. Aragon showed little enough interest in Sicily, and local independence could hardly have been difficult to regain had enough people wanted it; but both barons and cities were more interested in fighting each other. Cabrera defied the Queen Regent, and the country again dissolved into a chaos of factions, while in each region powerful feudatories reasserted themselves. Once again Messina and Palermo were openly at odds, and there was a succession of damaging raids on Palermo. Wheat exports were hardly possible. Revenue could not be collected, and Bianca had to rely on private borrowing.

While some of the barons might gain from such anarchy, the cities needed peace for trade; they wanted communications re-opened and fairs held again. Messina especially was soon agitating for the restoration of central authority. This commercial town had earned considerable privileges from both Martins, and for a time seems to have displaced Palermo as the normal home of the royal court and administration. Messina supported Queen Bianca, though its citizens prudently took advantage of the situation to occupy the royal castles at Catania and Syracuse. A parliament was convoked at nearby Taormina. Here it was agreed that a committee should be appointed with the duty of choosing a King, and that half the committee members should be Messinese. It was also proposed once again to place Sicily under the protection of the Church. Acting on this suggestion, Pope John XXII tried to veto any Aragonese claimant on the grounds that Aragon had defaulted in not recognising his feudal overlordship; indeed the Pope went further by declaring that King Ladislas of Naples was the rightful sovereign of Sicily.

Palermo, on the other hand, supported Cabrera and refused to accept the committee or the Pope's decision. There was even a widespread boycott of the Taormina parliament. Sicilians were so divided that it must have been generally welcome when a new King was selected on their behalf in Spain. Nine delegates representing the three kingdoms of Aragon, Catalonia and Valencia met at Caspe in Aragon, and out of a short list of six candidates elected Ferdinand, who came from a cadet branch of the ruling dynasty of Castile. Ferdinand in 1412, among his other titles, proclaimed himself 'by the grace of God King of Sicily'; though Sicilians had not even been consulted.

Shortly afterwards Ferdinand's envoys arrived to take over the government: one of them was a clothier of Perpignan who represented an industry which had a special interest in the Sicilian market. There was no need for a parliament to confirm this change of dynasty, nor for an invading army to compel its acceptance; and even when Ferdinand was excommunicated, this did not rally opposition against him. The country was too exhausted to react, or else foreign domination was positively desired as a deliverance from disorder. There was nothing novel about being governed from Spain; on the contrary, Sicilian barons of Catalan origin might have feared to lose their large estates if the Spanish connection lapsed. Naples and Milan were both ready to establish an alternative kind of alien rule, and the King of Portugal was preparing a fleet to make Sicily a Portuguese base in the Mediterranean.

When parliament met at Catania in 1413 there was some controversy, but mainly over who should have the honour of carrying to Ferdinand a message of humble submission. The King was reminded that his representatives had sworn to observe local franchises; but of course he never had any intention of respecting a law such as that by which Frederick III had obliged himself and his successors to reside in the island. In the name of the nobles, but also of the 'gentlemen' and 'citizens', parliament petitioned that the King would keep the administrative and legal system of Sicily separate from those of his other dominions and appoint local people to government offices. Nevertheless there was no power behind these requests, and in fact the Castilian dynasty was to apply local laws with considerable latitude.

Sicily was no longer a residence of Kings, but for four hundred years was to be administered by Viceroys, a centre less of politics than of administration, and with none of the per-quisites pertaining to a major focus of government. The term 'Viceroy' was at least some acknowledgement in theory that here was a distinct kingdom; but, of seventy-eight successive Viceroys, very few were Sicilians by origin, and none at all after the first fifty years. The first was Juan de Peñafiel, Ferdinand's son. Misreading the situation, a faction at Messina asked Juan to make himself an independent King of Sicily, but he refused, and few such proposals were ever heard of again.

Chapter 9

ALFONSO AND THE ECONOMY

Sicily's loyalty and her dependence on Spain were confirmed during the forty-two year reign of Alfonso of Aragon after 1416. The local nobility were persuaded without much difficulty to help him attack Corsica, and to let him make Sicily a base for the conquest of southern Italy, though in both cases this was a Spanish and not a Sicilian interest. Once he had captured Naples, Alfonso resided permanently on the Italian mainland; and when he referred to 'the two Sicilies', the island was in his view 'Sicily beyond the straits', while the much more important Naples was 'Sicily this side of the straits'. Subsequently he undertook an adventurous series of wars against Florence, Genoa, Milan and Venice, in which Sicily again gave help on a scale more generous than some other parts of his empire. Local merchants no doubt gained from providing for his wars, just as the luckier barons profited from ransoms and plunder; but the community as a whole must have lost rather than gained. War with Venice, for example, could only damage Sicilian trade, and the Venetians in 1446 even entered Syracuse harbour as a reprisal and burnt what ships they could find.

One reason for this devotion to Alfonso's dynastic interests was that he tied up these interests with increased privileges for the Sicilian aristocracy. Although titles and fiefs, in theory, had to be submitted on demand for royal confirmation, it was now allowed that estates or privileges held by a baron for thirty years were his by law even if illegally acquired; and thereby both the King and the towns lost many rights of taxation and property. The barons were allowed to administer oaths of allegiance to their own tenants as well as to impose private taxes on them, and when the nobility grumbled that the royal courts were too expensive, they were allowed to hear more cases in their own courts. In 1430, Alfonso gave to his favourite baron, Ventimiglia, the most prized privilege of all, the right to full criminal jurisdiction in his County of Geraci, and the right to leave this same authority to his successors. In this way the

94

leading barons established what must sometimes have been an uncontested authority over local government.

Alfonso's reign has been described as the period when Sicily emerged from the Middle Ages; and certainly in his affectation of humanism, as in his conduct of war, he seemed a new kind of sovereign. He was a generous patron of the arts and was given the appellation 'Magnanimous' by his Spanish and Neapolitan subjects, though he hardly justified this title in Sicily. Alfonso re-established a school of Greek at Messina. At Catania he set up the first Sicilian university so as to keep down the emigration of intellectuals. But his reign seems culturally interesting only by comparison with the desert of the two preceding centuries. Catania university did little for humane studies, but mainly confined itself to training lawyers and doctors in the practice of their profession. Sicily contributed few names to the Renaissance except Panormita, the humanist scholar, and Antonello da Messina, the painter, and both these were expatriates who spent their lives in Naples, Venice or Milan: to neither of them can one attach any noteworthy cultural environment in Sicily or any significant following there. Where necessary, artists and scholars were imported, as were the professor of Greek, Lascaris, from Constantinople, and the sculptors Laurana and Gagini from northern Italy.

Alfonso liked the reputation of being a great patron, but in practice had little money for artistic patronage. He provided the salaries for the professors at Catania; he gave Panormita the Zisa palace and an income from the Palermo customs. Yet the expenses of government were starting to expand in many directions, and they were not being met by new techniques in finance or administration.

The sources of revenue were still much as under the Normans. First there was the income from the somewhat diminished crown estates. The royal demesne no longer automatically included all the forests and mines, nor in practice all the sea-shore *ad iactum balistae*; but there were still nearly fifty towns not enfeoffed to the barons. A certain revenue came from selling cereals grown on crown land or given to the King as tithes. He also received a royalty from the valuable tunny fisheries: during the tunny season the fishermen were by royal order immune from any penal or civil action, and salted tunny in barrels was

95

a valuable export. On one occasion Alfonso personally seems to have cornered the market in sugar exports to Flanders. Less important now were the feudal taxes payable on the inheritance of fiefs, though military service was more commonly being commuted into a money payment which had a certain value. The trouble here was that the main feudal registers were defective and it was often extremely uncertain what obligations were due.

Duties on exports could be quite considerable. Sicily's surplus wheat and favourable export balance had usually produced enough revenue to cover ordinary expenditure, though merchants and foreign bankers had been asked in emergencies to lend money secured on future taxation. The chief peril was that after a bad harvest the wheat taxes would stop abruptly, and this made budgeting impossible. Alfonso now found normal revenue inadequate and this kind of uncertainty intolerable; to cover the deficit he had to borrow from barons and towns, and even once from the King of Tunis. But in most years a good deal of gold came from North Africa as payment for Sicilian cereals: low-grade African doubloons were then re-coined at Messina into good Venetian ducats and used to pay for Alfonso's expansionist policy in Italy. In this way the profits of Sicilian agriculture were lost overseas.

The *collecta* was a tax which by feudal tradition could be taken in certain emergencies. Strong governments had used this right frequently, though there was a general idea that parliament should be consulted or at least informed. Under the Spanish Kings the *collecta* appeared under its Spanish name of *donativo* to signify that in theory it was a gift by parliament. Alfonso collected such a tax when preparing for his expedition to Naples in 1442; then, in 1446, he obtained a regular *donativo* as an annual grant spread over five years and payable by the barons, bishops and citizens; when that was exhausted he was given a further sum for another eight years. In return he promised to use the money to buy back alienated lands and taxes of the royal demesne and so make extraordinary taxation less necessary in future; but the promise was not kept. Without anyone realising the fact, the *donativo* was becoming the largest single item in the regular revenue, even though each grant was thought of at the time as an emergency once-for-all measure.

Fountain and cloister, Benedictine abbey, Monreale

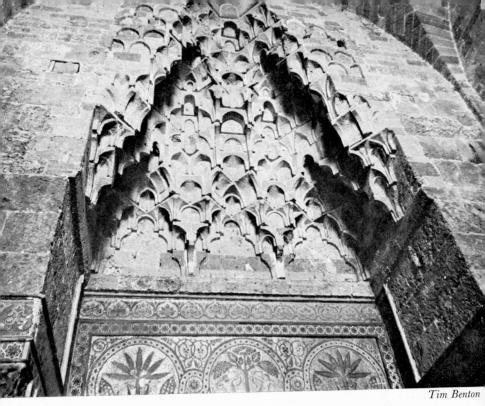

Detail from the main hall, Palazzo La Zisa, Palermo: 12th century

Domes of the 12th-century church of San Cataldo, Palermo

That of 1446 was still being paid in the nineteenth century. Nor did these grants stop Alfonso's continued alienation of crown property and prerogatives. No crime was so great that a criminal could not buy a pardon. New offices and taxes were instituted simply so that they could then be sold, and private people made large profits after buying permission to mint money. Alfonso's brother, the King of Navarre, and his son the future King of Naples, both received the valuable privilege to export Sicilian wheat tax free, and exercised this right even when Sicily was starving and the Viceroy tried to stop all exports.

This was the improvidence of a sovereign who had other things in mind than local welfare or prosperity. Not only did the drain of money to pay for royal policy cause a critical lack of coin, but the King was giving up prerogatives which had once been thought indispensable for the public weal. Efficient administration would be impossible as soon as barons knew that they could compound by money for any illegality, and a planned budget was out of the question when the very sources of revenue were sold outright to produce current income. The Sicilian economy, which had survived the anarchy of the fourteenth century, was thus brought close to disaster by Alfonso's political ambition. Among other things, an incipient growth of banking in Palermo was halted by government indebtedness, for the banks had not yet realised how much of their deposits should be kept as a reserve; and events were to show that any banker who did not obtain high office or move into real estate was in danger of ruin. After one bank failure in 1447, Alfonso's reaction was simply to order that his Spanish friends should be paid before other creditors.

Tax gathering, on the other hand, could be rewarding for a few lucky individuals, because keeping accounts was thought unnecessary, or else the books could be presented twenty years late without causing undue surprise. When accounts did not balance, the Viceroy or his subordinates could easily bury them in the archives; or sometimes they were audited without revealing the omission of tax revenue already collected. Royal officials must thus have appropriated large sums, and sometimes lent the King money which they had already stolen from him. The Viceroy Durrea almost certainly bought his own job from Alfonso, and lived in Spain for years while continuing to draw his salary. His son was put in charge of the cereal taxes at a considerable stipend though he was a permanent absentee. Occasionally some Sicilian tried to protest at misappropriations of the revenue, but others must have been making their fortune out of them and so kept quiet.

By the middle of the fifteenth century the economy was entering a difficult phase. Spanish imperial wars, the fall of Constantinople in 1453 to the Turks, the growing severance of trade with the eastern Mediterranean and Moslem Africa, all these made the island more vulnerable than before. Power was now going to be based more and more on artillery, on costly fortifications able to withstand gunfire, and a new type of warship which could also resist the recoil of broadsides: Sicily had neither the money for these, nor the craftsmen, nor the raw materials. Sicilian wheat was costing twice as much in the 1450s as at the beginning of the century and so was harder to sell. A favourable balance of trade was still apparently preserved, and Sicilian ships were found in the Adriatic and the Levant. A fair number of legal documents also exist which show that commercial loans, ship building, the hiring of ships and formation of trading companies were all matters of current concern. But although this was a period in Europe when great fortunes could be made, equally it was a time when lack of capital and enterprise were heavily penalised.

There is little evidence that much capital or enterprise were being applied to Sicilian agriculture. Away from the coastal cities the peasants had been accustomed for centuries to extreme conditions of either anarchy or semi-slavery. Some of them still dressed and spoke like their Arab forebears, remote as they were from the disturbances of time. Outside the towns the only effective law was the law of the strongest. Villagers had lost to the barons any say in choosing their own officials, and were also losing rights over the communal pastures and water supplies. The inhabitants of Termini protested in 1392 that the family of Chiaramonte had taken over certain common land, but their alleged proof of this fact was simply torn up in their presence by the baron. The aristocracy on their *latifondi* claimed a legal right to bind the peasants to work *di suli in suli*, from daybreak to dusk; and there were severe penalties against working shorter hours or asking for more money. Possibly the need for such penalties suggests that agricultural labourers were taking advantage of a fall in population to keep wages at least abreast of prices, and that employers were desperately trying to stop this by law. Wages were, at least in theory, fixed by regulation. Landowners could be fined if they paid too much, and there was a reward for proving any contravention.

Baronial landowners often were able to insist that their produce should be sold before that of their tenants; and it could happen that a whole neighbourhood had no option but to recognise the baron's monopoly on grinding wheat, making bread, slaughtering animals, pressing wine and oil; he, too, owned the village shop. Governments occasionally tried to protect the peasants from arbitrary exactions, but the barons had their own private courts and prisons to support their case. Occasionally, as in 1446 when the Baron of Calatabiano forbade shepherds to pasture their flocks on common land, the villagers repaired to the King's courts and won their case; but documents were easily destroyed, and several years of anarchy were enough to confuse the memory of old practices. Few peasants had the knowledge or the money and courage to appeal to the royal courts. Nor was parliament the kind of body to champion their cause; on the contrary, parliament tried to persuade the King that the royal courts were unpopular and ordinary citizens would prefer an enlargement of baronial jurisdiction.

There is little evidence of great poverty or unemployment early in the fifteenth century, but economic conditions soon became less favourable. Alfonso's extravagant foreign policy, apart from leading to more local power for the barons, required taxes on cereals which hit farmers and consumers alike. Insufficient money was left over for police and defence expenditure, with the result that piracy threatened the productiveness of the fertile coastal strip, and banditry encouraged the tendency for labourers to concentrate in large townships remote from their work. In the early fifteenth century the government seems to have been trying to make people return from the interior to the coast, if for no other reason than because taxes could not be collected inland; but at the same time there was a spontaneous movement towards the safety of the big towns.

99

Such rural depopulation was one reason why this one-time granary of Europe now began to suffer periodic famine. When the barons taxed the sale and carriage of agricultural produce, their tenants might prefer to reduce cultivation and either adjust to a more simple subsistence economy or even abandon the land outright.

An independent middle class never had much chance to consolidate itself in such a society. Partly this was because the laws of primogeniture resulted in fiefs not being divided and younger sons not being endowed with property. Some nobles in the fourteenth century had been well-known money-lenders, but there developed among the nobility a marked prejudice against trade and this helped to keep the classes separate. Few rich merchants existed outside Palermo, Messina or Trapani. Some of the peasants were able to rise above their fellows, and even reached the point where they could indulge in money-lending, speculation on price changes, or contracting to collect the local food taxes; but this small rural middle class had no independent political existence. The chief aspiration of the fortunate few was to buy land and join the world of feudalism, or at least to commend themselves to some great lord; and hence there was less interest in abolishing feudal abuses than in exploiting them. Nor were the lawyers an independent or innovating force, for they were entirely dependent on aristocratic clients; and this was another reason why parliamentary institutions took a very different path of development from that seen in England.

If the baronage was growing stronger in Sicily, it was partly at the expense of civic autonomy. Palermo and Messina alone had much civic freedom, and even this was largely an illusion. Control by either the government or the landed proprietors left little scope for a municipal third estate to develop with interests distinct from those of the baronage, and in fact the cities never formed a strong and independent force in parliament. Perhaps the continuous squabbling between various towns, to say nothing of faction fights inside them, made civic freedom seem less attractive than a government which could guarantee order, justice and effective administration.

Many towns had been, and went on being, alienated to the barons by Kings who needed money and who could often themselves provide no alternative to baronial administration. This was a somewhat different pattern to that found in Spanish Naples, and it suggests that special conditions were present in Sicily. Although the main strategic centres of the country remained part of the royal demesne, in the great majority of towns and villages the nobles and bishops had full possession, and they appointed civic officials and controlled taxation. Even in much of the royal demesne the barons took over effective power because they needed to control the market for the produce of their own estates. The government forbade them to intervene in city elections in these royal towns, but in vain, for they were the chief employers and the fount of patronage.

A strong monarch was always able to recover many of these lapsed royal prerogatives. Martin in the 1390s regained for the royal demesne Malta, Girgenti, Lentini, Licata and Corleone; and he laid down that the mayor of Palermo should be appointed by the crown and hold office for a single year. But only on rare occasions did towns work together in co-operation with the monarchy, and on their own they were ineffective. Palermo petitioned the King to enforce the rule that her other civic officers should be elected annually by lot from the well-to-do, but in practice election became a formality and the popular civic council went into abeyance. The monarchy had no overriding interest in civic freedom, just because all too often it saw no reason to build up an anti-baronial party; while on the other hand there was the temptation that ready money could always be obtained by selling a town with its taxes and profits of jurisdiction. Even when citizens could afford to buy themselves back, the King might sell them again, as Vizzini was sold seven times over: some towns remained permanently in debt as a result of purchasing their freedom, and this was one indirect manner in which the profits of commerce were taken out of beneficial circulation. Syracuse, Lentini, Sciacca, Corleone, Cefalù were all sold into feudal servitude by Alfonso, despite the fact that Martin had laid down that this would be illegal. In return for a loan to the King, the port of Marsala was given to a Spaniard and his heirs until the loan should be repaid, and this contract was specifically said to hold good even if by mistake the same concession should be made to others.

In every Sicilian town there were occasional revolts. These

were generally against defective food supplies or excessive taxation, and they almost never suggest that the various classes had any common interest in a revolution for municipal autonomy. Often they were a civil war for power. Control of civic administration meant control of tax allocation; it also meant control of appointments to jobs and of the communal lands and revenues. At Catania, between 1435 and 1451, the *popolo minuto* managed to secure some representation on the city council which controlled these matters, and this was not an isolated example. Messina was the most independent as it was economically the most advanced town in Sicily, and the most closely in touch with foreign countries; but although in the middle of the fifteenth century a few noble families and the silk and banking interests monopolised the city government, the lower middle class and artisans possessed a more articulate sense of their interests than elsewhere. Here, too, after a sharp conflict in 1448–9, it was therefore decided to grant popular elements a share in the apportionment of civic officers. But this kind of democratic reform was short-lived, because the democrats wanted direct taxes on income and land, while the patrician classes were determined to impose indirect taxes on food which would be paid chiefly by the poor.

At Messina the nobles and city fathers were able to redress the balance of power in 1462. They were opposed by a doctor named Mallone who had a large popular following. Mallone at one stage forced his way into a meeting between the mayor and his counsellors while the mob was in uproar outside. What little we know suggests that this was a serious conflict for power and the culmination of a long controversy. The popular leaders were evidently not irresponsible anarchists but were upholding the compromise of 1449 which had received royal approval. For a while they succeeded, and during 1463 Mallone was in power; but the following year he disappeared to an unknown fate in prison. Probably internal divisions had undermined the democrats, and the nobles may have bribed the Viceroy to restore their authority—he is known to have been open to bribes. The landed proprietors and merchants thus recaptured their monopoly of power and signalised the fact by making a special grant to the King. The old city taxes, removed by Mallone and the reformers, were reimposed in order to find the money for this grant and to consolidate the authority of the counter revolution.

Not only these internal divisions but also the rivalries between one city and another prevented the development of a middle class with common political interests. Catania and Messina in the fifteenth century both contended with Palermo for pre-eminence. For a time Catania seemed to be winning: it had the only university, and under Alfonso it was sometimes preferred as the residence of the Viceroy and of parliament. On the other hand, Messina in a number of parliaments between 1410 and 1478 claimed to be the true capital, and her representatives showed themselves ready to back their claim by force. Both Catania and Messina strenuously and successfully resisted the contention that Palermo should have a university of her own, and by so doing they caused Sicily nothing but harm.

A symptom of the lop-sided development of Sicilian cities was that foreign merchants took such a dominant place in their economy. These were mostly Spaniards, for Sicily was an important part of the Catalan economic empire and a market where Catalan cloth was exchanged for wheat. The King of Aragon not only paid some of his servants by giving them jobs and pensions in Sicily, but also settled some of his domestic debts by selling to Catalan merchants a privileged economic position there. Trapani, the nearest port to Spain, was built into a flourishing community by the Spanish connection, and this reflected a transference of wealth and population from eastern to western Sicily.

The Genoese were the next largest foreign element in the country. Being bankers as well as merchants, they could provide Alfonso with what he needed at Naples, and in return received special privileges in Sicily. Former Sicilian Kings had exempted them from local taxes and given their consuls extra-territorial rights. Frequently they quarrelled with Aragon over control of the grain trade, yet their privileged position survived just because everyone gained from it; and although Genoa itself no doubt profited the most, Sicily too benefited enormously in terms of good foreign currency. Not only the King, but also many of the landowners came to rely on Genoese credit, and so did the town of Messina itself. In some years Genoa took more cereals and cheese from Sicily than did Spain, and the rare occasions when we possess comparable figures suggest that, especially after 1450, their ships sometimes outnumbered Catalan in Sicilian ports. Their money and initiative also enabled them to outdistance Sicilians in the valuable coral fisheries along the North African coast.

Italian merchants and bankers played an important part in Sicilian history. Charles of Anjou had especially favoured those from Tuscany, and many Pisan merchant families came to live permanently in Sicily, while Venetian and Florentine galleys used to stop at both Messina and Palermo and put the country in touch with England and Flanders. Venice early had a church and a consul in Palermo. These Italian connections, encouraged as they were by the Spanish administration, helped to keep Sicily from being too exclusively absorbed into the world of Spanish culture, and Alfonso's annexation of Naples partly healed the breach of 1282. There were also English merchants at Messina as early as 1405; and in 1450, nearly half the contents of a shop at Trapani was made up of English cloth. In the sixteenth century the English merchants had a consul at Trapani and another at Messina (where the word *'ngrisi* came to mean 'foreign' or 'incomprehensible'): they took away silk and saltpetre, and in return brought tin, lead and herrings.

Even more important was Ragusa, the modern Dubrovnik, which for centuries continued to have a large colony of merchants in Sicily. Ragusan merchants possessed the advantage of political neutrality, being vassals of the Turkish Sultan yet also protected by the Pope. They therefore retained a favoured position at Alexandria and were a useful intermediary with the world of Islam. If Sicily had not compromised her neutrality through subordination to Spain, perhaps Sicilian merchants would have enjoyed a similar advantage. Sometimes in Messina harbour there were more ships from Ragusa than from anywhere else. They were not discouraged by Spain. Alfonso in 1438, and subsequent Spanish Kings, confirmed to the Ragusan merchants free anchorage rights and an exemption from customs duty.

Chapter 10

A PROVINCE OF THE CASTILIAN EMPIRE

In 1458, Alfonso died, bestowing Naples on his illegitimate son but his other kingdoms on his brother John. Sicilians were given no say in the matter. The straits of Messina once again became a barrier, and John divorced Sicily still further from the rest of Italy by proclaiming that the island should never again be a kingdom separate from Aragon. There seems to have been no active resistance to this revolutionary and wholly 'unconstitutional' proclamation. If there had been, John could hardly have overcome it, for he had no available forces to spare and his authority was gravely threatened in Spain itself.

Parliament met in 1458 at Caltagirone, and the King's weakness was such that political and economic grievances could be freely voiced. John was requested to allow that the King's eldest son should always be Viceroy. He did not accept this, but instead granted a petition of the barons which asked that their liability for military service should be reduced by two-thirds, and that *donativi* should not be imposed without parliamentary approval. He also agreed that no one except Sicilians could acquire lands and castles in the island. But where the direct interests of Spain were concerned he was less amenable. Parliament begged in vain for the King to make peace with Genoa and the Turks, or at least to negotiate a safe conduct for Sicilian merchants in the eastern Mediterranean; he could not permit the enemies of Spain to be allowed to trade in Sicily, nor that Moslem merchants should be free of molestation within sixty miles of the Sicilian coast. When it was asked that in that case Spain should at least guarantee defence against the Moors and restore the galleys which Alfonso had taken away, this met with no reply.

The big test of local feeling came when the nobles and merchants of Catalonia rebelled against John and sent to ask for Sicilian help. Their envoys found no enthusiasm. On the contrary Sicily provided men and ships to put down their rebellion, just as she had been glad to help maintain the Aragonese dominion over Sardinia and Naples. Parliament also made a grant to help Aragon subdue the Moors of Granada. A considerable amount of bullion was taken to Spain, so throwing the monetary system of the island into further disarray, and debts were contracted for the wars and then made a charge on the Sicilian exchequer. John had little to fear in doing this, because the feudatories depended upon him. Many of them in any case were involved financially with the Spanish government and did not wish to lose what they were owed.

Very rarely indeed did the Sicilian parliament come remotely near refusing a government request for taxation. But in 1478, some years after the Catalan revolt, there occurred one of the few direct confrontations in Sicilian history. The Viceroy wanted money for war against the Turks and to put down another revolt in Sardinia. He carefully (and quite unusually) prepared the ground by visiting the chief towns of the island to explain this emergency need, and clearly he anticipated trouble. Some towns agreed without demur, but some made difficulties, for the Turkish war could be considered a Spanish interest and against the commercial advantage of Sicily. When parliament finally met, the representatives of Messina created further trouble by claiming to take precedence over those of Palermo. Then the ruling elite of Palermo was persuaded to grant the tax, but for once ran into huge opposition from their fellow citizens. The Viceroy shifted parliament to the more favourable environment of Catania, and every means of bribery and intimidation were then used, without avail. The tax was never granted and the Viceroy had to be replaced. This one instance shows that at least the possibility existed of parliament developing some kind of counterpoise or check to the government and representing a broad front of Sicilian opinion; yet though dislike of taxes was enormous, it never took shape in any purposeful constitutional development.

In 1479, John was succeeded by Ferdinand and he, through his wife Isabella, united Aragon with Castile. The Spanish peninsula was becoming a single nation, and in the rapidly enlarging Spanish empire Sicily was inevitably condemned to take a small and diminishing place. Local interests were considered less and less, even though local taxes went on increasing. The conquest of Granada and war against the Turks both made demands on Sicily, and African gold which arrived in payment for Sicilian wheat was again used to pay for military provision. Ferdinand also decided to conquer southern Italy from his cousin, and hence Sicily had to aid yet another invasion of Naples. Gonzalo de Córdova set up his camp at Messina in 1495. By 1504 he had made Naples into a Spanish possession, so that once again the 'two Sicilies' owned a common allegiance.

Another sign of subservience was the introduction of the new Spanish Inquisition. From 1487 onwards the notorious Torquemada was sending Inquisitors to Sicily, and soon a permanent institution was properly organised with its headquarters in the royal palace at Palermo. Naples successfully resisted the introduction of the Holy Office; but in Sicily, though there was some initial opposition to it, to be enrolled as an Inquisition official was soon regarded as a great privilege by the Sicilian nobility. The chief Inquisitors were always, or almost always, Spaniards. Their devoted intolerance helped to keep Sicily orthodox and eliminate 'racial' minorities; but, at a time when the civilisation of the Renaissance was advancing elsewhere in Europe, the country was insulated from much of what was most challenging in contemporary culture. Messina towards the end of the fifteenth century was a minor centre of intellectual life, and books were being printed at both Palermo and Messina before 1480, but much of this spirit of intellectual freedom was subsequently lost in a world of moral and ecclesiastical censorship.

The expulsion of the Jews in 1492 further exemplifies the subordination of Sicily to policies decided in Spain. There were many Jews in Sicily: in some urban areas it is possible that they were a tenth of the population. In general they had kept a certain amount of religious freedom and their own schools and magistrates. Earlier laws had forced them to wear special clothes and forbidden them to hold public office or act as doctors to Christians, but often, despite ecclesiastical protest, they had managed to buy special favours. They had, for example, paid a subsidy to help the Spanish conquest of the Moors. They were active not simply in money-lending, but as weavers, goldsmiths and metal workers, and in every branch of commerce. Sometimes the only traders in the small country towns seem to have been Jews. They were especially celebrated as doctors. But occasional outbursts of racial intolerance grew suddenly worse after 1450, and these were made more acute by the fact that private individuals and the monarch himself stood to gain from the confiscation of Jewish property. From a parliamentary protest of 1460 we know that rates of interest were now rising above 10 per cent, and perhaps there was a wider crisis of credit underlying this development of anti-Semitism.

Although the citizens of Palermo protested that the Jews were doing no harm and their expulsion would hurt trade, the orders from Spain were firm. How many of them emigrated after 1492 and how many were 'converted' and allowed to stay cannot be said. Even converts forfeited much of their property, and probably a good deal of their wealth was taken out of Sicily. Many Jews left for Africa and the Levant; some even went to Rome and Naples, because other parts of Italy were less ready to accept the extreme intolerance of Spain. Even though many of them must have remained, the country lost some industrious citizens and no doubt a lot of capital too; and this lack of craftsmen and of organised credit were to rank among the chief weaknesses of the Sicilian economy.

A number of insurrections took place in Sicily between 1510 and 1525. These are still a little mysterious, though it is hard to follow those historians who think them to have been a kind of national resistance movement against Spain; probably they derived from a temporary disquiet among the baronage. For the last 250 years the barons had met little serious hindrance to their gradual encroachment on crown and communal property. Often, indeed, the government had abetted these encroachments, either in return for money, or else looking on this as a cheap price to pay for neutralising the main potential source of political opposition. Yet by 1500 this was changing; because the growing need of the state for revenue, together with new ideas about royal sovereignty and the need to make Sicily a strong military bastion, all gave the authorities the wish to halt this process. Sometimes there was merely a desire to revoke some past concession so that it could be sold all over again, but sometimes there was a more constructive desire to impose strong rule and eliminate the inefficiency which made government so difficult. By 1500, the King was becoming stronger in relation to the barons than he had been for a long time. Firearms were upsetting in his favour the internal balance of power, and a sharp increase of taxes had the same effect. When the County of Modica fell vacant, Ferdinand was able to override the claims of a prominent Sicilian family and give it to one of his own kinsmen. There was also a move towards bringing the nobles more under the direct jurisdiction of the royal courts; the government even proceeded against them *ex abrupto* and by using torture.

Eventually this reached such proportions as to seem an organised attack on baronial privilege, especially when Ugo Moncada arrived in 1509 as Viceroy to make Sicily a military base for the conquest of North Africa. Moncada had been a general with Cesare Borgia and Gonzalo de Córdova. As a military man he had no patience with traditional niceties; he simply needed large sums of money for his African war. Complaints were made by the victims of Moncada's firmness that he was loose-living and avaricious, but the more substantial objection was that he never took the barons' advice. He was haughty towards them and relied too much on either newcomers from Spain or else humble professional officials. By studying the royal archives, one of the Chancery secretaries, Luca Barberi, discovered that many overmighty subjects, ecclesiastical and lay, illegally held estates which belonged in law to the crown, and that many feudal obligations had over the centuries been conveniently forgotten. Fiefs therefore began to be confiscated and nobles imprisoned. Parliament protested violently that such acts were against 'the peace and quiet of the barons', and pointed out that Ferdinand had sworn to observe Sicilian laws, which presumably included Alfonso's law of 1452 which recognised the *de facto* possession of fiefs as evidence of ownership. Barberi was accused of every offence from taking bribes to killing a Negro slave; and some of the landowners, especially as they were beginning to face unexpected financial difficulties on their estates, were now emboldened to take a political stand before this monarchical revisionism had gone too far.

Other grievances also existed. The powers of the Holy Office were increased under Moncada, and, even though the chroniclers suggest that Sicilians enjoyed seeing people burnt alive, the occasional riots against the prisons and secret archives of the Inquisition indicate that its proceedings aroused great fear and hostility in certain quarters. Already the Inquisitors were reputed to be becoming rich from forfeited property (which they claimed in virtue of a blatantly forged document), and Moncada warned the King that deprived families were agitating to recover their confiscated goods. A new tax in 1512 on grain exports was also a blow to landowners and merchants alike. So was the Viceroy's attempt to suspend St. Cristina's fair during which Palermitans had had the valuable privilege of not paying customs or excise duty. In 1512 Moncada caused immense annoyance by calling in all the debased currency and requisitioning precious metals in order to issue a better coinage: this was perhaps a necessary act, but people did not receive the full face value of their money, and other interests thought themselves damaged when the King gave Messina valuable monopoly rights for minting coins. Finally there was enormous feeling against the Spanish soldiers when they arrived back from North Africa unpaid and began to commandeer food. When a mob riot broke out in which many soldiers were killed, Moncada executed the leaders, including at least one 'gentleman'.

Matters came to a head when the Viceroy called parliament in 1516 and made it clear that more money was required. Some nobles were still supporting him, but others were full of grievances. The sudden news of the King's death gave his opponents their chance, for they could claim that this automatically abrogated the Viceroy's authority; and when Moncada dissolved parliament, some of them reassembled at Termini on their own initiative. Once again parliament, this time under baronial leadership, seemed to be on the point of developing a life of its own.

Meanwhile a more popular revolution broke out at Palermo. This may have been touched off by the unemployment which followed the closing of parliament and the withdrawal of the barons. Moncada's story was that the revolt was organised by nobles who had criminal gangs in their employ—similar stories were told, perhaps truthfully, about every Sicilian rebellion from the Vespers to the movements led by Garibaldi and Giuliano—and he added that those who tried to stop it had their houses destroyed. Another ingredient was said to be a race riot against Jews who claimed to have been converted to Christianity, but this is doubtful: indeed, since the Spanish Inquisitors were attacked, very different sentiments may have been involved. At all events it was a serious uprising. Cannon were stolen from the city bastions and trained on the Viceroy's palace. Moncada in desperation reduced the food taxes and dismissed Barberi, but too late, and he himself was lucky to escape to Messina. The soldiers, after pillaging his palace, opened its doors to the citizenry: many of the archives were destroyed on this occasion, and an orgy of theft spread through the capital. The prospect of a tax-free holiday was irresistible. Other cities also gave way to rioting, and in some places a civil war broke out between rival families.

For nearly a year the government was in abeyance. Though the nobles at Palermo continued to protest their full loyalty to the Spanish throne, two of their number became presidents of an interim administration. The Messinese, on the other hand, supported Moncada and showed a familiar suspicion of anything that happened on the other side of the island. Eventually Moncada advised the King to try appointing an Italian Viceroy, and in 1517 arrived a Neapolitan, the Count of Monteleone. All now returned to something like normal: the food taxes were restored in order to balance the city's budget; a few of the magnates were banished and others imprisoned, while another close examination was made of baronial privileges.

Perhaps for this reason, another revolt broke out shortly afterwards. Its leader, Squarcialupo, had taken part in the previous rising. He was a minor noble, poor and in debt, but in the dim background of his rebellion were some of the leading families of Sicily. In the foreground once again were elements of the Palermo mob under a *capo popolo* named Zazara and several other gang leaders. There was remarkably little sign of any anti-Spanish feeling. Probably this was another mixed protest against inflation, government centralisation, and depreciation of the barons. Monteleone, too, was compelled to escape to Messina; his residence at Palermo was attacked, and some of his officers were castrated and thrown out of the palace windows on to the pikes of the populace. Again factions seized power in other towns. Squarcialupo managed to rule as a popular dictator for a few weeks, but as soon as it was clear that he did not possess the resources to win, some of his friends switched to supporting the Viceroy in a counter-revolution: in particular his somewhat doctrinaire republicanism and collaboration with popular elements did not appeal to others of his own class. He was eventually assassinated while kneeling at Mass, and Monteleone then carried out a severe repression. This revolt, like its predecessor, proved that the Sicilian aristocracy possessed little cohesion and were unlikely to be able to form a significant opposition to Spain; they had no leadership, no coherent political ideals or constructive suggestions for maintaining Sicilian liberties against the advance of Spanish centralisation.

There was a third revolt in 1523, this time instigated from France and involving Church dignitaries at Rome as well as a number of well-born Sicilians. These latter included the pretender to the County of Modica and others who had been highly placed in government service. But the conspiracy, which had little substance, was betrayed ahead of time. The brothers Imperatore were executed, and their quartered bodies were hung up as a warning in iron cages suspended from the palace walls. This was one of the surprisingly few attempts ever made by Sicilians to exploit the almost permanent state of hostility between France and Spain.

By this time there was a new King and a new dynasty. Ferdinand died in 1516 leaving no male heirs by his two wives, and since his daughter Joanna was out of her mind, he was succeeded by his grandson. Charles V was an Austrian Habsburg. He also ruled over Spain, but it was a Spain which no longer meant Aragon and Barcelona; the centre of gravity was now rather Castile and Cadiz; the Mediterranean would soon be less important than the Atlantic. Sicily thus found herself displaced from being a pivotal point in the Aragonese empire to being a relatively insignificant place on the periphery of something much larger; for the new routes to the Indies opened up by Portugal and Spain were to lose this island her profitable position on the main trade route of the western world. The process required some painful adjustment. Nevertheless Sicily proved one of the most loyal provinces of the Habsburg empire. Judging from Guicciardini's *History of Italy*—and Botta's supplementary volumes for the years after 1534—Sicily was hardly thought of any longer by other Italians as an integral part of their own community.

Photograph Mondadori Press

The 13th-century castle of Ursino, Catania

Palazzo Aiutamicristo, Palermo: 15th century

Tim Benton

Baronial stronghold at Caccamo

Ezio Quir

PART 4
Spanish Administration 1500–1650

Chapter 11

GOVERNORS AND GOVERNED

Spanish rule has sometimes been blamed for corrupting Sicily, for causing economic decline and social maladjustment, for perverting a healthy baronial class, setting Sicilians against each other, and giving an example of idleness and political apathy. But like all such historical accusations, the charge is not easy to prove or refute. It can be admitted that, as Spanish monarchs ruled Sicily for more than four centuries, the influence of Spain must have been extensive: the administration at Palermo was run by Spaniards and the ruling class became up to a point Spanish by origin. Nevertheless, many things ascribed to this alien influence were experienced in other countries which were quite outside the orbit of Spain, and that vague complex of qualities named pejoratively as *spagnolismo* sometimes seemed to characterise the Sicilian ruled more than their Spanish rulers.

Spanish policy admittedly aimed at conservation rather than improvement, and in this long period a great number of things changed surprisingly little. The Viceroys were not charged with devising fundamental reforms. They were chiefly concerned to keep the country quiet, to provide cheap bread, adequate fortifications, and wages for the army. They had instructions to maintain royal privileges, to put down banditry, and of course to collect as much tax as the country would stand. Twice a day at specified times they were meant to receive complaints and petitions, and they were told to be especially alert to prevent oppression of the poor. They were expected during their period of office to tour the island once or twice, though in practice they divided their time between Palermo and Messina and saw little else. Each Viceroy, when he returned to Spain, drafted a general report on his work, but these reports were surprisingly similar and often appear to have copied fairly freely from each other; seldom did they penetrate beneath the surface.

The grandees of Spain, from whose ranks came most Viceroys, regarded the office as very honourable. The salary was not at first lavish and there was plenty of costly entertainment;

but a good number of regular and irregular perquisites were available, and the appointment acquired the reputation of being one of the most lucrative in the Spanish service. Probably it was sometimes bought, and some incumbents are known to have done very well out of it. Medinaceli married off two daughters to rich Sicilians in the 1560s. Earlier, de Spes had married a local heiress and thus acquired a Sicilian county which passed to his family in Spain; he had also used his authority to arm several pirate vessels on his own account and press-ganged Sicilians to act as oarsmen. Other Viceroys, too, engaged in privateering, others in trade either personally or through their families. The temptations were such, and Sicilians were in some ways so difficult, that few Spanish governors survived without stirring up some kind of criticism. Almost all of them were faulted for being either too strong or too weak. Even honest efficiency was disliked; and no credit was given when, at the end of the sixteenth century, a Viceroy decided to be firm about appointing officials on merit and to make them keep fixed hours and work in proper offices at the royal palace; for the selling of jobs and justice was the common practice, and excessive zeal was not encouraged.

No doubt sometimes the wrong man was chosen as Viceroy, and too much weight was given to consideration of rank or even to the desirability of exiling a man temporarily from Spain. King Philip II, who succeeded Charles in 1556, was hard-working and had an over-developed sense of responsibility, but he never established effective bureaucratic control over Sicily. Vast quantities of paperwork submerged him in Madrid. He was slow to decide matters and temperamentally disinclined from taking radical solutions. Like his father, and despite protests from successive Viceroys, Philip liked to have his say in choosing even lesser officials in the Sicilian government. He frequently neglected to ask local advice. Yet despite this autocracy he could not make himself properly obeyed. Repeated orders to Palermo simply went unanswered, partly because letters took anything up to three months to arrive, but also because powerful Sicilians and local officials realised that unwelcome changes could, with care, be postponed indefinitely.

Philip set up a Council of Italy at Madrid to regulate the administration of his Italian provinces—Naples, Sicily, Milan,

Corsica and Sardinia. One Sicilian usually sat on this Council, though it was customary for a clear majority to be Spaniards. It tried to keep a fairly close control over the Viceroy. Its members sometimes used their influence to obtain jobs in Sicily for their relatives, and repeated regulations against bribing members of the Council show that bribery was often attempted. The Council of State in Madrid could override the Council of Italy and sometimes corresponded directly with the Viceroy. Both these councils were on the whole well informed about Sicilian affairs, yet they could not overcome the King's dilatoriness. All too often they neither controlled government effectively nor allowed the Viceroy enough initiative to act on his own.

The Spanish practice delighted in checks and balances. A slightly independent position was therefore given at Palermo to the *Consultor*, an invariably Spanish official who acted as the Viceroy's deputy. Likewise the Inquisition was for a long time outside the Viceroy's control, and sometimes the army and navy were too. These various organisations developed separate legal systems and tribunals with a jurisdiction distinct from the ordinary courts: so did the archbishops, the customs authorities, the Auditor General, and several minor tax authorities, to say nothing of the individual barons. A skilful offender could easily play one court against another, and the confusion made civil and criminal offences relatively easy. Every twenty years or so in the sixteenth century an official *Visitador* was sent from Madrid, who had to check that justice was being done, who investigated complaints, and confirmed that the Viceroy and other officials were not exceeding their powers. In 1562, after complaints had been made, the Marques de Oriolo arrived and virtually supplanted the Viceroy Medinaceli: he summoned parliament on his own initiative, dismissed magistrates, and even imprisoned and tortured the Viceroy's friends. Though in some respects beneficial, the arrival of a *Visitador* disrupted routine and undermined respect for the administration, just as it also encouraged tale-telling. A *Visitador* in 1607 took it on himself to give a free pardon to a man already sentenced to death for the capital crimes of banditry and sodomy: this may possibly have ingratiated him with the public, but it cannot have helped the Viceroy or increased the respect for public law.

One barrier to administrative reform was the Sicilian attachment to privileges and questions of protocol and precedence which, as the King warned one Viceroy, "mean so much to everyone in Italy". Sometimes a Viceroy was surprised by Palermo or Messina producing a privilege of which he had never heard; and if he questioned the matter, the town might be able to refer the matter straight to Madrid over his head. Another barrier to reform was that powerful people in Sicily sometimes bribed officials in Madrid to oppose change. Messina found it worth while to send an occasional 'ambassador' to Spain, while the city authorities of Palermo sometimes kept one at both Madrid and Rome; and the only functions of such an envoy were to preserve privileged immunities from viceregal interference.

A still greater obstacle was that native-born administrators were so often partisan in any dispute and bound by inveterate tradition to push the interests of their own kin and their own clienteles. Although parliament monotonously protested against giving jobs to non-Sicilians, the Viceroys regularly advised that local feuds, kinship ties and the corruption and bullying in local politics demanded the appointment of more foreigners. The Sicilian official class cannot in any case have been very large. Indeed it must have been seriously depleted in 1527 when, at a reception after a wedding between the families of Moncada and Ventimiglia, a floor collapsed and two hundred people died, the Viceroy himself and the bridal couple only just escaping. There was another serious accident in 1590, when the Viceroy's ship, returning from Messina, pulled away a jerry-built landing stage at Palermo and precipitated a substantial proportion of the Sicilian ruling elite into the water: the Viceroy again just escaped, but among the drowned were many senior officials and nobles in waiting.

The notorious weakness of the government was its corruption, a malady which was widespread in a society that regarded public office as predominantly a source of private advantage. Rich Sicilian aristocrats could apparently hire the Great Seal to authorise some private malpractice; and though evidence for such activities was fairly easily concealed, we know of salaries being paid to non-existent officials; we know that a scrupulous Viceroy might find that the Treasury had big gaps in its accounts, and probably this was not even so very unusual. Money could buy liberation from prison or the imprisonment and torture of a private enemy.

The sale of justice was frequently denounced, not only by the losing parties to an action; we have confirmation from parliament in 1523 that judges were purchasing their jobs and then selling justice to recoup the expense. Parliament also pointed out that public administration and judgeships were becoming inheritable private property. The King, though he replied by ordering that no one should buy their way on to the bench, could not enforce this kind of regulation in practice, for the sale of offices was a regular item in the revenue; and naturally the barons followed suit and sold public offices in their own fiefs. On several occasions Charles V forbade officials to receive presents, even of food; but the financial accounts of the aristocracy continue to show regular gifts to the judges, and probably suborning the law was normal. In order to discourage excessive litigation, the King in 1569 decided that judges in civil actions should be paid not by salary but by fees: this only led them to neglect criminal cases in favour of more profitable actions, and the prisons therefore became dangerously overcrowded. Under such conditions it is not surprising to encounter the assumption that individuals should obtain their own justice for themselves by their own strength, money or wit. That the laws were in any case impossibly confused was a subject of another parliamentary complaint in 1579.

Successive Viceroys, Italian as well as Spanish, were fond of expatiating in their reports on the character of the natives. Whether or not they copied from each other, the general conclusions remained much the same and received general confirmation from other visitors. There was admiration for a subtle inventiveness and sharpness of mind, as there was only praise for the loyalty to Spain, the friendliness to foreigners, and the readiness to obey really firm government. Yet Sicilians were criticised for being the most vengeful and passionate people in the world. Their capacity for false witness and bribery was notorious. Not only were they uncouth and ill bred, but they concentrated selfishly on their own good without consideration for the common weal. They had not the slightest interest in other countries. They were "a people greedy of honour, yet given to ease and delight, talkative, meddlesome, dissentious, zealous and revengeful"—that was the confirmatory verdict of the Englishman Sandys about 1610. They despised a gentle ruler, but would accept a good deal from the Viceroy so long as he listened to their complaints and maintained their precious privileges. The general advice was that a Viceroy ought to be absolutely firm in his orders, for he could get absolutely nothing done without using the threat of force; on the other hand he should also humour the leading citizens by inviting them to lunch or to accompany him at Mass.

Successive Viceroys agreed that the nobility had a vanity and status-consciousness which made them waste their energies in eternal quarrels about rank and precedence. However combative in private life, they were quite useless for service in the army or navy; and where possible they should be kept away from public business, at least in Sicily itself. Spaniards or Germans would be much more reliable and impartial. As Gonzaga said when asking for an Inquisitor to put down Lutheranism, a Sicilian would lack the necessary authority with his fellow citizens just because he was a Sicilian. In any case, the lack of education meant that there was no large enough class of intellectuals from which subordinate officials could be drawn. The single university at Catania was very small, and the examinations were so easy that a doctorate there meant nothing.

Many Sicilians were equally explicit about their own limitations, and hence they were grateful to Spain for providing a workable structure of administration. Some Neapolitan writers were later to lament the arrival of the Spanish in Sicily on the grounds that this island was thereby divorced from the Italian mainland with which she rightly belonged. To Sicilians, on the contrary, the Vespers and their invocation of Spain in 1282 became the very symbol of local liberties against the desire of Naples to dominate and exploit. Any government tended to be disliked and criticised in Sicily, but animus was directed much less against Spain than Naples. Spaniards were rarely treated as enemies and hardly even as foreign; intermarriage with them was frequent; and Castilian now replaced Catalan as the language of administration and of the social life which pivoted on the court.

Successive Spanish administrators realised that the cheapest way to hold the island with only a small garrison was to introduce few changes and as little challenge as possible to local susceptibilities and privileges. Sicily claimed to have voluntarily given herself to Spain, whereas Naples after 1504 could be treated more as conquered territory. The Neapolitan parliament disappeared under the Spanish administration whereas that of Sicily was retained. The royal bureaucracy in Naples had an easier task introducing reforms, but Sicily was more obviously a separate kingdom with its own laws. The Sicilian barons had to be flattered, and it was fortunate that their loyalty was cheaply bought. Social reforms, therefore, even where recognised as desirable, had preferably to be renounced in deference to baronial interests. So long as social revolution was exorcised by keeping the poor happy with cheap bread, the government merely had to perpetuate among other classes the illusion that their parliament and privileges saved them from Spanish exploitation. Far from being oppressive, indeed, Spain could more properly be accused of being too lax, too respectful of the antiquated feudal parliament and of the privileged immunities of nobles, clergy and the town guilds. If only Spain had been more oppressive, perhaps Sicilians might have been provoked into a greater political awareness and more sense of self-determination.

This is not to say that Sicily was completely supine and satisfied under Spanish administration. There had been three revolts against Moncada and Monteleone between 1516 and 1523. In 1555, two of the richest Sicilian aristocrats, finding it hard to approach the King through his ministers at Madrid, travelled to London to find Philip in his capacity as King of England, and persuaded him that the Viceroy was favouring the lower classes against the nobility—de Vega had gone so far as to have nobles whipped or imprisoned just as if they were ordinary mortals. To satisfy them, the Viceroy was withdrawn by being promoted to the presidency of the Royal Council at Madrid. Other complaints were laid against Viceroys for venality, lack of tact, or for sexual peccadilloes. Medinaceli was even attacked for his undignified habit of slipping away from his courtiers by a back door of the palace to go with his servants to the beach for a swim.

On several occasions it is recorded that people were bold

enough to shout abusive and ironic words at the Viceroy as he embarked for Spain after surrendering office; but even in their most obstreperous moments of opposition, Sicilians were seen carrying the royal flag and burning candles before the King's picture. If they rebelled, it was against individual afflictions— hunger, the aristocracy, badly distributed taxes, or a Viceroy whose fount of patronage was running dry. Several times there were serious outbreaks against the Spanish soldiers—not for being Spanish, but rather for their treatment of Sicilian women, or because of burnt crops, stolen animals and the usual billeting problems. People would flare up if ever they thought their privileges jeopardised, but only for a brief moment and without direction; and invariably there was a reaction in favour of Spain.

At all events there was nothing in Sicily remotely comparable to the patriotic revolt of the Netherlands against Spanish rule, or to the rebellions of Catalonia, Portugal and Lutheran Germany. On the contrary, when Catalonia in the 1460s and 1640s was imperilling the unity of Spain itself, Sicilians refused to join these rebellions and rather helped to put them down. Outbreaks occurred against the royal advisers, or against Sicilians who had bought up the right to farm the taxes, but almost never against Spain. Nor did they take place against the King, who remained the symbol of justice and the redressor of wrongs. In 1606, quite exceptionally, a Sicilian, the Marquis of Geraci, was appointed acting-Viceroy, but a large sum was offered to the King by other Sicilians to have him removed, which again suggests that Spanish rule must often have been positively welcomed as a corrective of local rivalries. By the same token, Messina repeatedly begged that their *strategoto* should be a foreigner.

Despite occasional restlessness, Sicilians seem to have been genuinely proud to belong to the Spanish empire; and when, in 1535, Charles V on the way back from Africa deigned to visit this remote province—the first sovereign to do so for a century and the last until 1714—his gracious condescension was warmly praised even though he loaded Sicilians with taxes. It was, indeed, this lack of political initiative or of rebelliousness which inhibited political development, much more at all events than any so-called Spanish oppression. Being ruled from Madrid relieved the barons of any necessity to transfer their family rivalries on to a political plane where the in-fighting would have been much more dangerous and costly.

The desire for independence was of course not absent, but it was personal rather than political or national. Each individual, like each class, had his own private interest to follow. On the other hand there was no feeling of general political coherence like that acquired by the Spanish kingdoms in their long struggle against the Moors or by the United Provinces against Spain. De Vega thus found that there was little feeling even for Sicilian national history, and one reason why he patronised the first two great Sicilian historians, Fazello and Maurolico, was to try to remedy this fact.

Sectional interests and loyalties were what really counted. When there was an insurrection at Palermo, Messina eagerly joined in repressing it, seizing the occasion to prove her fidelity to Spain; and likewise when Messina revolted, Palermo rallied to the crown, outraged at such disobedience. Some people relieved themselves from any responsibility for these internal rivalries by accusing Spain of deliberately setting the barons against the towns and the towns against each other; but Sicilians needed little encouragement to disagree among themselves, and the Viceroys were the first to be shocked by the way Sicilians wasted their energies on minor factiousness and sectional disagreement. Not only was city against city, but townsmen bickered with the country dwellers on whom they depended for food, and fear of either the town mob or the peasantry kept every other class in willing bondage to the government. Perhaps only the imposition of Spanish rule kept Sicily intact.

The most powerful people in Sicily, the *titulados* of the aristocracy, looked on the Spanish government as a guarantee of their privileged position. They had little to fear except social revolution; and it was because they feared social revolution more than Spain that the revolts of Squarcialupo and the Imperatore brothers did not receive general support. Having nothing much to gain by political independence, and being prudently allowed by the government to disobey the law within reason, the nobles made loyalty to the throne a point of pride. They went out of their way to celebrate the victories of Spain with clamorous festivities and fireworks as they tried to impress the ordinary people of Palermo with the uselessness of rebellion.

Chapter 12

PARLIAMENT

The composition of parliaments in the later Middle Ages had varied. Occasionally there was one assembly for east Sicily and one for the west. Despite the 'law' of 1296 about annual parliaments, many years could pass without any parliament being called at all, and sometimes the barons were summoned alone. By the fifteenth century, however, the Spanish Kings had introduced the custom of Aragon which consisted of fairly regular sessions of three separate *brazos* or Houses: the ecclesiastical, the baronial and the domanial. After the Viceroy's inaugural speech, these three *brazos* would meet separately to discuss his proposals, sending ambassadors to keep each other informed. According to Mongitore, who published the authoritative study on parliament in 1717, there was a strong tradition against raising contentious or 'frivolous' matters, since members knew they had come on the King's business. Some experts, he added, thought that a unanimous vote was needed. Voting was public, and a petition in 1562 to be able to vote by ballot was overruled.

The first House or *brazo* was that of the bishops and abbots, a privileged community who claimed exemption from many of the ordinary laws of secular society. Its leading members were a rich group, from whom any strong King would expect tax revenue, especially as most of their property had been a gift from previous sovereigns; and they also owed a special allegiance to the King in his capacity as Apostolic Legate. It was perhaps less easy for them than for the barons to pass their share of taxation on to others, and this made their House sometimes the least amenable to viceregal pressure. As the richer clergy were foreigners, this too gave them a certain independence, though the fact that they depended on the crown for their appointment and promotion kept their opposition within bounds. Absentee foreign prelates had only a limited interest in the liberties of Sicily. The archbishop of Palermo, almost always a foreigner, was usually their nominal head and the main spokesman for the whole of parliament:

later he was occasionally called the 'speaker' by those who tried
to invent a parallel with England.

The military or baronial House consisted of the leading
feudatories. These men were at first exempt from a good deal of
taxation in virtue of their liability to military service. In time
they were made to pay an increased share of some taxes, but the
accepted value of their estates was based upon defective feudal
registers and their own unchecked declarations to the authorities. As the King's policy was to indulge them in every matter
except political power, they were treated lightly, and in fact
their quota of taxation was easily passed on by them to their
tenants. Whenever they took the trouble, the barons were the
leading element in parliament, just because they were socially,
economically and militarily the most prominent people in the
island. They therefore could take the chief part in voting the
taxes paid by other people. But they were generally compliant
rather than nonconformist. In 1537 only two *titulados* out of
seventy thought it worth while making a personal appearance
in the baronial House; in 1540 only four; and the government
made non-attendance easy by the use of proxy voting.

The third *brazo*, as in Catalonia, was the royal or domanial
House, containing representatives from those towns which
remained directly subject to the King and were not part of any
feudal estate. A commission of parliament in 1398 listed forty-
five such places, though the number subsequently varied as
some towns were sold and others were re-acquired. A town could
possess more than one representative in parliament but never
more than one vote, unlike the barons who had as many votes
as they owned villages.

The domanial House showed some political awareness in the
fifteenth century, but little after 1478. Its members were
frequently selected by the government itself, and the representative of Catania, for example, came to be by tradition the
Viceroy's secretary despite a law of 1348 against the election of
government officials; even if they were technically chosen by
the civic council, this too could mean nomination by the local
baronage. Leading barons sometimes sat personally in this
House, and it became not unusual for a dozen noblemen
between them to control two-thirds of the membership. Most
representatives were in any case lawyers who needed to

ingratiate themselves with powerful people who could give them offices or advancement. One lawyer would often represent three or four towns at once. No member ever made any personal reputation in parliament until the early nineteenth century. The president of this House was usually the praetor or mayor of Palermo, who was always one of the greater nobility specially selected for this post by the government, a fact which helps to explain why the domanial *brazo* possessed so little vitality of its own. The election of representatives at Palermo was always a mere formality, and it was very rare for them ever to vote against the praetor's wishes.

The domanial *brazo* in course of time came to be compared to the House of Commons in England, but in fact the royal cities never stood together as champions of the third estate; they rather were more interested in trying to diminish each other and curry favour with the authorities. Some of the main towns were allowed to pay a ridiculously small share of the parliamentary *donativi*, and this reduced to minimal proportions any collective urban sentiment. Syracuse for five centuries claimed complete exemption by a privilege dating from 1298, and often for this reason decided to send no representatives to parliament. Palermo and Messina also sometimes claimed a special license, and sometimes they too sent no representatives, though usually they agreed to pay a certain sum so long as it kept a voluntary aspect and preferably was less than their fair share. Yet together the royal towns had to pay as large a quota of the *donativi* as the whole of feudal Sicily, even though the latter was by this time far more extensive and populous an area. Such an unbalanced tax system did great harm to the economy; and it could exist only because, in the domanial as in the baronial House, those who voted a tax were quite unrepresentative of the people who would carry the main burden. The various immunities established by the clergy, the barons, the richer towns and richer citizens in every town, meant that taxation fell chiefly on peasants and artisans who had no parliamentary spokesman; and hence parliament remained generally a willing co-operator with Spain and a conservative influence against reform.

Sicilians boasted that theirs was the only parliament apart from that of England to keep its old liberties. Some of them convinced themselves that it dated back to the fifth century before Christ. They cherished it as an embodiment of Sicilian nationhood and a recognition by Spain of the need to win local collaboration; nor was this entirely incorrect. Viceroys were recommended to respect parliamentary privileges, and knew that there might be trouble if they behaved without consideration or did not study the rule book. At certain vulnerable moments, as in 1478 against the Viceroy Prades, and in 1516 against Moncada, parliament briefly became a serious instrument of politics; and always it had a technical right of presenting petitions and approving the *donativi*. The need for increased taxation led to the summoning of parliaments every three years after 1500 and then almost once a year between 1531 and 1577; this gave every possible facility for the institution to develop politically. In 1539, after a disastrous harvest, there occurred one of the rare examples of the taxes proposed by the Viceroy being effectively reduced on a plea of poverty. In the 1560s parliament also sent a special ambassador to Madrid to protest against the Viceroy's behaviour. The sending of ambassadors to the King, over the Viceroy's head, became in fact a regular, if often pointless and expensive, operation.

Parliament, therefore, was one focus of any local discontent. There were occasional petitions against the Inquisition, against non-resident clergy, against militia service and the use of the Sicilian galleys for purposes other than defending the island. Just occasionally there may have been some genuine and perhaps even lively debates. In 1557 one man, the Count of Modica, was brave enough to give a contrary vote when the government tried to deprive him of his privileged immunity from paying export taxes on grain. In 1575 the Duke of Terranova obliquely referred to previous debates when he proudly informed the King that parliament had agreed to taxation "by an unanimous vote and had made their decision in a single day as has never been heard of before, since always there have turned out to be some delays and difficulties and sometimes the King's wishes have not been entirely carried out". Again in 1591, the Archbishop of Palermo told the ecclesiastical House that the grant of supply should be made conditional on the King's full acceptance of their privileges, and he even advocated that individuals should refuse to pay tax if further pressure were needed.

Such cases, however, were rare, and still more rare were occasions when an individual could carry his colleagues in championing a genuine public concern that went beyond private or sectional interest. Terranova had been careful to add that Sicily was the most obedient of all Spain's dominions, and in 1591 the Archbishop's opposition to the Viceroy was rejected by the representatives of the towns. Even the privileged elite in parliament was radically divided against itself. The 1591 parliament met at a moment which was quite exceptionally favourable to the development of an 'opposition', for there was an extreme food shortage, and an unpopular Viceroy had dared to attack both the Inquisition and the nobility: the baronial House eventually tried to hold up the grant of taxation, but they stood alone, and in this novel situation the government experts pronounced that the consent of two Houses would be sufficient to bind the third.

Parliament indeed seems to have been no more of a restraint on the government than was the Inquisition or indeed the Palermo mob. Although it could advise the Viceroy that the country was too poor to pay as much as he asked, nearly always the sum he demanded was at once granted, and those parliaments which lasted more than a few hours usually spent the time not resisting but discussing how to meet the King's wishes. It was quite exceptional when one parliament was allowed to continue for two months, and even on that occasion the representatives showed little sign of any desire to impose their will on the executive.

The Viceroy could anyway make laws on his own with no reference to parliament, whereas parliamentary petitions were frequently refused or given only qualified approval; often such petitions merely repeated requests of past years which, even when granted, had not been observed in practice. In any case parliament had to agree to taxation long before the King's answer to petitions could arrive from Spain, and this was another reason why money grants were never made conditional on redress of grievances. After 1600, these petitions seem to have been rarer, more trivial in substance, and less often granted than before. Parliament was to score another notable victory against a Viceroy in 1609, but, in fifty years, only on three occasions were there enactments of *capitoli* or parliamentary legislation, though there were numerous pragmatic sanctions which the Viceroy issued on his own authority: this does not betoken a flourishing parliamentary life or a widespread interest in affairs of state.

When parliament met, there were usually three sessions which stretched over about six days. This was too short for development of any corporate feeling, let alone of a regular opposition with a policy. Nor was there any fixed parliament chamber where members could meet and establish a sense of identity. Sessions could be held at Messina and Catania; and when they took place at Palermo they could be either in the royal palace, the cathedral, or in other churches, or even in private houses of the nobility. The result was that parliament was not thought of as a place for the manifestation of dissent. The poet Antonio Veneziano was imprisoned in 1588 for issuing a lampoon against the government, and was still in prison when in 1593 he was killed by an explosion in the arsenal; but parliament, unlike that in contemporary England, did not encourage such criticism. The clergy and the nobles had other means of political action. If there continued to be references to parliaments in contemporary diaries, it was chiefly to the solemnities attending their opening and closing, to the form instead of the substance.

A decisive fact was that the three *brazos* represented those classes which benefited most by Spanish rule. The nobles needed Spanish help too much to think of serious opposition except under an unusually tactless Viceroy, and it was easy for them to approve of taxation when they themselves had to pay relatively little. The barons' interest in parliament was therefore not as a political forum where the interests of Sicily could be debated, but as an occasion to obtain titles, jobs and privileges for their families and clients.

The Viceroy had nearly all the cards in his own hand. He appointed the heads of all three Houses, and had a preponderant share in choosing most of the ordinary members. One of his servants voted on behalf of any vacant diocese and for any fief where a baron had died without an heir, while of course he appointed the bishops and created new peerages. Royal officials had the advantage of knowing parliamentary procedure, and in each House they had a caucus of the 'King's friends' with whom conduct of business had been already discussed. Regularly the Viceroy wrote to the King with suggestions of titles, jobs and decorations to give prominent parliamentarians, or to ask that the King should merely write a few personal letters that would appeal to private vanity; and we know that such letters could be very effective. Alternatively, as in 1591, he could threaten a noble with punishment for his behaviour in parliament; but this was rarely necessary. If he anticipated opposition, he could even summon parliament in the rainy season when representatives of provincial areas simply could not reach Palermo.

Spain therefore had the best of both worlds: because parliament helped to raise taxes at the very same time that Sicilians believed it was jealously guarding their interests. The parliamentary *donativi* increased rapidly after a war crisis in the 1530s, and before long comprised between a third and a half of government revenue. The advantage of this kind of tax was its greater regularity than, for example, the wheat export licences which could completely stop after a bad harvest. It was more flexible and could be quickly increased. Furthermore, since parliament agreed to the *donativi*, and since a parliamentary committee collected them, their unpopularity did not fall entirely on the government.

As government expenditure grew, new *donativi* were introduced, and though the fiction was maintained that they were free gifts by parliament for special occasions, in practice once begun they continued indefinitely and were indeed spoken of as part of the *hacienda* of the King. One was introduced in 1555 for the repair of bridges, another in 1561 for the navy, and in 1564 there was voted the most considerable of all, the parliamentary *macinato* tax on the grinding of wheat. Others were subsequently granted for the militia, for the upkeep of the royal palaces, and the expenses of the Council of Italy at Madrid. Once granted, each of these was confirmed automatically by each subsequent parliament and remained a permanent article in the revenue.

The apportionment of the *donativi* between the various classes was sometimes admitted by the government itself to be unfair and uneconomic; yet the docility of parliament depended on a tacit compact by which the Viceroy, once the total sum had been fixed, left the privileged communities a fairly free hand in this highly sensitive field. How the money was raised was not his concern. By parliamentary decision, ecclesiastics were exempt from paying most of the ordinary *donativi* and on the rest paid usually one-sixth. A number of 'free cities' were also exempt. Palermo paid a nominal tenth. About a third each was allocated to the baronial and domanial Houses, in other words to the feudal and royal towns respectively. After a parliamentary committee had allotted each town and village its quota, either the local feudatory or a committee of wealthier citizens decided how to find the money, whether by a direct tax, or by borrowing, or—as was nearly always preferred—by indirect taxes or *gabelle* payable disproportionately by the labouring poor.

The unfairness of this system was obvious. Poor people in general, and especially in the royal towns, were worst hit. This was occasionally deplored by the authorities at Madrid, while even parliament itself frequently mentioned the need to exempt day labourers and introduce some measure of tax graduation. Public protests were on occasion registered against the bishops and against Palermo for tax avoidance. Non-residents sometimes took out nominal citizenship at Palermo solely in order to escape tax on their income elsewhere, and apparently they did the same at Syracuse, just as many people made fictitious charitable gifts to the Church so as to benefit from ecclesiastical immunities. An occasional objection was voiced against these procedures, but they continued all the same. The census, on which tax allocations were based, did not include the main privileged classes; and even a number of cities were excused from it. Census officials were also accused of corruptly favouring the barons against the towns. It has even been suggested, perhaps extravagantly, that the number of exemptions reduced the parliamentary *donativi* to a tenth of what they could or should have been.

One body which helped to create and preserve these exemptions was a committee of parliament copied from the Cortes of Aragon. The Deputation was an executive committee which continued in existence during a parliamentary recess and in theory was meant to act as a committee of privileges which could protest if the government ever tried to alter the 'fundamental laws' of the kingdom. This function soon became largely atrophied. The Deputation was also responsible for the allocation and collection of the *donativi*. At first it used to meet on its own initiative in a private house, but in the late 1560s the Viceroy Pescara brought it more under government control. He took over appointment of its twelve members, four from each House, and was careful to include some royal officials. Henceforward they were instructed to meet every Thursday afternoon in the Viceroy's palace, and their deliberations needed his ratification. The collection of most *donativi* was taken away from them, because clearly a good deal of the money had not been properly accounted for; but they were still allowed to supervise the census, and to continue administering some of the taxes, including those for bridges and public works.

These functions, supported by a considerable secretariat, aimed at protecting the privileged classes rather than maintaining Sicilian liberties or enhancing the prerogatives of parliament. The duties of the Deputation lay lightly on its members. For two centuries, so ran one complaint, not a single bridge was built or repaired in this land of mountains, valleys and torrential streams, and the tax money collected for bridges simply disappeared in accounts which no one could understand. The government knew that the deputies used their position to tax themselves and their relatives very gently. Subordinate officials exploited the committee for their own private ends. Meetings were held spasmodically, and membership became mainly honorific. Even the four representatives of the domanial House were regularly princes and dukes, and sometimes there was no one even so lowly as a baron among them. Nevertheless members took great pride in their office, and Viceroys encouraged this as a means of obtaining a modicum of unpaid service from Sicilian noblemen in the highly unpopular field of tax collecting. Without this Deputation, Spain's task in governing Sicily would have been much harder.

Chapter 13

FOREIGN POLICY, PIRACY AND DEFENCE

The King's interest in Sicily was mainly for the help which the local population could give towards Habsburg policy in Europe and the Mediterranean. When Charles V in 1519 became Emperor as well as King, he inherited interests which stretched from Africa to the Baltic, and soon as far as Mexico and Peru. Spain had to fight for long periods against the Turks and France, not to speak of shorter wars against Germans, Dutch, English, Portuguese and even the papacy. Sicily had no obvious interest in these wars except that against the Turks, yet was forced to contribute towards them until even Viceroys protested that the country could pay no more.

Quite apart from the fact that over half of the government revenue was ear-marked for direct military expenditure, there were other indirect contributions to the imperial interests of Spain. The Viceroy himself, though paid by Sicily, was sometimes away for years as a royal ambassador or in command of Spanish forces elsewhere, and the Sicilian galleys as well as soldiers from the Spanish garrison in Sicily were freely called away to fight with the *tercios* in distant Flanders or to put down rebellion in Naples. Loans contracted in Ferrara and Piedmont were sent for payment to Palermo, and an unknown amount of bullion was despatched from Palermo to Milan for the payment of troops. Great quantities of tax-free Sicilian wheat were also required to make ship's biscuit for the fleet and to serve as a bargaining counter in diplomacy, while cut-price Sicilian cereals compensated Venice for war damage done by the French to her shipping. Small amounts of Sicilian saltpetre and sulphur were used by the army (some was also exported commercially as far away as to the England of Henry VIII).

This military contribution was chiefly needed against the Ottoman Turks, who had annexed Greece and the Balkans and were busy occupying the North African coast. Sicily had once flourished when in close economic contact with North Africa. Under Carthaginians and Romans this connection had been a source of profit; so it had been under Arabs and

Normans. Under Frederick II, relations had been close enough for the island of Pantelleria to be ruled in condominium by the Christian Emperor together with the Bey of Tunis; and on several occasions in the Middle Ages the island of Jerba off Tunis was joined to Sicily. If economic ties continued despite political and religious differences, this was because Africa was a natural outlet for Sicilian wheat: cereals and cheese were exchanged for slaves and, above all, gold. Such Sicilian exports were in fact a not unimportant means by which Europe had replenished her supplies of bullion. By 1400, these mutually profitable ties were less than they had once been, but still the tunny fished off Sicily was conserved in the oil of Jerba as well as in the salt of Trapani, and the craftsmen of Trapani became rich on the coral of Tabarka. Christian settlements continued to exist all along the Barbary coast. Christians and Moslems even joined in occasional attempts to put down piracy.

Soon after the 1450s, however, the clash of Spanish and Turkish imperialism removed Sicily from her privileged position on the main trade routes of the Mediterranean. Henceforward, instead of living at the centre of a European-Afro-Asian complex, she was a border territory between two parties to a debilitating war. Parliament in 1458 and 1474 asked to be allowed to keep commercial links with Africa, but Spain was now protectionist and restrictive in economics as well as ultra-Catholic in religion. From 1480 onwards the growing severance led to frequent Moorish raids on the Sicilian coast. Ferdinand scorned to explore the possibility that the Hafsid dynasty of Tunisia might have more to gain from Christian Europe than from the Turks; and though more traffic continued between Messina and Alexandria than was once believed, relations with this non-Christian world were mostly conducted by smugglers, pirates and renegades, or else it was left to Venice, Marseilles and London to exploit a commerce in which Sicilians would have had a tremendous natural advantage. Ferdinand did speculate privately in selling Sicilian wheat on the Barbary coast, a speculation which in fact forced one of the few surviving banks at Palermo into liquidation; but the Catholic Kings, apart from wanting to increase revenue, had almost as little interest in Sicilian economic improvement as in constitutional reform. Not only did the interests of Spain lead to the drying up of a great source of precious metals, but existing stocks of bullion in Sicily were sometimes requisitioned, with inevitably harmful results on the import trade from the Levant which needed payment in cash.

In order to check the Turks and the Barbary principalities, Ferdinand and Charles used Sicily as a base from which to establish garrisons along the African coast: and the expense of successive expeditions, as well as payment of the garrisons, fell to a considerable extent on the Sicilian exchequer. Jerba was again annexed in 1497, and Oran and Tripoli in 1509–10— Messina sending six fully armed galleys and several food ships to help the Spanish. Conflict then moved to Algiers where a semi-independent state was being established by Khaireddin Barbarossa. This formidable fighter was a pasha of the Turkish Sultan, and in 1534 he expelled the Hafsid Sultan from Tunisia, so that nominal Turkish sovereignty extended over most of North Africa. Charles V tried to restore the dethroned Sultan and placed a Spanish garrison in Goletta, a fortress which commanded the narrows between Africa and Sicily; as Spain already had garrisons in Messina and Reggio, she now dominated the two main channels of east–west trade. The parliament at Palermo, while paying a good deal for these military enterprises, perhaps hoped that they presaged a proper conquest which would restore North Africa to the Sicilian kingdom. If so, it was money wasted; and anyway an effective occupation would have cost more than they could afford. A large amount of booty was taken, for the African cities were rich, but it went to the Spanish soldiers; and meanwhile Sicily had to endure many more raids in retaliation.

The government took some time to realise that this war was beyond the resources of Sicily, and although failure of the Sicilian harvest in 1539 helped to persuade Charles to drop his project of attacking Constantinople, still in 1541 another expedition was sent against Algiers. Military advice was against it, but the King insisted; the Viceroy was even told that it was chiefly for the benefit of Sicily and hence he must raise money by selling off crown lands and castles. Many Sicilian ships and thousands of Spanish troops were lost on this occasion. In 1551 the Turks recovered Tripoli, and allied with the French they devastated many coastal areas of Sicily in the next few years. In 1560 they scored a tremendous victory at Jerba and destroyed half the forty-eight galleys in the combined Spanish and Sicilian fleets—one Sicilian among the defenders built a remarkable apparatus for distilling fifty barrels of sea water a day.

This alteration in the balance of power was a process which not even the great Spanish victory of Lepanto could stop. Obviously the Turks could not be completely excluded from the Concert of Europe, and the resources of Sicily were proving quite insufficient for a major war in this forlorn cause. The Sicilian galleys took part at Lepanto in 1571, and the Viceroy continued to send food, charcoal and ammunition to Goletta; but this fortress and Tunis itself fell in 1574 to Ulucchiali, a renegade from Calabria who led the Turkish fleet. After sixty years of expensive effort, Spain held only Oran in western Algeria. She had involved Sicilians in a war from which they had lost considerably, and which, rather late in the day, was discovered to have been as unnecessary as it was beyond their means. North Africans were still anxious to import Sicilian wheat, and this might have been very profitable to Sicily; but Spain now needed Sicilian resources for other purposes and other wars.

Long years of fighting against the Turks and the Barbary states gave a special interest to other small islands off the African coast. Pantelleria was sixty miles south-west of Mazara, but only forty-five from Tunisia: disputed for centuries between these powerful neighbours, its predominantly Christian population had preserved Saracen dress and speech. Malta was a little over fifty miles to the south-east and for centuries had been a nominal dependency of the Sicilian King. Malta, too, spoke a language that was basically African. Spain regarded it as a vital advance post against the Turkish fleet, but the expense of maintaining this garrison island was considerable; and Charles V in 1530 therefore gave Malta along with Tripoli to be held by the Knights of St. John of Jerusalem as a fief under the Sicilian crown. The Knights were a military order and could be relied on to provide soldiers and ships. In 1551 they had to surrender Tripoli, but their heroic defence of Malta in 1565 was an important event for Spain and Sicily. Malta could not feed herself, so was allowed a certain amount of Sicilian wheat free of duty and received some help in Sicilian money and working labour. A falcon each year was due to the King in token of feudal subjection, but for all practical purposes Malta and Gozo were henceforward separate from the Sicilian kingdom. Although the Knights helped to curb piracy, they also provoked reprisals by the African states. Sicily suffered from these reprisals, and often found the Knights themselves to be the worst pirates and smugglers of all.

The protracted warfare against these other Mediterranean powers were something which hardly benefited Sicilians, yet the need for defence against retaliation made this outlying province in consequence doubly dependent on Spain. To secure local co-operation, the war was depicted not as a simple conflict for power, but as a struggle against Islam. Sicily was flattered by being called a bulwark of Christendom in the Mediterranean. The fallacy of this interpretation was shown by the fact that Christian France fought in alliance with the Turks, and many Christians worked actively in the Turkish arsenals and fleet. Sicilians too, though many of them served the Spanish cause with loyalty, sometimes defected in a significantly one-way traffic to the freer economic and religious world of North Africa: that may be one reason why raiding parties from Africa knew where to strike. Spain herself, while talking of a religious war, secretly negotiated with Barbarossa and Dragut to win them over as allies against the Turkish Sultan. At one stage Charles agreed to offer Algiers and most of Tunis and Tripoli to the terrible Barbarossa, but then ideology triumphed over practical politics; and later, when the Viceroy Colonna tried to champion Sicilian interests by opening secret negotiations with Ulucchiali, Sicilians themselves used this as an excuse to ask Spain for his dismissal.

By the 1580s, Philip had decided to cut his losses and partially to withdraw from the Mediterranean. The decline of Spain had begun. As he now needed to concentrate his military effort against the Netherlands and England, no more military generals were appointed as Viceroys of Sicily. Other Christian powers made peace with the Turks and so were allowed to buy wheat cheaply in the Levant, to the eventual loss of Sicilian farmers; but Sicily was left to fend for herself on this particular front. The Sicilian galleys were summoned to fight against Portugal in 1580, and when the Viceroy urgently needed a single ship for his own use he had to beg one from the Knights of Malta. Again the galleys went with vast stores of food and the 'Sicilian *tercio*' to be shipwrecked along with the rest of the invincible Armada against England in 1588; and raids inevitably became more frequent along the Sicilian coast when the navy and the Spanish garrisons had departed. There was no genuine peace, and the fact that open war changed into a war of irregulars probably spelt loss rather than gain to the island itself.

For the next two centuries the Barbary 'pirates' did great damage to external and even internal trade. These so-called pirates were often simply warships or privateers of a legitimate, indeed provoked, enemy power; nor were Sicilians backward in acting the pirate. Some Christian captives learnt the trade as prisoners in North Africa, and sometimes purchased freedom and prosperity by guiding African fleets to attack their own home country. Possibly most of the leading Barbary corsairs were of Christian origin. Either against them or with them, private Sicilian ships did a great deal of slave running along the African coast: they were licensed by the Vice-Admiral, who in return could demand for himself one in ten of all captured slaves and a fifth of the proceeds. Some of the richest Sicilian families built up fortunes out of piracy. A law of Charles V confirmed that any infidels taken at sea could be considered as slaves, and it was thought proper for the prettiest ones to be set aside for the King. One Negro slave in sixteenth-century Sicily was eventually canonised as a Christian saint. Even Viceroys took part in this lucrative trade, and in 1601 Maqueda probably died of plague caught from infected booty which his own private gunboat had captured.

Apart from Christian slaves, food was the main objective of the Barbary corsairs. The Spanish Kings, needing Sicilian produce for other purposes, had cut down the trade in wheat with Africa, and hence legitimate commerce was replaced by thieving raids. These were the more easy in that Sicilian castles had been built less against foreign enemies than for internal security. In any case fortifications had decayed during nearly two hundred years of external peace. Parliament complained that "every day, and especially in summer, these people make infinite incursions into the maritime places of this kingdom, and every year take a great number of Christian souls and ships belonging to your Catholic Majesty". In thirty years, over eighty attacks were recorded: any farmhouse within ten miles of the sea was in danger, and the main coastal roads were sometimes cut. In 1539 the acting Viceroy, when visiting his father at Taormina, had his galley with its whole crew seized under his very eyes. Barbarossa once sacked Patti, taking among other things the church bells for making cannon; Dragut built a winter base at Jerba, whence he sailed to sack Licata; in 1559 and 1574 there were landings even in the out-skirts of Palermo itself, and the island of Ustica became a pirate haunt only forty-five miles from the capital. Seven galleys were captured when escorting the Bishop of Catania to the Council of Trent, and Baron Valguarnera was once kid-napped and abandoned on a deserted island. In 1578 the Duke of Terranova, the doyen of the Sicilian aristocracy, was chased for seventy miles and forced to make a crash landing on the reefs of Capri: most of his retinue (including Veneziano the poet) were captured, though the Duke himself was saved by a strong swimmer who brought him to shore.

Spanish wars against France, England and Holland exposed Sicily to a different kind of predatory attack. It seemed at one point that France was preparing a full-scale invasion of the island, and dozens of Sicilian grain ships were captured by the French fleet. English vessels by the 1580s were selling Christian slaves on the Barbary coast, and their crews when caught were condemned by the Sicilian Inquisition to imprisonment and proper Catholic instruction. The Viceroy in 1604 asked parlia-ment for money against the English and Dutch on the grounds that they were introducing heretical notions of freedom of conscience: some of his ships on one occasion took an English merchantman and tortured its crew, but the next year a dozen Sicilian ships were captured in retaliation. About 1609 there were three English captains in charge of the Tunisian fleet, and a fourth at Mahdia had set up a Barbary state of his own.

The extent of piracy and privateering, as of internal brigand-age, were expressions of Spain's very limited commitment in Sicily and the islanders' inability to contribute much to their own defence. Here was one reason why Messina and Palermo could not compete commercially with northern cities. A siege mentality led to defence expenditure which, even though ineffective, was a hindrance to economic growth. On instruction from Spain, some fertile coastal regions had to be completely evacuated. There was a general move towards more easily defended (and less malarious) hill towns; and Carlentini, above Lentini, thus commemorates the name of its imperial founder. Stocks of food also had to be moved inland away from the ports, despite the fact that this had many disadvantages for trade. Yet the challenge did not have the beneficial effect of creating a community sense, a feeling of co-operation in active resistance. Those in danger preferred flight to the interior; and though pious citizens created a charitable fund to buy slaves back from North Africa, there was insufficient communal confidence for the organisation of a positive and collective military response.

Sicily was not easily defended, but the Spaniards did what they could afford. Gonzalo de Córdova repaired some fortifications; and then the young, warlike Viceroy, Ferdinando Gonzaga, employed Ferramolino of Bergamo, one of the foremost military engineers of the time, to make a thorough survey and build new fortifications in the years after 1535. They found that the north coast was not particularly vulnerable, because frequent unbridged water courses made invasion difficult. The south coast, with some over-optimism, was thought easily defensible because the only safe anchorages were well out to sea: having no proper port, it offered no place for a hostile fleet to collect, and for four months a year not even the grain ships could load.

On the west coast the one natural port was Trapani, which had prospered on trade with Spain and North Africa but whose sea defences had been left to decay. Gonzaga gave Trapani special attention, though its life as a commercial port had passed its peak. Lower down the west coast was Marsala, once the flourishing port of Lilybaeum, and here it was eventually decided to fill in the whole harbour with rocks to save the expense of fortification. Palermo needed special attention as the centre of administration and food distribution. So long as Palermo was safe, a Sicilian revolution would appear unthinkable. Every neighbouring village therefore had to send fifty workers to help build large bastions and ditches which now became a prominent feature of the town. Houses and trees all round Palermo were destroyed to eliminate possible cover for an enemy.

The east coast was much more vulnerable. Unlike Palermo, which was an open roadstead only partially protected by an uncompleted mole, Messina, Augusta and Syracuse had three magnificent harbours. At Messina, Gonzaga again conscripted everyone for labour, and pulled down houses, churches and monasteries, levelling orchards and vineyards to build new walls for the city. At Syracuse he used the ancient Greek monuments as quarries to strengthen Frederick II's fortress of Maniace against artillery. The great plain of Catania was one of the richest areas of Sicilian agriculture and very hard to protect from raids. Here and in other country areas Gonzaga relied on building or refurbishing a hundred watch towers round the coast, from which, either by smoke or fire, the whole island could theoretically be warned of attack inside an hour. Half of these were made the responsibility of parliament; the rest were charged to individual towns and barons. But the lack of corporate responsibility made this an impossible method of upkeep; some of these towers were never built at all, others soon fell into disrepair, and persistent gaps in the circuit rendered it very defective. A more bullying attitude by Spain might here have been in Sicily's interest.

The navy never recovered the importance it had possessed under the Normans, for the eclipse of central authority in the later Middle Ages compelled the government to abolish the tax for ship construction and to relieve the barons of any obligation to build vessels at their own expense. Despite Sicily's insular position at a veritable cross-roads of trade routes, any maritime tradition had therefore declined. There was a continual wastage of ships from war and weather. There was also an increasingly felt lack of the long oaks on which a shipping industry depended, as well as a lack of navigable rivers to make the inland forests accessible; in this respect Ragusa, Venice and the Turks were infinitely better supplied.

Sicily did not have quite the same incentive as did the Atlantic countries for developing new techniques of ocean navigation. Fishing was a big industry, but the fish were mainly tunny which were caught from rowing-boats off shore. Reliance was still placed on galleys and coastal traffic. Oared galleys kept the smaller ports alive, but the new northern sailing vessels had sufficient speed and seaworthiness to avoid the island if they wished. Moreover galleys were no longer adequate as fighting ships: in 1586 the Sicilian fleet failed to intercept a convoy of nine English merchant vessels returning from Constantinople, and they showed up no better in the Armada of 1588. Turkish ships could manœuvre unharmed just outside the harbours of Palermo and Messina. By comparison, Sicilian galleys were notoriously ill-made and expensive, and shipwrights were scarce. Charles V obtained money from parliament for the navy, and promised that Sicilians would be chosen as captains, though he did not keep his word. Philip III even had to appoint an Englishman, Sir Anthony Sherley, as admiral of the fleet in order to introduce the new techniques of naval fighting and ship construction developed in the Atlantic.

The Sicilian squadron varied in size between six and twenty-two galleys, some managed directly by the government, some privately owned, others hired out to private people. Palermo and Messina were expected to build galleys at their own expense. Providing ships, however, was sometimes easier than finding crews. A galley needed at least two hundred oarsmen, with preferably six men to each oar; and the tough life made galleys harder to equip than sailing ships. Sometimes about a quarter of these oarsmen were so-called volunteers, though their heads were shaven like the rest and they were chained night and day. Others were slaves from North Africa, for 'Moors' were more resistant than Turks and special raids were undertaken to replenish their number. A considerable proportion was also made up of convicts and the unemployed poor off the city streets. The barons who had private prisons of their own were thus well placed in manning their privateers, though the King tried to stop this abuse of their authority.

In some years, there was a 10 per cent mortality among the crews of these galleys. This was especially true among the 'volunteers', since in monetary terms they were less valuable than slaves who had to be purchased. It was also particularly true in the galleys hired out to private entrepreneurs, for such men did not have the same incentive to treat hired crews as well as they treated slaves who were their own property. In an emergency the sea ports were forced to recruit oarsmen by lot.

It seems that press gangs were sometimes able to work in the interests of foreign shipowners. We know also of occasions when oarsmen were simply thrown overboard when food was short. Genuine volunteers, perhaps for these reasons, were few, but fortunately the Jesuits justified the morality of conscripting people by lot. English sailors, Spaniards and Neapolitans, could sometimes be enlisted by the offer of good pay, but Sicilians rarely, and this fact takes some force out of the complaint that it was simply the fault of Spain if the coasts were left undefended.

Regular Spanish soldiers were the fighting element on these Sicilian galleys. A second line of defence was made up on land by Spanish and German infantrymen, their numbers being supplemented with mercenaries from the Italian mainland. During a campaign in North Africa, there might be seven thousand or more foreign soldiers stationed in Sicily; while at the other extreme, for example in 1545 when soldiers were needed in Germany, Sicily was left with almost none. In 1574 only eight hundred Spanish soldiers were said to be in the island, of which two hundred guarded the harbour of Palermo. Expert opinion estimated six thousand troops as a minimum for garrisoning the main island fortresses, but the needs of empire made this minimum unattainable.

These Spanish troops were occasionally mutinous when the Sicilian government left them unpaid and if local authorities would not provide food or billets. The main ports of embarcation were particularly exposed to military raids. In 1521 Marsala was almost destroyed. Again in 1538 there was a four months' mutiny over the lack of provision for winter quarters: the troops attacked Mazara and Messina and levied taxes on rich citizens; they ravaged the countryside, closing roads and gutting whole villages. The garrison of Syracuse mutinied in 1541. Though Sicilians had a bad name among the Spanish troops for overcharging, the soldiers were none too squeamish about requisitioning food and lodging. Individual soldiers often disappeared without trace. In 1575, after a Spanish captain at Sciacca had insulted a priest who refused to give communion to his mistress, there was a riot against the troops and eight were burnt alive.

As Spain became less interested in the Mediterranean she

would have liked to hand over more of her military responsibilities to a Sicilian force. Feudal knight service was in theory still owed by the nobility, and perhaps for as long as three months each year; the Prince of Butera had in theory to provide as many as 109 knights. But in long decades of being protected by Spain the barons had lost any appetite for the warlike living which had once been their *raison d'être*. Officialdom regularly lamented their lack of martial qualities. As Medinaceli complained, "the soldiers produced by the barons are quite ridiculous; they are undisciplined, and their weapons date back to the time of King Arthur". The government protested, but in the end was ready to accept payment instead of service, and though the barons went on being called to arms throughout the seventeenth and eighteenth centuries, this was just a roundabout method of getting money.

Since the barons were so unwarlike, the Viceroys tried to organise a popular militia. Spain was subsequently criticised for deliberately not training the local population in arms, but it is nearer the truth to say that Sicilians could not be persuaded to sacrifice their time and convenience. The Habsburgs tried but completely failed to recruit Sicilian troops to fight overseas, and they had only a limited success when they tried to train a militia for purely defence purposes. In 1532 the Viceroy explained that the King could not be expected to go on paying so much for Sicily's defence, and parliament therefore agreed to maintain a Home Guard of ten thousand foot and sixteen hundred cavalry. Its members were to be unpaid except for the captains and sergeant majors, and were expected to train twice a month and be ready for emergencies.

The scheme was unpopular from the first, and constant requests were made to revoke it. Medinaceli thought that Sicilians would prefer to submit to the Turks rather than to the militia, and Feria said that people thought it "the most odious thing possible". The militiamen did much damage to property, and no doubt many of them had been attracted by the immunity from arrest for debt which had been thrown in as an inducement. They were liable for service especially between May and October when pirates were to be feared, in other words at harvest time when labour was precious. Some of the baronage complained in 1563 that feudal rights and income were being reduced just because militia service was being given as an excuse to escape from servitude; other barons, on the contrary, became officers in this force and used the militiamen as a private army on their estates. Often there was a complaint that a captain would summon his men simply to receive bribes for letting them go home again. The force of sixteen hundred cavalry, recruited from richer people who could afford horses, proved completely unreliable. To supplement it, there was a more professional body of three hundred light horse guards, but even this became the subject of grumbles. Sicilians had to agree that any locally recruited force was likely to be either useless or dangerous, and in emergencies it would be better to rely on soldiers from Milan and Calabria. As Gonzaga complained, Sicilians would give their money gladly for the royal service, "but my one serious difficulty is that they will not become soldiers, since it is their nature to be unwarlike".

Chapter 14

DISORDER AND BRIGANDAGE

Sicily shared with the rest of Europe the social upsets associated with a long period of currency depreciation and increased prices. Inflation at the end of the fifteenth century was such that Constantine Lascaris, who in 1467 had become teacher of Greek to the Basilian monks of Messina, complained twenty-five years later that the value of his salary had depreciated by a third. The most obvious effect of this inflation on public life was the increasing inadequacy of ordinary tax revenue. Another was the growth of vagabondage. In the worst years many country dwellers were forced into the towns to find food and work, and this caused a problem of urban over-population and a lack of labour on the farms.

Much began to be heard of brigandage in official reports. Over a good part of inland Sicily neither royal nor feudal justice had normally penetrated, but individual family communities had for centuries tried to maintain their own laws and way of life. The bandits were often just these mountain folk, perhaps descended from peoples who had been chased into the interior by some distant invasion; or they were shepherds from the hill country who clashed with the settled agriculturalists of the valleys as increased population meant more arable land and so less winter pasturage in the lowlands. Tension in the countryside became worse when some of the sheep-runs were 'enclosed' along with commons and woodland; and every spring when the brigandage season opened, some of these men of the mountains emerged from their fastnesses to retaliate as best they could against the landlords and the cities of the plain.

The wild life of a predator on society had always possessed these attractions, and not only for these outlaws of the interior. When a bad harvest meant no food and no money with which to pay taxes, some farmers retreated seasonally into the penumbra of the *maquis*. Since Spanish-speaking officials had virtually no point of contact with the peasantry, and since the legal system was obviously *ex parte*, there were many people ready to develop a counter system of morals and politics. When a baron invoked the hunting laws to exclude shepherds and others from land which he had illegally enclosed, he generated a fierce if usually underground resistance. This is one way in which the notion gained acceptance that to cheat and steal successfully made one worthy of respect and admiration.

An underworld of secret fraternities was nothing new in Sicilian history. William II in the twelfth century had tried to eradicate a gang called the 'Avengers' who committed the most atrocious crimes and always by night. In the fourteenth century, Frederick III and Martin found that both rich and poor grouped themselves into kinship *conventicole* which were a law to themselves and aroused widespread fear. In the sixteenth century, Gonzaga encountered armed bands in the countryside which "prevented farmers leaving their houses to work the land. . . . We hear of nothing but killings, kidnappings, the theft of cattle, farmsteads burnt and women raped". Stealing sheep and cattle was, and remained, the commonest crime of all; sometimes it was designed to compel landowners into paying protection money, sometimes it was to feed the brigand bands, but chiefly it was to supply the illicit trade in smuggling meat past the excisemen at the city gates. Gonzaga saw that farmers were being frightened into inhabiting large concentrated villages remote from their farms. Some of them were abandoning agriculture altogether, with the result that exports and hence taxes suffered. "While things remain so, His Majesty cannot consider himself truly King of Sicily."

The detailed incidence of brigandage is hard to document, especially as vast amounts of the relevant material were destroyed by bombing in May 1943, yet some known examples in the sixteenth century are so similar to those in other periods that certain types of behaviour seem to have been habitual and repetitive. The gang of Agnello in the 1560s had its own flag with a death's head, as well as pipes and drums like the King's army; it was well armed, and could operate right up to the walls of Palermo. Rival delinquents working in Agnello's area without his permission did so at their peril. He could rely on people to tell him of police movements, and no doubt it was for this reason that he saw the propaganda value of giving to the poor as well as terrorising them; but clearly it was not only the poor who helped him. The bandit Saponara, who was caught in 1578, died of poison when in solitary confinement, and the authorities were not even very surprised, for they knew that highly placed individuals feared what he might disclose under torture. Already it appears that gang leaders in different areas had developed useful links between each other for the quick disposal of stolen goods. The local priest, who was almost the only literate man in the village, was sometimes browbeaten or otherwise persuaded into acting as a convenient go-between to whom ransom money could be paid. All these details might have been taken from any subsequent century.

Brigandage was common all over Europe, but the Spanish governors thought it especially characteristic of Sicily. They blamed the violent Sicilian temperament. Alba de Liste in the 1580s criticised excessive apathy and individualism for preventing the growth of public spirit and a sense of public law. De Vega was fascinated to discover that some Sicilians genuinely preferred to use corruption and violence even where honest means would have obtained the same end more cheaply; and he noted that ordinary legal procedures were completely ineffective in a society where false witness was the rule and ex-convicts were accorded special admiration. In popular legend the brigand was generally a sympathetic character, a rebel against society, a defender of the oppressed, perhaps even a fighter for Sicilian independence, though in practice his habitual reliance on false testimony sometimes took the not very sympathetic form of accusing some private enemy of crimes he had not committed. Almost every citizen illegally carried arms, simply because there was no belief in public law, and the Spanish policy of militia service (as well as the later practice of obtaining income from arms licences) ensured that there was always a plentiful supply of weapons.

One element in brigandage was the revolt of the poor against the rich. Another was the very reverse, when robber barons made their castles and town houses into a refuge for bandits who helped to keep the local peasantry in subjection. Yet another was aristocratic feuding. Three generations of the di Luna and Perollo families had contended for power at Sciacca. Each was supported by a private army of cut-throats and a retinue of slaves. The Viceroy in the 1520s appointed a special police officer to put an end to their rivalry, but di Luna's *bravi* killed this man, and his naked corpse lay in the street for days before anyone dared bury it; they then took over the town, burning the civic archives and slaughtering many of the Perollo. Yet this di Luna was son of an acting Viceroy and nephew of Pope Leo X, and he was still able to marry his son to a daughter of a later Viceroy, de Vega. The port of Sciacca, on the other hand, suffered severely from this protracted vendetta, and by the time that the quarrel was settled the town had been reduced to half its size and the countryside was littered with gibbets and quartered limbs.

The whole of Sicily at this period was convulsed by aristocratic factions on a smaller scale. At Catania, Agrigento, Trapani and Termini we hear of armed conflicts between rival families, and at Messina in 1518 one faction was using cannon in the streets. In Palermo, nobles could hire assassins to kill in broad daylight; there were pitched battles in public thoroughfares, and the courts were always reluctant to take action where barons were involved. The government was even asked by parliament to reduce the penalties on nobles who sheltered bandits, on the plea that any landowner risked terrible reprisals if he refused such shelter. Apart from fear, however, a landlord would have a positive interest in employing these *mafiosi ante letteram* to control his tenants and protect his crops; and if they were caught, there was still the chance that he had judges on a retaining fee. Medinaceli was worried that too many of the judges were Sicilians and hence exposed to intimidation or bribery, but there was no easy remedy for this. Strong government action was inhibited by the unwritten compact between rulers and nobles on which Spanish administration depended. When a bandit in 1547 took refuge over the 'frontier' of the County of Modica, he was safe.

The government knew that keeping roads free of robbers was important for social welfare, and, in so far as finance and baronial influence allowed, there was an honest attempt to enforce the law. Malefactors who ran away from justice were declared *banditi*, banned men. After another year of evasion they became *fuorusciti*, or outlaws, and could be killed by anyone. A third class was merely kept under surveillance: these were the *relegati*, turbulent characters who took care not to be caught *in flagrante*, men who must often have been not the perpetrators but the local bosses of misrule. Gonzaga tried the remedy of forcing people in this latter group to live in special places remote from their homes: but this was so effective that the feelings of outrage were sensed as far away as Madrid itself, and the Viceroy was obliged to state that he would never in future use such severity with mere crimes of 'honour'. Financial stringency moreover forced him to sell pardons, especially when the soldiers' wages were in arrears and they were threatening mutiny. The Marquis of Pietraperzia, found guilty of suffocating his father with a pillow, escaped very cheaply.

Gonzaga's successor, de Vega, tried the practice of setting fire to woodland to force outlaws into the open. In order to take the profit out of one lucrative form of crime, orders were also sent out that animals must be branded and that only controlled slaughter houses should be used, but these orders proved impossible to enforce. In desperation it was enacted that redress could be sought as far away as against second and third cousins for any offence committed by their relatives, and the penalty for false witness was raised to five years without pay in the galleys. A more successful method, however, was found to be the offer of pardon to any bandit who turned King's evidence: *omertà*, the honour among thieves upon which the underworld relied, was a code forced on the humble innocent by the powerful guilty who obeyed a very different moral law. The government therefore allowed that anyone who betrayed a known murderer could obtain not only freedom but the highly profitable right to reprieve other criminals as well. Many of the leading bandits in Sicilian history were eventually either caught (or reprieved) by these means.

Harsh repression occasionally succeeded, even though it often produced more irritation than gratitude among those whom it tried to protect. De Vega explained to Madrid that gentleness and indulgence had to be used with great care since clemency was interpreted as weakness. Medinaceli attacked the over-generous pardoning of crimes, since this only encouraged evil doers. Terranova, himself a Sicilian, likewise considered that fear was the best aid of the law, and that perjurors should be hanged. Don Juan once showed a nice sense of impartiality by making suspects draw lots for who should be hanged. Olivares believed it better to torture an accused before letting him know the indictment, otherwise it was too easy for him to produce false witnesses; and when this same Olivares defeated the two-hundred-strong gang of Lancia which had been terrorising Messina, he tied its leader by his four limbs to four galleys and tore him to pieces as an exemplary punishment. These successive Viceroys were more and more inclined to use summary measures and the *ex abrupto* procedure in their courts; for in a community where no reliance at all could be placed on witnesses, criminals otherwise had a guaranteed immunity, and this was considered far worse for society than the punishment of a few innocent people by mistake. All subsequent governments of Sicily were to learn this same lesson, just as they always met opposition from interested parties who preferred things as they were.

The official Captains at Arms had a mounted force of police to apprehend bandits; and it was found that if these policemen were compelled to compensate any victims of theft, this was an effective means of preventing crime and discovering culprits. The nobility objected that the Captains were altogether too intrusive and efficient in doing their job; and without doubt police powers of summary justice must often have been abused. Nevertheless, as the Messinese once informed the King, making secret agreements with a brigand might in practice be the best way for the government to keep crime within bounds. It might even be worth turning a blind eye if the police used their office to take revenge on personal enemies. Rough and ready law enforcement was better than no law enforcement at all, and there were no means of making policemen popular with people who either wanted their jobs or feared their efficiency.

Some of the more conscientious Viceroys appointed Spaniards to these Captaincies, since Sicilians were much too involved to be impartial and sometimes even tipped off the bandits they were supposed to be controlling. Once again, however, fierce local protests reached Spain against foreigners being given this particular office, and an indulgent reply came from Madrid that Sicilians should be appointed instead. Moreover the acting Viceroy Terranova, who among other things was the leading Sicilian landowner, not only preferred to increase the jurisdiction of the baronial courts, but liked to appoint his fellow barons to act as Captains at Arms in their own districts.

Chapter 15

THE BARONAGE

The King and his feudatories were only on rare occasions at odds with each other, for they had basic interests in common and yet largely diverse spheres of operation. The King needed Sicily for military bases and for its food supplies, whereas the barons were quite content so long as they controlled local affairs and were taxed lightly. On these terms the barons did not mind much if they had little political power and if Sicily lacked independence; whereas the Viceroys for their part accepted that there was no going back to the strong monarchy of Roger and Frederick II. Gonzaga strongly advised the King to give up the separate administration of Sicily, because it would be far cheaper if fused with Naples, but he was overruled. Both King and barons needed to preserve social order and wanted only a minimum of Spanish troops in Sicily. Spanish rule would have been much harder to enforce without a loyal and satisfied patrician class which was prepared to take over a good deal of police and judicial work.

Naturally the government tried to maintain what it could of the royal prerogatives, for among other things they had a cash value. Gonzaga tried to insist that, even though fiefs could in practice be inherited and even sold, the King still had some rights over such property; at least he must have an option on buying back any such land that came on the market and must have a tenth of the purchase price. Nevertheless the King's authority was a good deal less than, for example, it was in Naples, where under Charles V the legal rights of feudalism began to diminish noticeably. Barberi's researches into baronial tenures and obligations were purposely unpublished and left on one side in the archives, while at the same time the government gradually relinquished its former insistence on documentary proof of privilege. A number of Viceroys, for instance Prades, Moncada, de Vega, Medinaceli, were recalled because—at least, the nobility flattered itself that this was the reason—they went too far and threatened to upset the delicate balance of power between crown and baronage. The advice left by one

Viceroy for his successors in the 1590s was that "with the barons you are everything, without them nothing".

Powerful the Sicilian nobles certainly were, but it was a circumscribed power; and another Viceroy, Colonna, gave very different advice, insisting that so long as ordinary citizens had cheap food, the nobles would be no problem. Military service was no longer a privilege but an easily evaded duty, and with their antiquated weapons and armour the aristocracy were far more vulnerable in moments of popular disturbance than their fathers had been: this, no doubt, is one reason why after 1523 they were less willing to rebel. They had no monopoly of the great offices of state; on the contrary, orders came from Spain in 1569 that they were no longer to be given these offices, partly because they were not educated to understand the growing technicalities of administration, but also because it was prudent to concentrate their energies in local government.

Parliament continued to ask the Viceroy to use more barons in his council, but this was mainly a point of prestige, and the poor attendance of the barons in parliament showed their lack of interest in politics. The aristocracy lacked the will or the capacity to lead a separatist movement, a fact indicated by their own mutual jealousies quite apart from the often hostile attitude towards them of other Sicilians. Cut off from the ordinary life of the common people, they had acquired more and more of a vested interest in Spanish rule. One French observer noted with some scorn that, because of the disorganisation of their private affairs, they were obliged to accept government assistance and were even unable to resent the contempt with which Spaniards sometimes regarded them. By allowing them to play the petty tyrant in their fiefs, and by taxing them very lightly, Spanish domination was made easy.

Not every Viceroy had the same attitude in this matter; nor of course were the barons ever a single monolithic group with an identical interest. Occasionally some nobles were punished. Colonna in 1577 beheaded certain men of rank. Alba de Liste in 1591 put some in prison, and the Duke of Feria after 1602, bravely thought of introducing a more equitable system of tax allocation. Sometimes the government attempted to stand up for the poor by forbidding the baronage to demand taxation or oaths of homage from their 'subjects', and by forbidding landowners to exact free labour from tenants or to confiscate their animals and crops. A baron could, in theory, be punished if he stopped farmers selling wheat on the open market, or if he fenced the commons and excluded shepherds from pastures to which they had a legal right. But the very repetition of these prohibitions shows that the offences went on taking place. The truth was that no one except the wealthy could effectively petition the King about grievances. In 1578, when Colonna protested that the severe treatment of their tenants by Terranova and other nobles had been damaging agriculture, the King replied that the interests of the nobility must in the last resort come before everything else.

Despite their power, some of the aristocracy were quite poor, and most of them were learning to live on credit. Already in the fifteenth century parliament had begged the Viceroy to help nobles in distress. Some were in debt through bad farming, others through inability to administer their large estates, or through the stock family lawsuits which it was fashionable to drag out for decades. Fashion also imposed on those with any social ambition an expensive life in a palatial town house near the Viceroy's court. The consequent impoverishment of some of the old families was a worry to the government. For one thing, it was bad for agriculture. Landowners were sometimes paying well over half their agricultural income in mortgage interest; and sometimes a creditor obtained a lien on the income from an estate, in which case there was little incentive to cultivate it providently. Their cavalier attitude to debt payments, said Medinaceli, which went far beyond what was practised in Castile, bore very hardly on the class of poor artisans, and so did their lack of practical charity.

Any landowners of moderate ability and industry must nevertheless have survived inflation better than other elements in the community. What they lost in the devaluation of fixed-rent incomes they must have regained from the depreciation of their mortgage payments, to say nothing of the still more important fact that wheat prices rose fourfold between 1500 and 1650. Though some feudatories were poor, the 'states' of Modica, Terranova and Monreale were immensely rich. In 1540 the King himself was trying to buy Modica from the Spanish family which owned it, and he did not succeed. The Princes of Butera,

Trabia and Paternò were petty sovereigns. They paid relatively little in tax. The gross income of the Prince of Butera and the Duke of Terranova seems to have been in each case about 5 per cent of the whole revenue of the Sicilian government.

Marriage policy was carefully contrived to keep these fortunes intact: nobles did not scorn marrying beneath them for money, and intermarriage between cousins, even between nephews and aunts, was occasionally welcomed as a means of stopping the laspe of some rich family inheritance. In Sicily, much more than in Naples, aristocratic houses also took steps to keep up the splendour of their family by the entailment of property. Younger sons might have only a small inheritance which would return to the elder branch at their death. This expedient helped to preserve the *latifondi* during periods when it might have been profitable to divide them, a fact which in turn helped to maintain the predominance of an aristocratic class. In addition, four out of five of all villages and towns were under direct feudal control in the seventeenth century. Modica, Terranova and other leading baronies had private grain storages from which they could export wheat without paying the normal dues: this could be enormously profitable when famine conditions caused a general embargo on other food exports, and, once they had made a profit out of scarcity, these 'grain barons' then could sometimes beg for official relief to keep their starving peasants alive.

Most of these men had purchased jurisdiction over their estates, often for quite large sums, and this gave them the right not only to punish criminals, but to enjoy a revenue from fines and confiscated property. Ferdinand, Charles and Philip II were each petitioned by parliament that all nobles should automatically receive this franchise, but they refused, and not until 1621 did the government sacrifice its most tangible symbol of sovereignty by allowing the privilege of possessing private courts to be purchased as a matter of right. On one interpretation of the law, ecclesiastics were not meant to hold fiefs with criminal jurisdiction, but in fact bishops as well as barons obtained this privilege. In strict law, too, there was a right of appeal from feudal courts to the crown, but rarely was it invoked, "for the baron would take such offence that any vassal who resorted to the King's court would be persecuted to the point where he would leave all his goods and flee"—so one official reported. The baron appointed the judges; he possessed the notorious *dammusi* or underground prisons; he could legally use torture as well as condemn to death.

The diminished importance of knight service meant that the aristocracy rarely performed the main duties to society which had constituted the original justification of their privileges. They liked to blame Spain for fostering their own habits of idleness and snobbery, yet Spaniards rather looked on these as peculiarly Sicilian characteristics. A Spanish grandee such as Olivares deplored the laziness and extravagance of the aristocracy and their lack of public spirit. While the aristocracy of Genoa and Florence were active in industry and commerce, Sicilian nobles left new economic developments to depend on foreign capital; and when they decided that trade was shameful, this was an attitude which was copied far down the social scale. One official in 1622 saw this as perhaps the main problem of all—how to convince people that gentility was not lost through hard work. Even many of the tradesmen in Palermo were foreigners: the grocers, for example, were known generically as 'Lombards'.

Most important of all, the nobles lacked any practical interest in agriculture even though agriculture was the source of their wealth. Disdaining an active economic role, they became absentee landlords attracted by the glamour of the court and the comforts of Palermo. Once there, according to a Neapolitan observer in the 1590s, they took on the prevalent affectation of indifference to making money, and preferred to mortgage their estates and hand over management to a new class of *gabelloti*. Anyone who remained on his estates and tried to introduce agricultural innovations risked incurring the disapprobation of his peers. The productivity of the soil thus did not go back into the land; it went into the towns, into the building of palaces and churches, while provincial roads were neglected and the farming community was abandoned to malaria and brigandage.

Income derived from the land was often spent unproductively on buying the mere prestige which went with the right to call oneself a 'grandee of Spain first class', or to keep one's head covered in the Viceroy's presence. This selling of titles and privileges may have seemed one way of making up for the fact that the nobles paid so little towards the ordinary taxes, but if so it was self-defeating, since nobility carried privileges of further exemption from tax, and indeed it was deliberately sought with this in mind. As more and more rich people became barons, the older families were eager to buy themselves out of such company, and this naturally touched off an emulous spirit of competition which could go on for ever.

Alfonso in the fifteenth century had created the first marquis not of royal blood. There were seven counts in 1500, eleven by 1550, and twenty-one by 1600. Charles V created the first dukedom in 1556 for the same di Luna family which so devastated the town of Sciacca. To keep up this profitable rivalry, Philip then let the Geraci rank alternately with the di Luna as the chief titled family in Sicily. To outdo these, in 1563 Butera bought the first title of prince, and only ten years later there were four princes. By 1621 the number of *titulados* swearing fealty to the new King was over double that of sixty years before, and yet the real acceleration in this process was only just beginning. Altogether, in the ten years of the 1620s, there were created seven new dukedoms, seventeen marquisates and twenty-seven new princedoms; and of these twenty-seven, eight were in 1627 alone. As the fashion caught on, a hundred and two princedoms were created in the course of the seventeenth century—and this out of a population of about a million.

Each baron, as he bought his way up this hierarchy, thought himself obliged to make ever greater expenditures on outward show, even though this almost invariably had to be done on high-interest credit. Each new title acquired would bring with it the need for a more numerous body of retainers. There was a special market at Palermo where slaves could be bought: a Negro could cost about three times as much as a horse; many slaves, however, were white, and there was no legal difficulty in enslaving Christians. Clothes and liveries also became more lavish. Spanish habits created a mode of dress which, though at first ridiculed for artificiality and even effeminacy, was later adopted with enthusiasm. Tightly fitting clothes, very short coats, beards and long hair, had been an early sign of Spanish influence. Foreign visitors could not make up their mind whether Sicilians dressed in the Italian or the Spanish manner, but it seems that Spanish fashions were increasingly propagated by the habits of court life. People took to using oils and perfume. By 1565 the government was trying to curb the vogue for stuffing doublets with cotton wool, because mounting a horse was already becoming difficult. The expensive fashion for using carriages had by now begun to catch on. Sicilians became celebrated for their hand kissing, cap doffing and gaming. Their preoccupation with precedence, decorum and ceremonial went on being ascribed by themselves to the example of Spain, but in practice a code of gallantry, gravity and etiquette was taken to such an extreme as to appear odd even to the Spanish.

The Viceroys were pleased to indulge the taste for buying titles and privileges, and we know that there was a deliberate policy to bring the aristocracy to Palermo where they could be kept under supervision. Yet the ruinous predilection for excessive luxury was repeatedly deplored by the government. At least three sumptuary laws date from the sixteenth century, though this was a department of life where legislation had a minimal effect. Limitations on ostentatious mourning and on dowry payments would perhaps have been welcomed by the nobility if only they could have been enforced; but no one could be expected to stand voluntarily aside from a code of competitive pomp which had become the outward mark of a man's status in life. Parliament itself, realising that this rivalry in splendour threatened to ruin nobles and their creditors alike, petitioned for the government to stop it. Gold and silver were therefore by law forbidden to be used in dresses. Liveries were not to be of silk. No man could be attended by more than two grooms and three pages, the intention here being to leave more labour for agriculture and defence. Probably the nobles were glad to have this excuse not to go on competing for prestige; but, on at least one occasion, tradesmen and artisans marched on the royal palace to complain that restriction on carriages and clothes would result in unemployment, and the government had to relax its provisions.

Another expedient by the Viceroy Maqueda in 1598 was the setting up of a commission empowered to take over and administer the property of the most indebted barons, giving them a regulated allowance, endeavouring to run their estates more efficiently, paying interest on their mortgages and trying to settle some arrears of debt. This showed that baronial extravagance and inefficiency were becoming a matter of serious national concern. Maqueda seems to have been more concerned with getting creditors paid than with keeping up the social position of the aristocracy, though in a sense the two went together. He was also interested in increasing agricultural production on the *latifondi* by taking these estates away from idle and inexpert hands. His edict, however, was far in advance of the administrative capacity of the times. The commissioners were sometimes corrupt and often too permissive; occasionally a baron deliberately used this kind of suspended bankruptcy to escape some of his financial obligations, and he could sometimes illegally appoint commissioners of his own choice. Several attempts had to be made later to control these abuses and give the commission more power.

The amount of time and effort spent by the ruling elite in striving for social position is a fundamental fact in the political and economic barrenness of this society. Instead of making suggestions for improving the economy or making Sicily more self-reliant, the shocked protests smuggled out by the barons to Madrid were rather against Viceroys who did not treat the *titulados* with sufficient respect, or against mere commoners who used titles to which they had no right. The grandees begged that the Viceroy should be ordered to address them as 'Excellency', and that ordinary barons should not be given the same consideration as themselves. Several times they tried to establish their own precedence over the prelates in court ceremonial.

Normally the Viceroy tried to be indulgent to their more harmless requests, but there was no need for him to yield on any point of substance. His authority was strengthened when the King ordered that no longer should the money of the poor (who paid taxes) be wasted by the barons on expensive parliamentary deputations to Madrid; and this proclamation was a clear sign that parliament and the barons were less of an independent force in the seventeenth than in the sixteenth century. In one sense it was an advance in civilisation that inter-family fighting was softened into a conflict over who should walk first in a procession or who was entitled to four horses for his carriage; yet it was a time-wasting and sometimes expensive pastime. As late as 1574 a full-dress treaty of peace had to be drawn up between two notabilities of Licata, in which they promised not to fight, nor to use disrespectful language about each other, nor even to resort to the courts without first asking the Viceroy's permission; and a century later, squabbles for precedence ruined more than one state ball in the palace.

Unfortunately these men were the leaders of society and their standards of behaviour were widely copied. Different orders of friars excommunicated each other over points of status, and the Archbishop of Palermo once refused to let parliament be inaugurated because of the most petty point of protocol. An impasse was reached sometimes in the narrow streets of Palermo when neither of two carriages could give way—a fine for the nobleman and forty lashes for his coachmen was thought preferable to any loss of face. But equally there were bitter contests for precedence between towns or between the various artisan corporations inside a single town. The government just tried to minimise conflict. It also charged as much as possible for any concession of privileges, trying, however, not to cheapen each new dignity before it could be replaced with another even more grand. By diluting the once highly select Order of the Golden Fleece, and multiplying the extravagantly coveted Key of the Bedchamber, Viceroys not only obtained a considerable revenue, but at no expense save that of dignity they won the backing of all nobles who had a lively expectation of favours to come.

Chapter 16

CHURCH AND STATE

Younger brothers and younger sons of the Sicilian aristocracy had few prospects of an independent career in a world where politics was taboo, where soldiering and practical agriculture were unfashionable, and where entails and primogeniture were almost universal. Some of them, and their sisters, were placed *faute de mieux* in the Church, where they formed a powerful support of the established order. One reason for the placid acceptance of Spanish rule was that Sicilian churchmen were in general submissive and dependent on the crown; because although subsequent Popes whittled down Pope Urban's grant of legatine powers to the rulers of Sicily, and on occasion claimed the island as a papal fief, it was the King's pretensions to ecclesiastical authority which generally prevailed. Sometimes he continued to be thought of as in a loose sense a spiritual as well as a temporal ruler. Appeals to him in this capacity could even address him as *Santissimo Padre*. The Spanish prelate who represented the King's ecclesiastical authority in Sicily, and who sometimes was referred to as the 'Vice-pope', was above archbishops and bishops, and he it was who had ultimate jurisdiction in ecclesiastical cases.

Not only were Church affairs supervised by a government department, but the Inquisition looked to Madrid and not Rome for its authority. It was the King, moreover, who denounced usury and tried to dissuade the impoverished parish clergy from their traditional practice of selling the sacraments. Papal religious supremacy was of course recognised, but within limits. It was the Viceroy who effectively ensured that priests behaved with proper decorum. He insisted that the citizens should hear Mass regularly and reverence the sacrament in the streets; his regulations required that they should observe the sabbath and close their shops on Sunday; by his order, doctors were forbidden to treat patients who refused to make their confession. The King had originally created and endowed all the Sicilian bishoprics, and hence the appointment of bishops was for the most part effectively in his hands; there were also periodic enquiries to see if any rights of patronage had lapsed, and a very substantial income from selling lenten indulgences and raising money 'for the crusades' was regularly added to the King's ordinary revenue.

This remoteness of papal authority was one reason why the Church in Sicily was in some ways lethargic, why so many clergy for example were married, or why, to take another practical case, regulations had to be issued more than once against the serenading of nunneries by monks. It also helps to explain the lack of a special kind of stimulus and conflict which elsewhere contributed to the development of a more sophisticated political system.

Inevitably there were some instances of friction between Church and State. At least three times in the first half of the sixteenth century riots took place against the Inquisition; twice Sicilian rebels were sheltered by the Pope, and more than one Viceroy was excommunicated. In the 1550s, Christendom even saw papal troops in active hostilities against the Most Catholic King. Pope Paul IV attacked Philip as a heretic and a "drain full of filth". He once 'confiscated' Sicily and awarded it to the Venetians; and in pursuance of this empty sentence the papal galleys began sinking cargoes of Sicilian grain and silk. But Philip II, for all his piety, resolutely maintained his inherited rights over 'the Sicilian Church'. The edicts of the Council of Trent were refused admission to the country, and when Cardinal Baronio wrote a book arguing that Urban's bull could never have existed (just because no Pope would ever have given away so much), this volume too was made forbidden reading under the most dire penalties. Moreover most Popes had too much need of Spanish political help to question the King's pretensions, and Rome needed the Sicilian wheat which friendly Viceroys sent on specially advantageous terms.

Under royal patronage the wealth of the Sicilian Church had become notorious, even though it was mostly enjoyed by only several dozen bishops and abbots. The Archbishop of Monreale at one point possessed seventy-two fiefs: his annual income in 1580 was perhaps 40,000 *scudi* and was increasing. Titular incumbents of this post with such illustrious names as Medici, Farnese, Borgia and Barberini, show that many Popes were glad to have this rich sinecure in their family, and

therefore were ready to play down any potential source o
conflict. The Archbishop of Palermo and the Bishop of Catani
each had about 20,000 *scudi* a year, which was more than th
Viceroy's salary. It made little difference that there were lav
dating from the thirteenth century to stop the Church acquirin
property. Ecclesiastical estates continued to grow and n
monasteries to be founded, as pious legacies to the Chur
gradually removed land into an area where it was partially
even entirely exempt from taxation.

Ecclesiastical immunities, financial and judicial, arouse
good deal of hostile feeling. Clergy were exempt from
secular courts in both civil and criminal cases. The Vic
could not legally override ecclesiastical rights of asylum, des
the fact that in Palermo alone there were as many as t
hundred churches where criminals could take refuge,
bandits sometimes used them as an active base for fu
activity. The clergy had a general exemption from excise
for their own farm produce, and lay property was some
improperly registered as ecclesiastical to take advantage o
One device was for a family to transfer its goods to a s
brother who was an ecclesiastic. Servants and sometime
tenants of the clergy were able to obtain the same imm
for themselves, and the number of 'servants' therefore b
greatly inflated. By becoming a tertiary of some men
order, or by attachment to a quasi-religious organisati
the heavily over-staffed department for the crusade ta>
rich people were able to claim not only tax exempti
freedom from the ordinary courts; and bishops were ac
deliberately enrolling affiliates so as to increase th
jurisdiction and revenue. In addition the clergy were
free from many parliamentary taxes, and Archbis
Monreale were sometimes even more favoured than
After 1535, moreover, the King allowed ecclesia
privilege of first asking the Pope for permission before
their reduced quota, and though this was thought of
formality, it resulted in their tax payments being s
many years in arrears.

Royal control over the Church was made easier b
that the more politically important ecclesiastical post
only in the King's gift, but were regularly bestowed

foreigners. Repeatedly parliament was promised that on
Sicilians would be given episcopal appointments, but in practi
Sicilian sinecures were too useful for paying off political deb
and as salaries for Spanish civil servants; bishoprics were som
times offered to a nephew or grandson of the Pope as part of
political alliance, or were used to win a cardinal's support in
conclave electing a new Pope. For many centuries it seems tha
no native-born Sicilian held the archbishoprics of Monreale o
Palermo. Naturally there were many complaints at this, an
not only from frustrated careerists; because these foreign clergy
again despite many royal promises, were often non-resident
and, quite apart from its disadvantages for religion, an appreci
able proportion of the earnings of Sicilian agriculture was thu
siphoned overseas. It also meant that the senior member o
parliament and some of his episcopal colleagues were shadowy
characters who had little interest in Sicilian affairs but a great
need for royal patronage. One further consequence was that
there was little contact between rich and poor clergy, since so
many of the rich were regularly resident elsewhere; and this gap
eventually had important social and political results.

The Inquisition was an additional means by which the
Church was harnessed to the State and became another buttress
in the elaborate edifice of checks and balances. The Inquisitors
were directly responsible to the King who appointed them, and
were sometimes used by him to counteract the Viceroy and to
obtain private information about other royal officials. Until
towards the end of the sixteenth century, the Viceroy and the
judges could even be made by an Inquisitor to do public
penance if ever there was a serious conflict of jurisdiction, and
several times a secret report to Madrid by the Holy Office
helped to secure a Viceroy's recall. People at every level of
society, but especially the higher aristocracy, attached themselves to the Inquisition as lay familiars. One incentive was that
this carried with it freedom from customs and excise as well as
the right to bear arms. Familiars also could claim an immunity
from the ordinary courts even in cases of murder; and in a world
where the ordinary judges were learning the need for more
summary *ex abrupto* measures to control brigandage, this could
be invaluable to many men of rank and authority.

Viceroys protested that the Inquisition was protecting "all

the rich nobles and rich criminals of the kingdom," and that not only was this tax immunity seriously reducing the revenue, but under cover of belonging to the Inquisition the nobles were arming bands of delinquents who could then break the law with impunity. Di Castro, a Spaniard who had been born in Sicily, said that it was not even worth hiring a lawyer in any case where the Inquisition was interested. From the King's point of view, however, this authoritarian organisation with its secret and even terroristic methods had some advantages, since it helped to maintain religious and political orthodoxy. For him it was an ancillary spy system, and its separate police force and prisons were a means of inculcating fear and submissiveness. In a country where he could afford only a small military establishment but where fear was an essential ingredient of political power, this was a cheap instrument by which he could recruit Sicilians themselves to keep other Sicilians in subjection.

In such a good cause the Inquisitors were allowed to use torture, and their instructions encouraged them not to stop the torture "until the truth should be told": if their victim died in the process, it was held his fault and the judgement of God. Cursing might earn a hundred lashes or a pierced tongue; bigamy could be punished with lashes but also by three years in the royal galleys without pay. In 1553, however, a Spanish soldier was buried alive for reviling God and being in treasonous relations with the infidel. Another man was cremated alive for asserting that Islam and Christianity had certain fundamentals in common. One notorious sufferer at the hands of the Inquisition was an Augustinian monk, clearly out of his mind, who was first condemned to the galleys for heresy but then had seduced other galley slaves: when visited in prison by the Inquisitor General, somehow this prisoner managed to kill his tormentor with his handcuffed fists, and was then burnt alive as a warning to others. This punishment became the ultimate reward for impenitent heretics, male and female. About one person a year on average was handed over to the secular authorities for execution, and the choreography was always carefully devised to make each occasion entertaining and instructive for as many spectators as possible.

Sicily was a frontier territory very close to areas of dangerous spiritual infection in North Africa and the Near East. The fanatical excitement of the counter-Reformation encouraged the Inquisition to persecute even those Jews or Moslems who were converts to Christianity. Evidently some of the best doctors in Sicily were converted Jews, and sometimes a jealous rival would allege that one of them had poisoned some honest Christian patient. There were also many Christian 'Moors' living in Sicily, perhaps the descendants of slaves; at least a hundred of these existed at Trapani in 1534. Reasons of expediency sometimes demanded that heterodox merchants should be allowed permits of residence, and in the 1560s the Viceroy expressly allowed such aliens to stay provided that there was no concealment and they paid a special tax proportionate to their wealth; but Jews had to wear a badge, and 'Moors' a fez or turban. They were forbidden to entertain Christians. Any of them who left the country were closely supervised on departure to see that Christians did not escape too, and if it turned out that they had been baptised they could be sent to the galleys. Subsequently, in another wave of intolerance, there were more rigid decrees of expulsion: the only exception was for slaves; indeed Moorish slaves, since they were private property belonging to rich Sicilians, were liable to execution if they tried to go home.

A certain degree of intolerance was shown by the Inquisition even to the thousands of Greek-speaking Sicilians. Far more hated, however, were the various protestant heresies, which had especially infected some elements of the clergy and the merchants of Messina. By 1546, according to Charles V himself, Lutheranism had contaminated "certain of the principal personages" of Sicily. No doubt there was some exaggeration in this remark: the Inquisitors once even accused a Viceroy of Lutheran heresy because they disliked him, and it must have been tempting to blacken personal enemies with this most all-embracing, misunderstood and unanswerable of epithets. Nevertheless some 85 Lutherans, including 43 priests and monks, were denounced by the Inquisition in the ten years after 1547; 7 of these were burnt in person and many others in effigy.

By trying to eliminate heresy, the Inquisition was helping to attack a dangerous source of independent and sometimes revolutionary thought in politics as well as religion. Along with Jesuit control of education, this contributed to keeping Sicily orthodox and obedient. Barely a glimmering of the 'scientific revolution' was allowed to penetrate, and literature had if possible to be preserved as a courtier literature, full of conceits and ingenuity and affectation, but preferably devoid of any stimulating content. The Holy Office censored books, and foreigners on arrival might have any dangerous literature confiscated. On a number of perilous occasions, for example in 1516, 1560, 1585 and 1647, the chief Inquisitors, who had the interests of Spain as well as of orthodoxy at heart, helped to subdue popular riots and political rebellion. For their part, the Viceroys, despite political differences, were not ungrateful for this help, and strongly advised Madrid to keep Spaniards and not Sicilians in the chief inquisitorial posts.

The Inquisition and the ecclesiastical courts had supervision over morals, and here again they helped to underpin an important sector of state authority. They judged matrimonial matters. One disturbing example of an inexplicable change of sex was thought so challenging that the subject had to be sent to Spain for the King's personal inspection. Witchcraft, bigamy and sexual perversion seem to have been the most frequent offences which came before these courts. Perhaps Sicilians had been accustomed to the more lax traditions of the Greeks and Arabs. Homosexuality, for example, which particularly offended the government, was apparently rife: Charles V persuaded himself that it caused the frequent earthquakes that plagued Sicily, and Philip II thought of sending a special officer from Spain with greater powers than the Viceroy to take drastic emergency action. Comprehensive orders were published describing in extravagant detail various categories of homosexual practice and the requisite scale of penalties. A person who could afford 15,000 *scudi* might possibly buy himself off from the most serious of these, but the tariff was higher than for murder. The worst offenders, or at least those unable to pay, were liable to be burnt as an example, and a special *piazza* in Palermo was set apart for punishing these most offensive of all sinners and criminals. The chief hangman of Palermo, who had carried out some of these executions for homosexuality, was himself executed for the same offence in 1608.

Only their fierce regard for moral and religious orthodoxy could have made successive Kings overlook the manifest abuses of this system and allow the Inquisition such power. The Holy Office became extremely rich through benefactions, but especially because it confiscated the possessions of any victim. Such confiscations were, of course, a strong incentive to zealous persecution, and people complained that not even tradesmen who were owed money by a heretic could collect once the Inquisition had marked him for their own. Informers, on the other hand, might obtain one-tenth of the proceeds of any successful prosecution, and since the anonymity of informers was kept, many people must have found this an effective and profitable means of paying off private scores. One result was that all over Sicily the Inquisition owned property, and this property was untaxable and outside state jurisdiction.

The Viceroy sometimes reached the point of complaining that Inquisitors used their position for personal financial profit and spent too little time on matters of faith. This criticism can in part be discounted as partisan, but disgraceful frauds were on one occasion established and admitted. Certainly their wealth was considerable, and equally it assisted the recruitment of laymen as assistants or familiars. Ferdinand in 1510 had said that there should not be more than twenty of these lay officials in each large city, but in 1577 the Viceroy put their number at over twenty thousand and it was still growing. One Neapolitan observed "that all the nobles and gentry of Sicily have become familiars of the Holy Office in order to escape from the ordinary courts and the Viceroy's authority". Even the wives and widows of these nobles proudly and prudently wore the cross and lilies of the Inquisition on their breasts. Obviously far too many people were financially interested in an institution which, once it had got rid of Jews, Moslems and heretics, spent a good deal of time feathering its nest and undermining the Viceroy's authority.

By the 1590s, after a succession of ugly brawls, the King at last realised this. Henceforward the Inquisition's jurisdiction was not to apply to barons, nor in cases of homicide, nor to tax collectors and those who owed money to the state, nor indeed to anyone involved in public business or to cases "which concern the public good". Even higher officials of the Holy Office could no longer be protected from the royal courts if they were themselves accused of homosexuality. From this moment onwards the Inquisition played only a minor role in religion and politics.

PART 5
The Economy 1500–1650

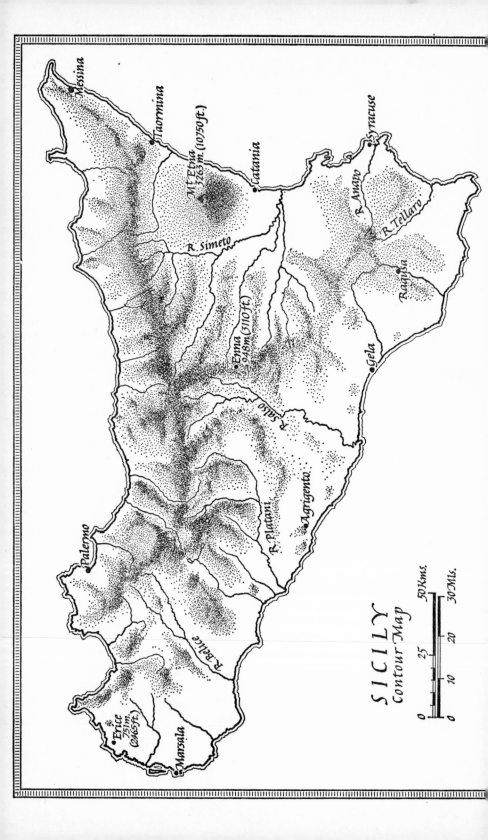

Messina

Taormina

Mt Etna
3263 m. (10750 ft.)

Catania

Syracuse

R. Anapo

R. Tellaro

R. Simeto

Ragusa

Enna
948 m (3110 ft.)

Gela

R. Salso

Agrigento

R. Platani

Palermo

R. Belice

Erice
751 m.
(2465 ft.)

Marsala

SICILY
Contour Map

50 Kms.

30 Mls.

0   10   20   30

0   25   50

Chapter 17

ECONOMIC POLICY AND THE REVENUE

Spain both helped and hindered the expansion of the Sicilian economy, but how far it did so and in what directions are questions not easily settled, nor is it possible to be confident when tracing the fluctuations of growth in different fields of the economy. Despite many appearances of decline, one foreign observer in the 1550s described Sicily as the richest of Spain's Italian possessions, and late in the sixteenth century a Viceroy reported that it was flourishing as never before. This must have been either a deliberate falsehood to comfort or deceive the King, or else a mistake by someone familiar only with the subtropical coastline, for the revenue of Sicily was only half that of Naples or Milan. Nevertheless, even when pauperism and vagabondage were obviously increasing, it is as well to remember that some Spaniards continued to speak of Sicily as a paradise where the wine was perfect, where game abounded, where the best wheat in the world was produced as well as abundant sugar, silk and fruit. Visitors, just as six centuries earlier, were greatly impressed by the irrigated orchards and the mills round Palermo. They could even comment that the nobles wore richer clothes here than anywhere else in Italy.

What was more difficult to determine, however, was whether fine clothes were or were not a sign of economic health. Not every visitor could observe that the nobles were heavily in debt, and that this expenditure on foreign luxuries was both a burden on the balance of payments and a loss to productive investment in Sicily itself. It took time before people could make a pattern out of such tell-tale signs as emergency food imports, a regular shortfall in tax revenue, and special measures to relieve poverty, but the signs became increasingly obvious after 1535. In a bad year, Colonna wrote in 1578, "there are few kingdoms poorer than this one"; and the bad years were apparently becoming more frequent. If rents went unpaid, landowners and their creditors suffered alike.

When things went wrong, one explanation in retropect was to blame Spanish misgovernment. Even though Sicily escaped the trade monopoly practised in Spain's New World dominions, this was still colonial rule of a kind: commodities were exported raw, navigation was run by foreigners, communications remained antiquated; and even if this was as much a Sicilian as a Spanish responsibility, undeniably agriculture was made to serve imperial policy. Some Sicilians undoubtedly gained from the commercial connection with Spain, yet others lost because Spanish interests caused a decline of trade with Africa and the East, and the result was a shortage of precious metals and a barrier to capital accumulation. If only there had not existed this plausible excuse for blaming Spain, perhaps Sicilians might have had to seek out more fundamental reasons and remedies; they would have had to consider such unwelcome subjects as land distribution, tax allocation and social inequality; and it might have been recognised that most local problems had deep roots in the social structure of Sicily itself.

Taxation was of course the chief complaint against the government, though we now can see that taxes probably rose less fast than the incomes of the rich. How much was actually collected and how much sent to Spain can only be guessed, so that the balance sheet of the Spanish connection is to this extent obscure. One view, namely that Sicily took a major part in financing Spanish policy in Europe, is quite implausible; for one thing, sometimes money was brought from Spain to pay for the local military establishment. Some foreign visitors could even conclude that Palermo contributed nothing to the King's expenses elsewhere, but this too was quite incorrect. In 1580, to take one example, despite the fact that the Sicilian ministers tried to argue that money should not be sent to Spain, a great deal of bullion accompanied the ten Sicilian galleys when they went to fight against Portugal.

Sicily was often desperately lacking in coin, and though much of this must be explained by the legitimate or smuggled import of foreign luxuries or by the profit to foreign ship-owners—Sicily's so-called favourable export balance was often a complete illusion—a good deal must surely be ascribed to direct or indirect payments to Spain. It is unlikely that there was ever much surplus on the ordinary revenue, and often there was a heavy deficit. But some dues were collected for the King personally and not included in the national budget: these were sometimes, and perhaps regularly, taken out of the island. The proceeds of the crusade tax were often sent to Spain despite the complaint that they were originally intended for the defence of the Sicilian realm against Islam. One set of figures from the 1590s shows that, quite apart from a good third of the total revenue earmarked for defence, another fifth was for emergency expenditure 'on His Majesty's service'. Parliament could even be requested to pay *donativi* in Castilian money, presumably so as to make transfer more easy. An unknown amount of cash also went overseas to expatriates or foreign owners of Sicilian property, for a good number of the richer aristocracy were non-resident. Another unknown amount went as bribe money to be used at Madrid. Palermo and Messina spent a great deal in Spain on buying privileges against each other, and other towns and private individuals must often have done the same.

Considerable sums were also transferred in the form of salaries. For four hundred years parliament went on complaining that important jobs were held by foreigners. That the Viceroy and the *Consultor* were never Sicilians was not questioned, nor was the fact that the Queen or a royal prince sometimes had a large income from Sicily, but it was not much liked that local army leaders and the castle commanders were foreigners, nor that the Treasurer, the chief customs officials, the senior judges and Inquisitors were commonly Spaniards. Some leading civil servants at Madrid were paid by the Sicilian taxpayer. So were Spanish generals elsewhere in Europe. There were certain payments made by the clergy to Rome and by the Holy Office to its mother institution in Spain. Many pensions were also paid to residents abroad. In the 1540s the Viceroy remarked that 60,000 *scudi*, or not far short of 10 per cent of the national revenue, went annually to pay pensions and grants, much of it probably abroad; in 1602 the amount was 43,000 *scudi*, compared with only 69,000 on salaries, and much the same proportion is found in other figures for 1634 and 1663. Most of the higher prelates were foreigners who must have taken all or part of their salaries overseas, and quantities of valuables are sometimes known to have left the island in an archbishop's baggage. Moreover, the King had a right to the personal possessions of bishops who died and to the revenue of vacant bishoprics, though these spoils may often have remained in the island.

Everywhere in Europe the sixteenth century brought a crisis in government finance, and Sicily in addition had special problems of her own especially after Gonzaga's expenditure on re-armament in the 1530s. "The ordinary income of the government does not cover even basic everyday expenditure," reported the Viceroy bluntly in 1546. As administration became more complicated, as wars became more frequent and more expensive, the budget was completely unbalanced, and on one occasion under Charles V more had to be borrowed in a single year than parliament was willing to grant over three. In 1546 the Viceroy could borrow at 8 per cent and even tried to lower the rate to 7 per cent, but lenders were already asking for 10. Four years later the shortage of coin forced his successor to offer 12 per cent on any silver sent by private people to the mint. In 1565 the government debt was quoted at only two-thirds of its par value. The Viceroy took theological advice on whether he could reduce the rate of interest, but in practice by 1574 nothing could be borrowed under 15 per cent, and in 1591 people would not lend on any terms. There was consequently a default on interest payments, to the great loss of monasteries, charities, town councils and many baronial families.

Despite government credit being frequently shaky, income from government bonds was usually thought more assured or at least more dignified than the returns on agriculture and trade. Rich families and corporate bodies habitually immobilised their capital in this way and so contributed to make a static and conservative society in which capitalistic undertakings were shunned. Just as the vast extent of mortgages on feudal property associated many people besides the baronage in the perpetuation of feudalism and the *latifondi*, so this habit of lending to the government gave moneyed people an additional vested interest in loyalty to Spain. If parliament never developed a 'constitutional opposition', this was because there was not sufficient readiness to limit grants of supply or make them conditional, and this in turn is not unconnected with the fact that parliamentarians had to approve taxation if they wanted what was often the greater part of their income paid on time.

The tax system was by now growing impossibly complicated. Taxes varied from place to place and from year to year; they were collected in many quite different ways, and another complication was that the official year in some government departments began on 25 March, in others on 25 December. The dozen or more *donativi*, taken together, were the Viceroy's main standby. The various customs and trade taxes were usually the second largest item, followed by the crusade tax. Miscellaneous minor sums were obtained from the sale of offices, from the tunny fisheries, the revenues of vacant bishoprics, and so forth. Viceroys continued to complain of the slackness and corruption of Treasury officials and of the many mistakes made over payments. Often it was convenient for a tax to be capitalised by the government when a lump sum was accepted from a professional tax collector who then was allowed to recoup the sum or improve on it as best he could.

Where public finance bore most heavily on economic life was over the taxation of exports—wine, cheese, meat, silk, but above all cereals. The *tratte* (*ius tractae*) were licences which had to be purchased before selling grain overseas, and they were controlled by the *Maestro Portulano*. The *tratte* could be most remunerative in years of abundance so long as outside demand was maintained. They had the great virtue of being easy to collect at the storage pits or *caricatoi* to which landowners were obliged to bring surplus produce. The government incidentally obtained a bonus of about 2 per cent of these deposits, being the average amount by which humidity expanded the grain between deposit and sale. Furthermore, management of a *caricatoio* could be sold for a lump sum to people who realised how it could be exploited for gain.

This system grew up gradually. After a period of completely free trade, Alfonso in 1423 imposed an *ad valorem* duty on exports to be fixed every three months after a survey of current prices and stocks. King John increased the tax until it made up a third of the cost price of wheat, though this was dangerously discouraging to agricultural production. In 1450 there were hunger riots in Palermo, because, quite apart from this tax question, the town was growing in size, and the purchase and storage of reserves was becoming a real problem. On this occasion the Viceroy was out of town because of the plague and so unable to control events. Fearful of infection the city banned all supplies from the countryside. The terrified town mob was easily persuaded that the store-keepers had been behaving corruptly and that the city patricians were privately hoarding food while awaiting a still higher price; storehouses were broken open and the wheat was found to be putrid; wine and oil were soon pouring down in rivers to the sea.

This was an early instance of something which was to give the government increasing concern. There were five popular risings at Palermo between 1512 and 1560. Soon almost every official report to Madrid referred to current estimates about the harvest and their effect on grain prices. One emergency remedy for shortages was to impose an embargo on export. Another less urgent remedy was to discourage exports by imposing an additional export tax if wheat prices ever exceeded a certain limit. Sometimes the Viceroy resorted to direct price controls to hold down the cost of living; but, at a time when devaluation and tax policy were acting in an opposite direction, this was always difficult and sometimes impossible. Landlords were also ordered to reserve one-third of their produce for local consumption in the villages, and Palermo in 1474 was empowered to requisition supplies: this too was very hard to enforce.

The government had other interests to consider than just those of the Sicilian consumer. In order to produce revenue, too many *tratte* were sometimes sold, with disastrous results. Provision for the army and navy was another important priority, and they got supplies at cut rates. Favoured foreigners too were allowed to export wheat without paying duty or observing embargoes. The Pope by ancient privilege had the right to export some wheat freely from Sicily, and was quite ready to excommunicate those who delayed his supplies. Similar tax concessions, in the interests of Spanish foreign policy, were made to Venice, Naples, Malta, Genoa, Savoy and Monaco, and sometimes these concessionaries used this valuable right simply to buy wheat tax-free and sell it at a premium. Gonzaga asked the King for the same privilege for himself, to supplement his own salary, and some cardinals also asked for it. A considerable amount of Sicilian wheat was thus pledged by decisions taken at Madrid, and it was nearly always foreign interests which gained from this.

Sicily, on the contrary, generally lost by it, and sometimes heavily. First there were occasional famines caused by government miscalculation over exports. Secondly, the cost of living rose excessively. Thirdly, tax concessions to Spaniards and other foreign powers had to be balanced elsewhere in the revenue. Fourthly the Sicilian exchequer was charged for supplies consumed either in Spain or by Spanish troops elsewhere. There were also severe repercussions on agriculture, for, as taxes increased, foreign customers looked for cheaper sources of supply. Already in the fifteenth century Genoa was importing cereals from the Black Sea. Venice sometimes found it cheaper to bring wheat from Flanders and England, and later in the sixteenth century there were large imports to the Mediterranean from Poland and the Baltic. High prices and duties, and the variation in duty from year to year which made the Sicilian trade so unreliable, this was what persuaded foreign merchants to "avoid Sicily like the plague", so the Viceroy wrote in 1544.

The government was partly, but by no means only, responsible for this: the attempt to control such an enormous industry and make it the basis for national taxation was bound to pose problems of control which no government of the time could perhaps have solved. The *caricatoi* were sometimes so badly kept that the wheat rotted. Officials in charge of them—usually Sicilians—had their own separate system of courts and an immunity from the ordinary laws: evidently they sometimes took the job just to make money out of it, and then employed junior officials to do the actual work. Fraudulent certificates were issued by them and their subordinates for consignments never deposited; or else non-existent wheat was sold which was subsequently declared to have been stolen or spoilt. Some officials covered themselves by going into spurious bankruptcy. Foreign merchants found that bribery was often necessary to obtain export permits; and, once their ships had docked, they had little option but to pay or go home empty.

From 1515 onwards there were parliamentary protests that increasing export duties were making wheat less profitable to grow. Consumers in particular stood to lose by this. So did landed proprietors—though it is fair to add that they themselves helped to raise prices by imposing their own local *octrois* on the transport and grinding of wheat. Farmers had come to rely on advance payments by foreign merchants before they would undertake to sow, but now these were lacking. Even the government lost potential revenue, so that its policy in the end proved self defeating. This was already clear when the usual purchasers of *tratte* in 1537 offered the Viceroy much less than he asked and astonished him by their "dishonest and impertinent conditions"; but the imperious needs of Spain prevented the obvious remedy. One result was a great increase in the smuggling of cereals out of the country, and perhaps this alone managed to save Sicilian agriculture. Even more controls were then applied, until smuggling reached the point of being deemed as severe an offence as heresy or treason. Desperate orders were renewed that not even the grower himself could consume his own wheat until it had been declared. But this did not work, and in 1541 the Viceroy had to tell Charles V that "the greater part of this kingdom is dying of hunger".

Unfortunately the authorities could diagnose only part of the malady and had no effective remedy to suggest. All over the Mediterranean there was now a pattern of irregular and sometimes insufficient harvests, but in Sicily conditions were especially bad just because the King had inherited this substantial and easily collected tax on exports which he was understandably reluctant to forgo. Gonzaga eventually advised reduction of the tax as the only way to restore commerce and increase revenue, but the King overruled his advice. Since the government's creditors were demanding repayment, the Viceroy was ordered to raise the *tratte* still higher until they cost more than the cost price of wheat itself—this at a time when Charles was in some years giving his friends and allies as much as one-third of Sicilian cereal exports duty free. The *tratte* thus for a short time became the largest item in the revenue; and since city taxes, too, were largely based on wheat and flour, the increasing burden of public finance fell on this one staple commodity which was an essential requirement of everyday life.

What made such a policy particularly short-sighted was that cheap food was a basic necessity for the smooth working of the Spanish administration. It is equally true that increased production would have been very useful for Spain and her armed forces in Europe. Indeed already by 1540 the inability of Sicilian agriculture to keep pace with demand was forcing the Habsburgs to curtail their military commitments. It was not only that growers were tempted to produce less; Sicilian ship-owners who had taken wheat to Spain, and who had been promised by the Viceroy that they would be paid on arrival, found this promise dishonoured; furthermore, merchants who had lent money to finance these exports were never paid, and they did not mean to be caught again. Perhaps the King regarded such services as a proper payment by Sicilians to-wards the expenses of empire, but, as a result, not a single ship could be found in 1546 to take another cargo. When, at long last, the Viceroy was given permission to reduce the tax by one-third, foreigners were learning to fight shy of this unpre-dictable Sicilian market. When the next bumper harvest was gathered, the previous year's stocks even had to be dumped because there were no buyers. Yet in 1557 the export tax was increased yet again, and in 1564 a new parliamentary tax was imposed on the grinding of flour. This *macinato* was easy to collect and difficult to avoid, but for the next three centuries it was to prove a grave burden on agriculture and on standards of living.

Yet another example of the way a food crisis could be exacerbated by official policy was in 1588–90 when too much wheat was allowed to go to Spain (among other things to victual the Armada against England). Again it was not entirely the government's fault, for both growers and grain exporters regularly tried to deceive the government into cheapening export licences by overestimating stocks, and this time they succeeded all too well. Too late a shortage was recognised, and the first rumours were enough for farmers to begin hoarding and merchants speculating on scarcity. The result was that prices soared and shortages quickly became an artificial famine. The government forbade exports and ordered everyone to declare their stocks, but this gave growers a further inducement to bury their grain. Tens of thousands died of starvation, and some of the dead were found with their stomachs full of grass.

Very few years were as bad as this, yet in general the standard of life must have fallen since the later Middle Ages. Food was becoming more expensive. Perhaps there were already begin-ning to be more mouths to feed. This was a world where hunger riots were never far away, where in the grim months before the harvest people might attack the storage pits, and where emergency bread rationing was often necessary. Here was an intractable problem for the government, and on its solution could be said to depend the future prosperity of Sicily. Contemporary economic theory thought in terms of embargoes and price controls, even though these sometimes made shortages worse than ever. To economise on wheat flour, the Viceroy tried ordering that fashionable gentlemen should not use starch for their cuffs and collars. But how to tackle the fundamental question, how to procure adequate tax revenue and yet encourage wheat growing, was more than economists and civil servants knew.

Chapter 18

CHANGES IN AGRICULTURE

Everything in Sicily in the last resort refers back to agriculture. Agriculture provided the raw material for whatever commerce and industry existed. It provided most of the taxes and far the greater proportion of all personal incomes. It was a factor in foreign policy, as well as providing the basic cause of every political revolt for centuries. Every Viceroy found questions of land tenure, wheat exports, domestic food supplies and possible harvest failures to be inescapable matters of daily preoccupation.

In the early sixteenth century, Sicily perhaps exported two million bushels of wheat in a good year by official reckoning, and possibly as much again through smuggling which evaded the official statistics. She still had some claim to be what Braudel called the Argentine of Europe. But increased taxation, together with her growing city population and the cropping of marginal lands, posed a challenge which was too difficult. In northern Europe, the stimulus of increasing population and land shortage eventually led to the discovery of improved methods of agriculture and crop rotation, but in Sicily there were too many physical and social obstacles to overcome. The cereal areas of Sicily were hot, dry and had a heavy clay soil; hard wheat grew here quite easily, but higher yielding varieties and more profitable crops would have called for new methods, more labour, and heavier monetary investment. Part of the trouble, so people said, was that rich Sicilians were too rich to have much incentive for the changes which would have been required; or, at least, social custom was against it. The dam built by the Pignatelli above Terranova was quite exceptional. Landowners found it socially more acceptable to buy new estates than to improve old ones; for land meant prestige as well as being a hedge against inflation, whereas improvements would have needed thought, work and money, and still would have been difficult to carry out.

The peasants were therefore left to cultivate the land as they always had; using the most primitive tools, they were accustomed to exploit one area to the point of exhaustion and then move elsewhere. The traditional simple rotation of wheat and fallow resulted in land still being idle every other year, or even two years in three, and the lack of an alternative crop not only brought all the disadvantages of monoculture but meant a gradual lowering of the yield per acre. Two successive years of bad weather could suddenly throw the whole economy into disarray. High wheat prices would occasionally encourage farmers to plough up scrub and woodland, but then a temporary glut would reverse the process, except that goats and erosion prevented the trees from growing again and the hillsides were left denuded. At the same time a trend towards *métayage*, or share-cropping, discouraged improvements, just because neither land-owners nor labourers were anxious to invest in the land so long as the other party received half the proceeds from any unilateral investment. Moreover this kind of contract could drive a tenant into permanent debt if one bad harvest left him with no margin in reserve.

Agricultural improvements depended only to a small extent on government action. It was easier to legislate against usurious loans than to stop them, easier to penalise cattle thieving than to enforce the penalties. The Viceroy in 1601 did make another attempt to standardise the many different systems of weights and measures which hamstrung inter-village commerce, but it was thought enough just to issue a decree without setting up precise master measures, and in any case there was tremendous and effective opposition to such a revolutionary step. Messina, for instance, could not have endured to change its measurements and adopt those current at Palermo.

Likewise any improvement in communications would have required more local co-operation than was conceivable. The fact that all wheat had to be carried to the ports on muleback helps to explain why other countries increasingly found Sicilian produce too expensive. Funds were allocated to build bridges over the torrential streams which hampered traffic, and the work was placed under the supervision of a committee of nobles; but some of the money was spent on other things, and some not spent at all, while there were many rumours of frauds and profiteering. The committee was ordered by the government to be more careful in checking estimates and contracts and in prosecuting those who tried to set up monopolies in the department of public works; and yet a bridge over the river Belice, one of the few new ones built, was a crumbling ruin within nine months of its construction, and the Viceroy had to report that he could find not a single competent engineer in all Sicily. It is likely indeed that communications became slower rather than quicker during the course of the sixteenth century. Even the main Palermo–Messina road was dangerous and sometimes impassable, and hence this journey was usually made by sea. One outside observer was surprised to find that the inhabitants of Messina hardly ever ventured into the interior more than a few miles outside the city gates.

Probably the climate was becoming drier and more extreme than it had been in Arab and Norman Sicily. As late as the fifteenth century, Alfonso regularly had Sicilian rice sent to him on his expeditions, and we also know that cotton and sugar then grew freely in areas which later could support only dry farming. In the sixteenth century some springs and water courses failed, and occasionally mills changed to using oxen instead of water power. There were sciroccos from North Africa so oppressive that windows had to be kept shut in the fierce heat of July, and rich people liked to excavate a special 'scirocco chamber' to which they could escape. Sand storms not only ruined harvests but could make it impossible to see across the street at Palermo. Whether these storms were worse than before can only be surmised. The fact that diarists mention terrible winter rains as well as heat to explain harvest failures can be interpreted more than one way. No doubt an increasing population would have meant that harvest failure had a more devastating effect than before, and hence drought and storms could be expected to receive more attention in the documents, but growth of demand would also lead to more predatory methods of agriculture, and these could not help but upset the hydrography of certain areas.

Sicily must have remained well wooded throughout the Middle Ages: venison and game had been common in the markets, and the King maintained huntsmen and foresters in districts where later we find no trees at all. When these forests disappeared is not easy to say. In the thirteenth century Sicily had still been providing timber for the shipwrights of central Italy, but by the seventeenth century there was hardly enough for local consumption. Firewood and charcoal were the only available fuels for domestic and industrial use. Large areas of forest must also have been burnt down, either accidentally by the charcoal burners, or deliberately in war time and as a police measure against brigandage.

Most of all, however, fire was used to burn stubble and to clear new ground for planting wheat. One seventeenth-century diary which has survived at Palermo refers to "the fires which the peasants light between July and September in order to clear the rough growth on the sterile mountainsides and make them fertile, with the result that when the wind catches the flames they spread everywhere and cause irreparable damage to vineyards and sown crops". Whenever a harvest failure sent cereal prices rocketing, virgin territory could thus be cleared, just for a few profitable seasons, after which it could be abandoned before the tax collector discovered what was happening. Even olive groves were sometimes destroyed for this purpose in a fatally improvident sacrifice of capital for income; and although, after a parliamentary protest over the lack of olive oil in 1566, the King made cutting these trees illegal, such a decree was no more than a pious hope. Foreign observers were astonished how little regard Sicilians had for olive trees or for making olive oil, and there was a widespread conviction among local farmers that tree cultivation was unproductive and unrewarding.

By the middle of the sixteenth century, de-afforestation was showing its usual effects. As the soil dried out, avalanches occasionally destroyed roads, cutting off villages or even burying them, and sometimes killed hundreds at a time. Soil erosion gradually began to upset water control, changing the course of rivers and creating regular annual floods. Fertile valleys were being crippled by the spread of marshlands and malaria; and this fact, together with the insecurity caused by brigands and pirate raids, resulted in cultivators being pushed further up the hill sides where steep inclines made the cycle of soil erosion still more severe. Rivers which had once provided irrigation now disappeared for most of the year; in the wet season they became torrents which carried away bridges, destroyed mills and houses, and sometimes broke down city walls and devastated whole areas of Palermo and Messina.

A possible change in climate is also inferred by the decrease in sugar growing. Sugar cane had been a flourishing crop for many centuries, and processed sugar had been exported as far away as Flanders and England. Cultivation was expensive, since it needed copious but not excessive irrigation; for best results it needed replantation every few years, and extraction also required costly milling machinery. About 1410 there had been thirty sugar refineries in Palermo alone, and at Syracuse there was a 'gate of the sugar workers'. Special traffic regulations had been needed for the transport of firewood and cane. So valuable was sugar for the economy that the law allowed compulsory purchase of land for it, and water could be taken from whatever source; workers were also bound to the industry by law and were free from arrest during the season when the refineries were working.

The subsequent decline of this trade meant a serious loss of foreign exchange. More than one cause was at work. Supplies of wood fuel became exhausted near the refineries and would have been simply too expensive to bring by mule track from more than a few miles away. Perhaps irrigation and water power became too scarce except near the Simeto and Anapo rivers in the east. Sometimes, as at Termini in 1517, a popular rising against the local baron destroyed a factory and its plant. Clearly production had also become inefficient. This was a kind of industry which needed constant investment, and there was always a temptation to go for immediate profits at the expense of assets. Some evidence suggests that cane was cut immature and the replanting cycle was not maintained. The process of boiling the sugar apparently went on for months, and it is unlikely that much experiment was done to find quicker and better methods; nor was the residue used productively. At all events, by 1610 it could occasionally be cheaper to export the raw sugar and then reimport it once refined. The government also taxed sugar exports. Parliament protested in 1515 that export taxes were damaging the industry, and for ten years they were remitted. Charles V further tried to help growers by freeing them from legal compulsion to pay their debts between November and February, the period of greatest strain; but the result was to make borrowing more expensive in an industry where credit was indispensable. By this time both the Azores and the Canaries were exporting sugar, and after 1580, when Portugal was united with Spain, Brazilian sugar began to be increasingly imported into the Spanish colonies. Yet the taxes on sugar exports from Sicily were raised even higher in 1651.

The Spaniards introduced some important new crops. There was the tomato from Peru, maize from Mexico and tobacco. The spiky sisal took its name from a port in Yucatan. The potato also arrived in Italy at the end of the sixteenth century but was not easily popularised in Sicily. Most useful of all was the prickly pear cactus, whose local name, Indian fig, reveals its derivation from the West Indies: before long the prickly pear was to transform the Sicilian countryside, for it could tolerate great dryness, and since it was easily propagated even in crevices of rock, it was deliberately planted to break up lava on the fertile slopes of Mount Etna. Not only was this an admirable hedge plant, but its fruit made an important dietetic contribution in the daily lives of both rich and poor.

Animal husbandry was declining in the sixteenth century as more pasture was ploughed up. Large areas had until now been kept for permanent rough grazing, and over a great deal of Sicily this might still have been the most efficient form of agriculture. Cheese, meat, wool and hides had all been exported. But a growing population and a probably decreasing yield per acre brought with it a land hunger which was bound to be at the expense of the wandering shepherds. Advancing civilisation inevitably led to more laws and more property, and this in the long run would make nomadism more difficult.

The government was especially anxious to keep enough horses for the army. From the time of the crusades until that of the Crimean war and 1915–18, Sicily bred horses for military use. Alfonso depended on them for his campaign in Naples, Lorenzo de' Medici wanted them in Florence, and in 1457 the Earl of Worcester exported some to England; but the breed lost its old importance once the barons were opting out of military service. Moreover, the peasants preferred mules for farm work. The government tried to reduce the number of mules despite the complaint that this would cripple internal transport. Ferdinand and Charles V renewed an old prohibition against the taking of horses in settlement of civil debts, and Philip II gave some help towards improving Sicilian bloodstock.

A decline in cattle rearing is suggested by the fact that meat was sometimes hard to procure, and there was a lack of draught animals needed for the wheat fields "whence Your Majesty's revenues chiefly come". Repeatedly it was said that stealing sheep and cattle was on such a scale that livestock did not pay. The inducement was offered of allowing owners of more than ten cows to possess firearms (so long as the guns were over three feet long and difficult to conceal); immunity from militia service was offered to possessors of twenty; those who had fifty cows or more were freed from the horrors of billeting and from being held to account for offences committed by some bandit relative. It was laid down that animals should not be pawned or taken for debt, and that they should not be killed except by public officials in licenced slaughterhouses. Prohibitions were also made against the slaughtering of heifers for meat; though probably this had an opposite effect to that intended, since it took away some of the profit from legitimate cattle rearing and made the theft of animals more likely.

An even more significant reaction was the stern official disapproval of the excessive consumption of meat by wealthy citizens, ecclesiastics, and Spanish soldiery. The Pope had to be asked to stop the clergy eating so much, and each company of Spanish troops was rationed to four sides of beef a week. An attempt was also made to centralise all meat selling at Palermo, a fact which suggests that the selfish interests of wealthy consumers and the Palermo meat market possibly underlay this serious threat to the prosperity of agriculture. It is possible, indeed, that there was no absolute decline in meat production, but just an increased consumption: not only were there more mouths to feed, but Sicily had the reputation in the sixteenth and seventeenth centuries of being a meat-eating country where the Lenten fast received scant attention from the upper classes. When taken in conjunction with heavy excises and controlled prices for meat, this might help to explain the growth of organised syndicates for stealing animals and selling on the black market, and these syndicates in turn were becoming a major reason for the deterioration of the Sicilian economy.

Chapter 19

INDUSTRY AND URBANISATION

Sicilian towns and industries were of course so closely involved with the world of agriculture that no clear distinction can be drawn, yet their interests often deviated from those of the farming community, and they soon presented the government with very special problems of their own. Wool, cotton and silk had all been cultivated in Sicily during the Middle Ages, but it was always hard to create a flourishing textile industry. Cotton, linen and hemp manufacture seem to have largely or even altogether come to a stop by the fifteenth century, and several complaints were made between 1514 and 1526 that, apart from rough cloth woven by peasant families for their own use, the woollen industry was dead. Spain was accused of discouraging higher quality textiles which might rival Catalan cloth. Nevertheless this criticism was not entirely fair. Government help was forthcoming after 1515 to set up a factory at Palermo, though good workers could not be found and sales were so slow that the manager went bankrupt; eventually the building was converted into a pawnshop. In the 1550s, the administration was trying to encourage a merchant from Lucca to introduce skilled labour and capital, and again in 1608 the Madrid authorities were offering government action to restart the Sicilian cloth industry and open up markets in the Levant. These instances were almost certainly not isolated.

All such attempts, however, came up against the fact that local money and labour shied away from industrial enterprise. Sicilian wool was probably not good enough for fine cloth, but domestically grown cotton was of adequate quality and yet continued to go overseas for manufacture; then the finished goods were imported, in each case through the agency of foreign merchants. In 1622 it was said that a million *scudi* a year was spent on imported cloth, in other words about as much as the government's total budget.

Much the same happened to silk. Perhaps silk weaving never recovered from the exodus of Arab workers in the twelfth and thirteenth centuries and of the Jews after 1492. At all events 90 per cent of Sicilian silk was exported raw—another official about 1600 thought that this export trade was worth about a million *scudi* a year. The demand for the raw material from local manufacturers was surprisingly small, though foreigners were glad to buy it. In the early sixteenth century merchants from northern Italy were trying to reinvigorate the weaving industry at Messina and Catania, but their task was not easy. Sandstorms and the volcanic ash from Mount Etna occasionally spoiled the silkworms. Sumptuary legislation also reduced demand, and it was even made illegal for silk to be worn by artisans, countrymen, domestic servants or prostitutes.

Once again the government's financial policy did not help, especially as manufactures were taxed more highly than exported raw material. The duty on exported silk was sharply increased in 1562. Messina resisted this as discriminatory, but then spent an enormous sum buying a privilege which forced the silk exporters of eastern Sicily to use this one port only. Such restrictionism was bound to harm the industry. Instead of wanting to reduce the silk taxes, Messina was merely hoping to be able to levy them on her own account and then pay the proceeds personally to Philip II instead of in tax to the government at Palermo. Parliament objected, but in vain, and nothing shows more clearly the impotence of parliament in any serious matter. Instead of trying to make the silk industry cheaper and more efficient, the Messina merchants relied on injuring their competitors in Palermo and Catania. The silk trade continued to be reasonably prosperous, and indeed the growth of luxury spending in seventeenth-century Europe gave it a new lease of life; but a tell-tale sign was that the increase was rather in the export of raw material to be manufactured in countries where risk capital was available and profits were sought in industrial efficiency rather than restriction and privilege. The desire for monopoly privileges was a sign of weakness, and it was one symptom of a growth of restrictive practices which left the silk interest unable to meet competition from France and Genoa. Even in Messina itself, foreign merchants and shipowners took most of what profits there were.

The biggest city of Sicily was Palermo. Its population about 1500 has been estimated at anything from 25,000 to four or five times as many, but whatever the true figure it was expanding fast. The Viceroys made periodic attempts to assess the population for tax purposes. The first census of which we possess details was in 1501, and others were taken at about fifteen or twenty year intervals to keep pace with changing population distribution; but they had to be based on information volunteered by heads of families, and the anxiety to evade taxation and militia service made them untrustworthy. Ecclesiastics and nobles had valuable privileges of exemption from the census, and so had the inhabitants of Palermo and Messina. Whether the population of the island was more or less than a million by 1500 is therefore still in some doubt, though probably it was less. Palermo was estimated for tax purposes as a tenth of the whole.

One reason for Palermo's growth was that the rich wanted to escape from the discomforts and insecurity of life on the farm. They needed to get closer to the Viceroy so as to obtain favours, pensions and titles, while exemption from the census made residence in Palermo a useful means of tax avoidance. The result was that the territorial aristocracy were, except for very very brief periods, in undisputed control of the town and its large revenues. The mayor, or praetor, was invariably one of the great magnates, and despite the law he sometimes remained in office much longer than a year. The six senators who assisted him were also almost invariably noblemen. After 1584 they, like the praetor himself, were chosen by the Viceroy, and frequently there was at least one Spaniard among their number to act in the government's interest.

The landed proprietors, by dominating the main towns, helped to create an environment unfavourable to economic development. A Venetian ambassador in the 1570s reported that Palermo was a parasite town where almost all the aristocracy now resided, a town which consumed most of the revenues of the island and yet despised the country districts which made its luxurious living possible. In their wake these noblemen brought domestic servants and tradesmen from the countryside, and other farm labourers followed them in order to live off monasteries and civic charities. This urbanisation of the peasantry was variously explained, whether as a flight from brigandage, from feudalism, or from enclosures of land by the baronage. Several times in the mid-fifteenth century there had been complaints that country-based landowners were using every legal and illegal means to stop this desertion of the countryside, and clearly it had become a danger to agriculture; but the interest of the towns, short-sighted though some people might have thought it, was bound to prevail.

The existence of an urban proletariat at Palermo is shown by the endowment of special hospitals and workhouses, and by the foundation early in the sixteenth century of a municipal pawn-shop which apparently was intended to lend money at as little as 1 per cent. Some Viceroys and some Sicilians were already expressing their horror at the growth of slum conditions. The shopkeeper and artisan classes had for a long time formed guilds or *maestranze*; there had been over forty of them as early as 1385. Parliament begged the King to bring these democratic organisations under firm control, but in general they were thought useful or at least harmless. Each guild was presided over by a consul. They supervised and laid down standards for each industry, excluding competition and regulating the admission of apprentices; and sometimes they were given a small share in civic government as a reward for good behaviour.

The growing population at Palermo caused a severe problem of food supply, and it was not unusual for the praetor and senate to meet each day to discuss it. On instructions from Spain they had to stockpile wheat, and if a bad harvest sent up prices they could then sell bread under cost price; indeed they were obliged to do so. Sometimes, if farmers in an emergency held out on them, the city was allowed to use force to requisition food supplies. In 1560, even that did not suffice and the size of the municipal loaf had to be reduced. On this occasion the by now unfamiliar device of a popular assembly was employed to justify the decision of the city patriciate, but the consuls of the *maestranze*, who were usually consulted over food prices, refused to agree and warned that a bread shortage would mean trouble. Hunger riots soon began to occur, and some of the leading citizens had their palaces broken open and arms stolen. The guilds eventually helped to re-establish law and order. There were a few exemplary executions, and, to prevent a recurrence, more grain storage pits were excavated outside the Viceroy's palace.

Another instance of official intervention was the setting up of the *tavola* at Palermo in 1552–3. This early example of a public bank was designed to help remedy the lack of commercial credit resulting from the collapse of private banks, and to make up for so much of the country's financial business being in foreign hands. It was soon being used for private deposits from all over Sicily, and these were guaranteed by the town. The government and the parliamentary Deputation also kept their liquid funds in this bank, and it was of course widely used by the city authorities. For example, in 1593 the bank advanced a large sum to the municipality at a low rate of interest to celebrate the arrival of the holy relics of St. Ninfa, which had been acquired by the town, and to help pay off part of the accumulated civic debt. Two noblemen and one merchant were appointed governors of the bank. The praetor was also charged to examine the books each week because of possible frauds.

Among other public works, the municipality undertook expensive improvements in water supply and drainage; especially after 1557 when a flood (caused unwittingly by the anti-contraband police when they stopped up a sewer running under the royal palace) drowned hundreds—Fazello said three thousand—and devastated a large area of the capital city. Special overseers were put in charge of water supplies: they were instructed to see that there was enough flow for the flour mills and that private people did not take too much for irrigation; in fact, however, these officers illegally conceded too many permits, and before long there were complaints that the whole area was being made to suffer because of their corruption or inefficiency. Work also continued, though very slowly, on a large breakwater to make the port of Palermo safer.

The Viceroys were at pains to embellish the city, no doubt guessing that their reputation would depend on this more than anything else. One of them commissioned a splendid Florentine renaissance fountain, which his family then persuaded the town authorities to buy from them. Two of the finest town streets in Europe took their names from Viceroys, the via Toledo in the 1560s, which ran from the royal palace to the sea, and the via Maqueda in the 1590s: together these streets cut the town into four roughly equal sections, and ten years later another Viceroy built a fine baroque octagon at their intersection, the Quattro Canti. A good deal of new urban development, coming after the big fortification work of Gonzaga, destroyed much of the

Town hall and the Pretoria fountain, Palermo: 16th century

Anders

The Quattro Canti, one side of the octagonal Piazza Vigliena
in the centre of Palermo: early 17th century

medieval city, and the several hundred aristocratic families who
now converged on Palermo needed room for their *palazzi*. An
old law was revived which gave them rights of compulsory
purchase over urban building sites at one-third above 'the just
price'. In the interests of security, building was forbidden for
half a mile outside the city walls, but in fact the shanty towns in
the suburbs were growing faster than problems of overcrowding
could be solved. The flight from the countryside soon created a
fertile seed-bed for plague and revolution.

Messina was a smaller but more mercantile and potentially
richer city than Palermo, and its geographical position was far
more promising. It was a great emporium for the whole
Mediterranean, an ideal watering place and supply base. Its
inhabitants, according to an official writing in the 1590s, were
industrious and "skilful in acquiring and keeping money", and
the revenue of the town and its population was kept secret even
from the government itself. But Messina, despite its marvellous
port, had some physical handicaps which other major Mediterranean ports escaped. Once in each century the east of Sicily
was devastated by earthquakes. Messina was also especially
vulnerable to any diminution of trade with the Levant brought
about by the Turkish wars and the Greek and African pirates.
Its hinterland was mountainous and poorly provided with
communications, so that the town depended on seaborne
shiploads of grain and suffered badly in any period of dearth.
Yet the sixteenth century was a great period of municipal
expansion here; many new suburbs were built as the population
increased. Supplies of local timber were running out, but the
ship-building industry could still use wood from Calabria; and
the mulberries of north-eastern Sicily led the flourishing silk
trade.

The *strategoto*, or mayor, of Messina was appointed by the
Viceroy, but, unlike those of Palermo, the senators were elected
by the citizens each April and seem to have possessed a greater
degree of autonomy. They jealously kept numerous documents
proving their privileges, and dozens of these documents were
blatantly manufactured in the 1430s at a time when forgery
had been raised to a high art. Messina was proud to possess a
letter written by the Virgin Mary from Jerusalem in her own
hand: the Spaniards were excessively curious to know more

about this document, and a Viceroy was once allowed to kiss it, but the King could never obtain more than a translation; Palermitans of course maintained that it was a fake, and when the Jesuits of Messina loyally tried to proclaim its authenticity they ran into trouble with the Inquisition which took Palermo's side.

Against the Palermo-oriented history of Sicily published in 1558 by the Provincial of the Dominicans, Fazello, Messina helped to sponsor the somewhat different version by Maurolico in 1562; for an appeal to the past was now becoming a funda-mental element in what was a permanent civic squabble. Messina even managed to claim exemption from the parlia-mentary taxes, but in order to maintain this privilege she in practice paid *ex gratia* sums which were probably higher than the tax would have been. Apart from being free from the census, her imports and exports were also free of duty during the month of her annual fair, and this immunity was of considerable value. The citizens claimed, and usually were allowed, that their town should have the exclusive and lucrative right to coin money, as well as the privilege of appearing only before Messinese judges. Their town asserted the right to appoint all Sicilian consuls overseas. They also arrogated to themselves valuable jurisdiction and taxation privileges over nearly fifty villages between Milazzo and Taormina, and this helped them to control their own supplies of food and raw silk. Sometimes they were able to enforce the right of *contra privilegio* through which they could refuse to obey an order by the Viceroy until they had had time to appeal to the King against it.

This kind of behaviour ran into a good deal of opposition elsewhere. One Viceroy in 1565 called it "pure childishness" that so much energy was being devoted to questions of civic precedence. Another in 1577 complained that bandits took advantage of Messina's privileges to escape out of governmental jurisdiction. Taormina deplored the subordination of north-eastern Sicily to the interests of this one town, while democratic elements in Messina itself protested that the so-called privileges of their city were merely a cover by means of which a narrow oligarchy protected their private wealth. Above all, Palermitans utterly repudiated Messina's pretension to equality, let alone her claim to be *caput regni*. Nevertheless the land-owning and mercantile aristocracy of Messina controlled ample municipal revenues with which to back their case, and in 1591 they bought not only a virtual monopoly of silk export, but also confirmation of all other past privileges and a wide exemption from the jurisdiction of parliament. They also won the right to have a university, though Catania put up a most strenuous opposition to this infringement of her profitable monopoly in the field of higher education.

One further privilege won by Messina was that the Viceroy and his court should live there for half his term of office. The result of this attempt to perpetuate earlier practices of ambulant government was a considerable disruption of state business. The administration with its archives was obliged to move periodically from place to place, and it made government very difficult if decisions or lawsuits were pending at a time when the move took place. Messina in any case did not have enough office accommodation. Moreover, mislaid records must have hindered administration quite apart from creating irreparable gaps in Sicilian history. In 1607 a barge carrying these archives had barely left Messina for Palermo when it foundered on a reef— the sailors were accused of paying too much attention to the prostitutes on board. Many noble families and towns on this occasion lost proof of their privileges—or were able to say they had done so—and one can imagine the loss to government efficiency and to the revenue. Nor was this the only disaster of its kind.

Alongside the expansion of the two biggest cities of Sicily there was a remarkable development of new towns and villages. One element in these was immigrant labour from overseas. Sicily over the centuries had absorbed a long succession of immigrant peoples, and the latest were Greeks and Albanians fleeing from the Turkish occupation of the Balkans. Landowners and government alike, recognising their usefulness as farmers, helped to settle these newcomers on uncleared territory. In return, the settlers would usually agree to cultivate so much land and accept the local baron's feudal jurisdiction. Of seven main villages created by these immigrants, the largest was Piana dei Greci where Archbishop Borgia of Monreale had allowed some of them to settle in the fifteenth century. These Albanians were mostly Catholics of the Greek rite, and they kept their own priests.

Right down to the twentieth century they retained a distinct identity, with their own language, folklore and fashions of dress.

In building new villages, the Albanians gave an impetus to a movement which by 1600 was changing the Sicilian country-side. Normans, Hohenstaufen and Angevins had all founded new villages in Sicily. The leading barons followed suit, as the Chiaramonte for instance had built Mussomeli and Siculiana and held out inducements to encourage settlers to populate these deserted areas. There were at least 9 new villages which had been founded in the fifteenth century, and over the next two hundred years about 150 more were established, almost doubling the number of village settlements previously in existence.

One probable reason for this remarkable process was a growth of population which increased the need for food and so encouraged enterprising landlords to plough up virgin land. As prices rose, so grew both the need to make more money, and the increased domestic demand for wheat which satisfied the need. Some indebted landowners clutched at this straw, for with little expense they were able to improve their estates and increase their income. Since the large *latifondi* were sparsely inhabited and thinly cultivated, a landlord who wanted to meet the cost of city life would divide parts of his estates into smaller farms on attractive long-term leaseholds which would appeal to tenant farmers; and such leaseholds would increase his income.

The foundation of new villages simultaneously conferred on the baronage prestige and the illusion or reality of power. Social status among the magnates was largely measured by the extent of their territory and the number of townships where they held powers of life and death. There was prestige for the Tomasi family in obtaining the barren island of Lampedusa, and for Requesens in colonising Pantelleria. Founding a village with more than eighty families usually brought with it a seat in the baronial house of parliament, or an extra vote if its owner already owned this privilege. In this way the parliamentary barons increased from 72 in 1556 to 277 by 1810, while the other two Houses of parliament remained barely altered. Yet some of these prestige hamlets never grew large enough to carry the expense of public administration and eventually ceased to exist.

Another motive for internal colonisation was provided by

raids on the Sicilian coast, which drove people away from their farms and forced them to look for less accessible land elsewhere. Brigandage and agrarian discontent likewise made it unsafe to live in isolated farmsteads. Government policy also helped, because there was profit in selling licences to create new villages, apart from the fact that increased food production meant more customs and excise revenue. One Viceroy thought of compelling feudatories to sow at least one-third of their *latifondi*, because increased cereal production was also urgently needed for the balance of payments, quite apart from keeping the expanding population of Palermo fed and happy. At the same time there was a positive need to resettle people on the land in order to reduce the pauperism, overcrowding and disease of the cities, and to curtail the revolutionary feelings which bred in the Palermo suburbs.

Once a landlord had a licence, he would build houses, almost certainly a church, and usually a mill and oil press for general use. There was not much return at first, because to attract settlers he would have to promise freedom from dues for perhaps ten years. Villagers would invariably be given certain communal rights, the use of water, of wood for fuel, perhaps timber for building and making ploughs, so long as they did not cut down the oak trees. To take one example, the government in 1518 allowed the Lord of Castelvetrano to build a village at Menfi. Settlers were slow to come, and in 1536 colonists were offered the added inducement of an eight-year moratorium on debts. Even this did not help, so a hundred years later the family broke up their fief and offered small farms on long leases to anyone who promised to build a one-roomed house and reside there permanently; and by 1652 there were 576 inhabitants. Casteltermini was licensed in 1629 and within twenty-five years boasted two thousand inhabitants. These settlers had to help pay for the upkeep of the church and the priest; they had to provide six rooms for the baron and his officers; and he retained a monopoly on the slaughter of meat, as well as on the milling of flour, and certain preferential rights over the retail trade. Each family owed him so much produce. At Vittoria and Santa Ninfa, not only debtors but other criminals had to be promised immunity, and perhaps delinquents formed a considerable element of the population there.

The new residents came in part from the open countryside, in part from baronial villages where the landlord was accustomed to demand unpaid forced labour or where the baronial courts were notoriously unjust. Many came from the royal demesne. Since the royal towns and villages had to pay an unduly large share of the *donativi*, they had often accumulated considerable debts, and this was reflected in high local food taxes. By comparison, the new village settlements offered lower taxes, lower ground rents and greater permanency of tenure. Taormina for this reason lost half its six thousand population between the censuses of 1583 and 1653, and Castrogiovanni nearly half of its nineteen thousand inhabitants.

The economic results of this redistribution of population cannot be known precisely, but one social benefit was the increase of copyhold contracts or *enfiteusi* in certain favourable areas. Although most agricultural workers remained day labourers or share croppers, landlords who wanted to attract settlers would have to offer permanent or long leaseholds, and these were a stimulus to hard work and investment in the land on the part of the new tenants. Probably these copyholders did not receive a great deal of land; but wherever there was a ready market and enough water, there the planting of vines, olives and citrus trees became worth while, and sometimes was expressly stipulated in the lease. This type of contract was usually found near existing towns. For various reasons which are not entirely clear, it was particularly common in eastern Sicily; and, by its means, tens of thousands of acres on the slopes of Mount Etna were transformed in the seventeenth century. The large County of Modica was eventually leased out in *enfiteusi*, and so were dozens of fiefs in the possession of the Archbishop of Monreale. In some select areas, and for a few decades, this may have seemed like the dawn of an agricultural revolution, but the next century was to show that it was a false dawn.

Chapter 20

ECONOMIC DIFFICULTIES AFTER 1600

The reign of Philip III (1598–1621) was a time of exceptional economic difficulty, for new trade routes were being developed elsewhere in competition with those of the Mediterranean, and all over Europe there were continued problems of currency depreciation and a deficiency of government revenue. Prices were rising because of American silver and an increasing population; yet Sicilian trade was simultaneously inconvenienced by a shortage of money. What had once seemed to be a favourable balance of payments was threatened by increasing foreign competition to Sicilian wheat exports and also by excessive spending overseas on the part of public authorities and private citizens alike.

One result of this money shortage was that coins were being clipped, even to a point where they could no longer be identified. The government blamed this practice mainly on the friars, the clergy and the Knights of Malta. In order to obtain more silver, laws were published against anyone keeping more than one spoon and plate, and any slave who reported his master for breaking this law could win freedom and obtain one-third of any confiscated property. But the good coins continued to disappear, and foreign merchants were increasingly reluctant to accept what was left. Finally the Viceroy panicked and made things worse by forbidding the use of clipped coins altogether: burning to death was made the penalty, but in vain, and eventually even the Palermo pawnshop had to close.

In 1607, urgent requests were made for Spain to send more silver. Yet in 1608 the Viceroy despatched a consignment of silver objects and coins back to Spain, presumably made up of tax money and perhaps gifts to him and the King by individual Sicilians. We might never have known about this shipment except that the Viceroy's illegitimate son was on board and he and the cargo were captured by a Flemish privateer from Tunis; but it suggests that the government may well have been in large part responsible for the lack of precious metals. Parliament offered to help the Viceroy buy back his son's freedom, and indeed redemption of Christian slaves from North Africa was another regular channel by which bullion left the country; but this particular captive became a Moslem and refused to return.

In the same year a report went back to Madrid that in the last five years the cost of farms had trebled, and most of the land had been falling into the hands of a few nobles. Another dangerous sign was that most of the aristocracy were increasing their indebtedness, and it was fashionable and easy for them to default on these debts: money-lenders and mortgagees could put in a receiver to secure at least their interest payments, but there were various means by which a noble could frustrate this; moreover the class of town artisans had no such redress against the rich clients on whom they entirely depended. Countrymen sometimes could not find grazing because of enclosures. Some of them were dying of hunger because they could not afford high-priced food. Everyone complained of taxation: the growers singled out the taxes on cereal exports, while consumers blamed everything on the grist tax. Nevertheless, apart from silk, there was no conceivable alternative to cereals as the main source of revenue.

The government suffered as much as anybody from this rise in prices. In 1602 the Viceroy reported that expenditure was running two years ahead of taxation; he was having to withhold salaries even though incomes had depreciated to the point where they were worth only a quarter of what they had once been. He made another effort to reduce luxury spending by wealthy citizens. An attempt was also made to put a larger share of taxation on the rich, but he lacked the strength or perhaps the courage to make it succeed.

The Viceroy who arrived in 1607, the Marquis of Villena, tried further palliatives. He succeeded in replacing the defective coinage, but only by making the bank of Palermo pay half a million *scudi* to cover the difference, so bankrupting it for years. By borrowing from the municipality, he managed to pay the Spanish soldiers, and he also introduced a further element of bread rationing. In desperation he encouraged that implausible English charlatan, Anthony Sherley, who was not content to be appointed High Admiral, but also claimed to know a secret alchemical process for making silver and how to conquer the fabled gold mines of Timbuctoo. To meet Sherley's expenses, new taxes were decreed, in particular a tax on lawyers which Messina at once claimed was a violation of her municipal privileges. Parliament protested that the country was too poor to pay, and the ecclesiastical House was especially riled. Mention was made of possible excommunication. A notice was even put up in Messina calling the citizens to arms. Obviously the Viceroy had made the mistake of offending too many people at once. Having to contend simultaneously with a tax strike by the rich and hunger riots by the poor, he now went to the unusual length of arresting two aristocrats who had tried to organise a parliamentary opposition; but, under threat of another mob revolt in Palermo, he had to release them and withdraw the taxes which caused most offence. This was an almost unprecedented defeat for the administration.

The next Viceroy, the Duke of Osuna, was a man of different mettle who had little patience with local privileges which stood in the way of good government. Cultured, cynical and unscrupulous, this young Spanish grandee was appalled by the effects of government inaction. He discovered that assassinations were common all over the island, since murderers were cheaply procured and easily protected from the law by their aristocratic employers. Everyone carried weapons, and the bribing of government officials was accepted as normal practice. "No one is safe even in his own home", so he wrote to the King. "This Kingdom recognises neither God nor His Majesty; everything is sold for money, including the lives and possessions of the poor, the estates of the King, and even justice itself. I have never seen or heard of anything to compare with the crimes and disorders here."

Osuna quickly showed what a strong hand could do. A week after his arrival in 1611, the Palermo streets were cleared of vagabonds. Within a fortnight, forty suspicious characters had been banned from the town, and others were imprisoned or expelled from Sicily. Arms licenses were cancelled, and the wearing of short knives was forbidden even to the privileged classes. Osuna set up a special confraternity to reconcile families and stop the endless vendettas which were clearly one of the main problems of this society. He refused to respect the rights of criminal asylum in churches and in the houses of *titulados*. He gave up the practice of allowing criminals to buy their freedom, though he promised reduced sentences for any who voluntarily surrendered. An English visitor noted that "there is no travelling by land without a strong guard", but he added that "this Viceroy hath well purged the country of banditties, by pardoning of one for the bringing in or death of another". When a cashier of the city bank absconded with a large sum and could not be found, Osuna threatened to punish the Palermo authorities if the man were not produced within a week; he was found at once. Osuna also attacked a regular but dangerous practice when he tried to insist that no one with a criminal record should join the police.

Defence was an equally urgent problem. The Sicilian galleys were quite unseaworthy and their officers had not been paid for over two years. Osuna had once visited England to study the new English ships at first hand, and he now ordered the building of twelve vessels, expressing a preference for French sailors where possible. It was his policy to undertake a serious and profitable war against the Barbary states, as a result of which Sicily began to capture more slaves than she herself was losing into captivity. Osuna even managed to make the city militias turn out for drill—it is interesting to find that the Genoese residents at Palermo mustered the surprisingly high number of 1,300 men as their contribution. In retrospect, the few years until this Viceroy left in 1616 were sometimes recalled as a golden age. He set up committees to look after schools and orphans, and revived the practice of every morning and afternoon keeping an hour for open audiences and complaints. He genuinely travelled round the island to see things for himself. Withal he was a notable patron of architecture and letters. It was at his instance that the new Italian theatre of Tasso came to Palermo, and by his permission they could perform on Sundays and allow women on the stage. He strongly encouraged the carnival festivities, and indeed took his enthusiasm to the point of trying to make mask-wearing compulsory.

Problems of finance were also faced by Osuna with vigour. He discovered that not only was borrowing necessary every year to cover even normal expenditure, but a sum of 340,000 *scudi*, or about a third of the annual revenue, had recently been unaccounted for in the receipt books. About 200,000 *scudi* a year had to be spent on the infantry, and 130,000 on the galleys, while 250,000 were required for interest on the national debt: altogether over a million *scudi*, bearing interest at 14 per cent, was owed to the municipality of Palermo itself. Osuna was acutely aware of the need to maintain government credit and lessen the deficit. He stopped some pensions, and secured a quarter of a million *scudi* on loan from the Genoese. To cut down abuses, everyone was instructed to produce documentary evidence about any tax concessions or salaried jobs they claimed to enjoy.

Only one branch of taxation could be quickly increased, namely the *donativi*. Parliament was therefore called in 1612. After considerable discussion, agreement was reached "without any person dissenting", for Osuna had gone to much more trouble than his predecessor in using the traditional methods of parliamentary manipulation. His task was the more easy in that the baronage were of course specifically exempted from having to pay. Moreover they, together with the ecclesiastics and the towns, largely represented the debt holders who by special provision were to have a first call on the money. As a concession to Palermo and the wheat interest, a good deal of the new taxes were shrewdly placed on silk; other exports in general were also to pay more tax; so would firearms and hunting licences, and here again the barons were exempted. Parliament petitioned that, if these taxes should prove insufficient, then the Deputation, on which the leading barons of Palermo had an absolute majority, could raise the extra money any other way they wished.

Osuna was able to report to the King that this virtual doubling of the *donativi* restored government credit. The Palermo and Messina banks re-opened, salaries were increased, and foreign merchants were assured that debts would be settled within the day. The Messinese, however, protested strongly. They had paid an enormous sum in 1591—in Castilian *escudos*, moreover, which were worth much more than Sicilian—to be free of the silk taxes which Palermo and the landowning aristocracy had been trying to impose. They had tried to reserve their rights by not sending representatives to the parliament of 1612, and they now repeated their claim to be free from parliamentary control and from any taxes levied without their consent. To support their case, they offered 20,000 *scudi* as a solatium to Osuna and a large grant to the government. We know that the Viceroy was not averse to receiving presents, but on this occasion he advised the King to make a stand, pointing out that six times in fifty years the Messinese had refused to pay taxes, so much so that they were becoming almost an independent republic. Alone and unarmed, so his supporters said, he personally went to face a riot in this disobedient town and brought back the city fathers bound with chains to Palermo, where he imprisoned them in solitary confinement at their own expense.

Several years later, however, the King was desperate enough to accept Messina's offer and the tax on silk was temporarily remitted; a *Visitador* was sent from Spain, and Osuna was censured for exceeding his powers. The right to monopolise nearly all silk exports which Messina had purchased in 1591 was reaffirmed in 1616, and yet further large grants to the King had to be made by the city in each of the four years 1620–3, and this continual need to repurchase her 'rights' showed them to be shallowly based. In thirty years Messina spent two million *scudi* on securing a privilege that was not properly observed in practice. In 1629 she even offered an additional million *scudi*— equivalent to the total annual revenue of the government—if Spain would agree to divide Sicily in two, with Palermo and Messina as separate capitals each with a Viceroy of its own.

This drastic suggestion could be recognised as a confession of weakness. Despite her theoretical claim to be the true capital of Sicily, Messina saw the interests of Palermo gaining, as more and more nobles went to live there. From the Viceroy downwards, officials did not like having to move with their families periodically to Messina. On the contrary, rich Messinese tended to follow the court and become Palermitans by citizenship and residence; rich Messinese heiresses went to marry in Palermo; the lawyers found it prudent to be nearer the Palermo courts, and shipbuilders discovered that more contracts went to the Palermo arsenal. Meanwhile parliament and the parliamentary Deputation ever more solidly came to represent the interest of western Sicily at the expense of the east. It was claimed, at all events, that more and better bridges were built in the west.

Messina may have been free from paying the *donativi*, but in practice she had to borrow heavily from the Genoese so that she could offer frequent bribes to Spain. Her suggestion to divide Sicily at the river Salso was therefore a desperate move to secure some independence. A fierce propaganda war was opened in Spain against Palermo. Pamphlets were published there to point out how Messina had always been far more loyal to Spain (the Palermo rebellion of 1516 was freely quoted). The complaint was also made that Palermo, while exempting herself from taxation, deliberately placed a disproportionate burden on other regions of Sicily and on the poor in general.

The King was tempted by the million *scudi* offered at this most extreme moment of Sicilian internal quarrelsomeness, but Palermo's influence in parliament, and a counter monetary bribe, persuaded him to refuse. The expense and inconvenience of a duplicated administration was a powerful argument for refusal, and Palermo showed that *donativi* of 21 million *scudi* had been granted over 34 years without Messina contributing a single *maravedi* to them. Parliament begged the King always to consult the Deputation before granting any further favour to Messina, and Palermo followed this up by sending so many of her own privileges to Madrid for confirmation that the Council of Italy indignantly refused to read them.

One calamity which gravely damaged the economy at this time was bubonic plague, and in both these towns the process of rapid urbanisation created slum conditions which encouraged that terrible scourge. Messina with its large maritime traffic was the commonest point of entry, though poor land communications could keep outbreaks localised, and sometimes Messina had the plague but Palermo escaped. In 1575 both cities had suffered badly, and a no doubt exaggerated account spoke of half the population being killed at Messina. On such a desperate occasion, road blocks were set up to stop all movement of population, and anyone who tried to evade them risked being thrown to death from the castle walls. All dogs had to be killed except the hunting dogs of the well-to-do. Wheat export always ceased, and the collection of taxes became impossible.

Another serious infection arrived at Palermo in 1624 on ships carrying Christian slaves redeemed from Tunis. The whole life of the town came to a halt. The relics of St. Cristina and St.

Ninfa were endlessly carried in intercession through the streets, so spreading the infection. Many people died, including the Viceroy himself—Van Dyck, who was painting the Viceroy, escaped overseas in time. Cardinal Doria condemned to death a Greek doctor whom he judged to have deliberately propagated the plague to obtain extra fees, but a more empirical remedy was found to be the burning of infected goods. When all else had failed, miraculously the bones of St. Rosalia were discovered in a grotto near Palermo; the Cardinal Archbishop seems to have been doubtful at first, but public opinion was insistent, and after six months of careful deliberation by doctors and theologians he agreed to demote her rivals and make her the principal patroness of the town. Palermo was delivered from the plague, and the elaborate festivities for St. Rosalia henceforward became the great social occasion of the Palermo year.

When the Thirty Years War began in 1618, Sicily was of course required to help the Habsburg cause, and it was this fact which eventually nullified the achievement of Osuna. The temporary 300,000 *scudi* a year granted by parliament in 1612, instead of redeeming the national debt as had been hoped, was spent as income and had to be renewed in 1621. A special rider was then added asking that the Deputation should have full powers to use this money in paying the debt-holders (particularly those in Palermo) without the Viceroy being able to pre-empt it for other purposes. In practice, however, without realising the fact, parliament had created another item of normal revenue over which the deputies had little if any control.

Meanwhile every kind of office and tax had to be either sold or pledged to creditors of the government. The perquisites of office must have been considerable, and even the man who distributed coal to the various rooms of the royal mint evidently found it worth while to buy his job. At the other extreme the *Maestro Portulano* in charge of the customs bought his position in 1634 for the huge sum of 20,000 *scudi*, and the headship of the Treasury once fetched 35,000. The collection of customs at Palermo was leased out continuously through the century; and it did not help trade that the lessees naturally made what profit they could. To be in charge of grain distribution in Palermo, or of the municipal pawnshop, could bring a fortune. Snobbery was taxed increasingly, and the real inflation of princely titles began in 1620. When anyone who paid a mere hundred *scudi* could obtain the title of *Don*, many 'plebeians' eagerly took this first step up the social ladder. In 1623 the official rate of interest was lowered by 2 per cent. This saved payments of 100,000 *scudi* a year, but it also reduced the income of many important people and hence caused the kind of reduction in personal expenditure from which shopkeepers and artisans also suffered; yet parliament made little protest and continued to vote the taxes demanded. New borrowing, however, could not easily be effected at the reduced rate.

Despite complaints that the country was being exhausted in the service of Spain, despite the fact that many aristocratic families were undeniably living well beyond their means, the strange fact becomes evident that some people had plenty of money. More and more the towns were forced to pay their taxes by borrowing, but at least there were people to borrow from. Notwithstanding all the complaints of poverty, this was a century of grandiose civic buildings, baroque palaces and churches. It was a period when scores of new villages were built. Though lack of capital was restricting economic development, more accurately it could be said that what was really lacking was not so much actual money as the habit of profitable investment. Buying titles was preferred to building ships. Messina's offer of a million *scudi* in 1629 was hardly a sign of poverty, and an even larger amount was spent by the same town in the 1620s on its civic theatre. Indeed Spanish observers were shocked at the lavishly competitive entertainments by which both Palermo and Messina tried to win each Viceroy's favour. Terranova could lose 50,000 *scudi* at gambling in a single evening, a sum which would be more than all the taxes on wheat export even in a good year. The Count of Modica had once been fined 60,000 *scudi* for his misdemeanours. In 1638 the Stella family spent 60,000 *scudi* acquiring a tunny fishery near Trapani and its baronial title—in a year when parliament complained of grave financial prostration. The Bishop of Girgenti spent as much as 156,000 *scudi* buying feudal dominion over the towns of Girgenti and Licata.

It was mainly because of the Thirty Years War that these sums were needed, and eventually the extent of the demand was such as to bring the island as near as it ever came to rebellion against Spain. Sicily had to send 70,000 *scudi* a year to help the Emperor in Hungary, and in 1620–1 the enormous sum of a million *scudi* was allocated for expenses in Germany. Soldiers and galleys regularly went, at Sicilian expense, to fight against the enemies of Spain, and vast amounts of food furnished the Habsburg armies in Lombardy and Alsace. Special grants were paid to Spain's ally, Savoy, and for other secret operations in central Europe. The Viceroy was even told in 1638 to recruit Sicilian troops, but had to reply that this would be impossible. Explicit orders arrived to say that in the existing emergency the interests of Spain must come first. Yet although there were sometimes only a few hundred Spanish troops in the whole island, and although Sicilians were being asked to pay heavily for a war in which they had no interest, there was surprisingly little evidence of rebelliousness. At this moment of grave emergency for Spain, Sicily even helped the Habsburgs to put down revolutions in Portugal and Catalonia.

As Spain approached the moment of her defeat by France, her demands on Sicily became greater than ever. The silk tax was again increased in the early 1630s. Parliaments had occasionally to be called twice in the same year. Sometimes they were summoned to meet in Messina and the Messina representatives were given precedence over those from Palermo, for this might lead to an extra burst of generosity. In 1639, just as thirty years previously, extra stamp duties were placed on official documents and a 2 per cent on leases and contracts of sale; but at this point there was a concerted opposition from rich people, lawyers and clergy, so that these particular taxes had to be withdrawn. An alternative levy was then imposed in 1642 on olives, mulberries and vines, though this too proved impossible to collect in the face of opposition from the landlords. There was an occasional windfall, as when the Egadi islands off Trapani were sold for 160,000 *scudi*. Pardon for all crimes except treason was put up for sale on a sliding scale varying with a man's income. But finally the Viceroy reported that no more revenue could be found. Commerce was at a standstill, and the normal taxes were yielding less and less. At last even parliament was emboldened to say that further demands could hardly be met.

Portrait by Antonello
da Messina, Cefalù:
15th century

The Triumph of Death: wall painting, probably 15th century, Palermo

Catania partly destroyed by the eruption of Mount Etna in 1669 : fresco in the cathedral, Catania

PART 6

The Disintegration of Spanish Sicily
1640–1713

Chapter 21

THE PALERMO REVOLT OF 1647

In Sicily, as in many other parts of Europe, the last decade of the Thirty Years War was a time of political and economic crisis. In 1641 the English ambassador secretly informed Spain that certain Sicilians with French help were plotting to win independence. Others were said to be negotiating with the Turks. When the war turned in favour of France, the Viceroy was startled to find that even the common people showed signs of pleasurable anticipation, and he therefore began digging trenches round Palermo. The Marquis de los Velez was not the man for an emergency. He was a mediocre politician who boasted that he had become Viceroy only to make his fortune. Soon he was sending urgent requests to be allowed to resign.

The growing agitation was due less to any sense of political injustice than to social upheaval and economic distress. Too much money had been sent overseas to pay for the war. At home, after 1630, there had been cuts in public works and in expenditure on the police: the Viceroy noted with astonishment that once again it was unsafe to travel anywhere without twenty or more companions as an escort. Too many people were living on credit, and the frequency of bad debts destroyed confidence and made loans expensive. At last the policy of over-taxing the poor threatened real trouble, and parliament itself in 1642 and 1645 was forced to admit the desirability of trying to find taxes which were fairer and would fall on those who could afford to pay. Even when parliament agreed to such taxes, however, they could not in practice be collected. So long as the leading citizens in each town allocated the main financial burden in their area of jurisdiction, the results were almost bound to be negative.

Administrative and political grievances certainly existed, but it was not these that would cause revolution. Spanish rule faltered only when the mass of ordinary citizens was driven by real hunger. Two bad wheat harvests in succession were the danger sign, especially as the available storage capacity was not keeping pace with the growth in population. An unexpected deterioration of stocks in one single *caricatoio* could be a disaster: this could easily happen through dampness, either accidentally as the muleteers waded through rivers with their wheat, or deliberately as a load was soaked in order to increase its weight. An unexpectedly dry spring could do even more damage; so could locusts, for a plague of locusts always lasted two or three years, and they could easily ruin a whole harvest. The practice of monoculture resulted in there being no alternative food and often no alternative employment. Since the bulk of taxation fell on cereals, not only was the revenue imperilled in a bad year, but food prices might rise to the point beyond which men would risk attacking the grain pits and so perhaps touch off a major revolt.

Remedies were not easily found. The Viceroy was always ready to fix prices by law, or he would perhaps distribute money to the poor so as to offset the rising cost of living, or he might issue a decree to stop landlords and moneylenders distraining on the wages and tools of those in debt. He could temporarily reduce the food taxes, but Palermo would then have to default on its bi-monthly interest payments, and this very quickly led to a drying up of commerce and so to widespread unemployment. In every real emergency he would forbid wheat export, but that only led people to hoard supplies and so could be self-defeating. The overcrowded population of Palermo might then break out in revolt against the landowners and wheat brokers who were thought to be, and sometimes were, creating an artificial scarcity in order to procure higher prices.

In 1644 the quality of the bread in Palermo had to be lowered, but 1646 was a far worse year, especially as in the interim there had been an over-sanguine calculation of stocks and too much wheat was exported to Spain, Venice, Crete and elsewhere. At Messina the city authorities blockaded the straits and impounded every food ship they could seize. Syracuse also claimed to be able to do the same in virtue of a legitimate civic privilege. This behaviour, though understandable, was self-defeating since it drove Apulian grain supplies off the market, but each town argued that if they did not do it another would. Messina was also forced to reduce the subsidised bread ration, and this led to riots. Fearful of a similar outbreak, Palermo tried hard to keep the municipal loaf at its old price and weight, though this only resulted in the starving peasantry flocking into the city to obtain cheap food, so creating an impossible pressure on supplies. The bread subsidies also imperilled the financial stability of the city bank. In February 1647, heavy rains rotted the seed, and sowing had to be done again; but few peasants can have had any seed to spare. Then there was a savage drought in March and April, and, fearing requisition, many growers hid their remaining stocks. In the countryside there was sometimes nothing to eat except wild plants. In the towns there were beggars by the thousand sleeping in the open; disease began to spread, and dozens died of starvation each day.

The Archbishop of Palermo ordered a public penance. Crowned with thorns and bearing skulls, lacerating themselves with iron chains, citizens spent days in continuous procession. One observer saw men pulling ploughs in the streets, harnessed like animals, pretending to eat baskets of hay, and showing many other "admirable signs of penitence"; and a special procession of prostitutes was graciously given refreshment by the Princess of Trabia in her house. Mercifully some rain fell, but it was followed by another suffocating scirocco which withered what was left of the crop. When finally, in May, the bread ration could no longer be maintained, another less penitent procession marched on the cathedral, and one of the smaller loaves stuck on a pole was thrust insultingly at the image of Christ on the altar. There were shouts of "Long live the King and down with taxes and bad government". As church bells summoned people onto the streets, los Velez shouted from a window of the palace that he would lift the food taxes, but the City Hall was already alight, the prisons were being opened and the excise offices demolished. The terrified Archbishop armed his clergy. Some aristocrats tried throwing money to the mob, but most fled to their country estates, so causing additional unemployment and leaving the forces of order leaderless.

This riot was the work of the really poor, instigated perhaps by petty criminals who wanted to release their friends from prison and to destroy the police records. If they acknowledged any leader it was a certain La Pilosa, an escaped convict and murderer who seems to have linked the underworld of Palermo with that of the surrounding villages. Against such a spontaneous movement, the government and the well-to-do were powerless. When La Pilosa was eventually defeated, it was by the artisan guilds of Palermo which represented the privileged working class. These *maestranze* may have included as many as a quarter of the working population. Their members tended to live close to each other in crowded areas in the town, where they were usually a law to themselves and where policemen were rarely seen. No doubt these guildsmen often resented the patrician administration of the city, but most of them depended on the aristocracy for employment and had good reason to fear mob rule; nor had they any country estates to which they might escape.

The consuls of the artisan guilds eventually helped to capture La Pilosa, and under torture he confessed to have planned the rebellion with the assistance of the Albanian settlers in the near-by hill villages. He admitted that he had meant to make himself King and distribute the money of the Jesuits and the city bank to the poor. He was then placed on a public platform and, after being comforted by the Jesuits, pulled to pieces by red hot pincers. Los Velez in gratitude handed over public order to the *maestranze* and let them take charge of the city fortifications. At his own expense he employed a personal guard of forty fishermen, and he put the consul of the coppersmiths in charge of the police. The leading guildsmen were also allowed to elect two representatives to the city government, and it is not without interest that they chose rich citizens from among the Viceroy's friends. They then celebrated their victory with a great feast. But all this made the nobles more reluctant than ever to return to Palermo, and, seeing himself alone, without the main prop of Spanish rule, los Velez panicked and fled.

There is little evidence that the revolutionaries thought of appealing to a nationwide revolt, let alone to such a conservative and inanimate institution as parliament. Some other towns remained quiet through these events; they may have had more grain stocks or been less torn by social divisions than Palermo. Far from feeling a common nationality and opposition to Spain, some of them opposed the revolution or treated it as an occasion for private gain. The citizens of Catania used the chance to annex land which they claimed that the crown had wrongfully taken. Messina, faced with social troubles of her own, curried favour with the Viceroy by giving him money and soldiers to put down the Palermo revolt and offering to house him and his court.

Palermo, however, was far from being entirely alone, for food supply and the cost of living were also problems elsewhere. Some villages inside the jurisdiction of Messina rose against the food taxes which the Messinese imposed on them. At Sciacca a hunger riot developed into an assault on the town hall which led to destruction of the communal archives; after which the nobility enrolled armed bands of peasants to restore law and order in the town. At Girgenti the Bishop barricaded himself in the episcopal palace to avoid giving up his stocks of food, but the mob broke open his prison and terrified him into surrender; he even revealed where he kept his money buried in the garden. The most angry scenes occurred at Catania where a shoemaker raised the cry of "Down with the food taxes and long live the King of Spain". The peasants invaded Catania and behaved just as they had done at Palermo. Some of the nobles barely had time to escape by rope over the city walls, and the mob moved in procession around the town with the heads of their victims on sticks. A young member of the patrician Paternò family tried to put himself at the head of the rioters and restore order, but here too it was the artisan guilds who succeeded in saving the day.

Back at Palermo, few people had any idea what to do once the Viceroy had gone. Administration was almost at a standstill, and the cessation of the municipal *octrois* left the city penniless. The guilds made another attempt to involve the rich in taxation, and levies were imposed on balconies and windows, on carriages, tobacco, snuff, wine and beef. Of all these guilds, the fishermen and leather workers showed themselves to be the most united and forceful. The fishermen were nearly a thousand strong and they had learnt in their trade the need for cooperative effort. Most of them would have been absent at the tunny fisheries during the May riots, but in August they had a decisive part to play.

By now there was a new revolutionary leader, d'Alesi, a goldsmith who lived in the leather workers' district and was related to their consul. He too had once escaped from prison, and his well-born enemies spoke of him as a hired assassin, but he was a much more romantic and generous character than many of the aristocracy liked to pretend. He had a genuine wish to improve the condition of the poor, yet he was surprisingly moderate and thoroughly loyal to Spain. D'Alesi had lived abroad, and at Naples had already learnt something about popular revolution. Although he was a man of the people, he also wanted law and order. He tried to stop the rioting and make young children give up the weapons they had stolen. Indeed he forbade keeping firearms in the city and proclaimed the death penalty for looting. Such was the immediate gratitude to him for stepping into this vacuum of power that suddenly he found himself a man of authority, and for a brief while the richest people competed in pressing gifts on him. The Grand Inquisitor, Trasmiera, took advantage of d'Alesi's strong religious sense. Along with some of the nobles, d'Alesi and Trasmiera began treating with the Viceroy, and persuaded him to accept certain moderate reforms: these were mainly concerned with reducing the food taxes, increasing the share of the artisan guilds in the city government and allowing more local autonomy.

Adulation seems to have been deliberately employed to turn d'Alesi's head. He used to ride through the streets in a costume of silk and silver, or in full armour with a gun in each hand and a train of followers. He was given the titles of *Illustrissimo*, Captain General and Mayor of Palermo for life. But there was no disciplined party behind him, no experienced advisers, no money. He could not solve the economic crisis. Others among the popular leaders were offended by his attempt to control crime, and still others by the studied moderation of his demands. As soon as the Viceroy, at d'Alesi's request, had returned to Palermo and promised reforms, the rebellion lost all its momentum. Shopkeepers wanted their debts paid, just as the privileged classes wanted their bi-monthly interest payments and their old monopoly of the city government. A good deal of money was soon being spent to incite a vendetta of the fishermen against the guilds who supported d'Alesi.

When fighting broke out later in August 1647, the fishermen were apparently led by some of the nobles and supported by a mob of the *basso popolo*. D'Alesi, caught hiding in a sewer, was killed along with the consul of the leather workers; their houses were destroyed, and their heads impaled on railings in the central square. The Grand Inquisitor and his colleagues, armed and on horseback, urged the people to slaughter in a counter revolution more bloodthirsty than the original revolt. Within hours, however, there was born the legend of d'Alesi the betrayed hero and social reformer. The Viceroy had to confirm the reforms already agreed with this *capo popolo*: popular representatives were to be kept on the civic council; uncultivated *latifondi* were to be sown with cereals as d'Alesi had particularly insisted in order to provide more food and employment; the excise duties were not restored to their old level, and less use was to be made of the underground *dammusi*. This charter of liberties was all that remained of the revolution, and it was a collection of paper promises which meant nothing.

This insurrection of 1647 understandably caused panic, but there had never been much danger to Spain. No support came from overseas, and the popular leaders had other objectives in mind than national independence. The divisions inside Sicily, geographical and social, went far deeper than any presumed national solidarity, and in the end the revolt was put down largely by Sicilian action. A decisive fact was that the *maestranze*, though they possessed some collective feeling and political sense, were divided, as they were also frightened of losing their own few privileges. Once they had agreed to act as a police force against the populace, they had destroyed their only leverage on the government. Being entreated by the Viceroy to save Spanish rule was fulsome flattery, but it nullified them as an independent force, and d'Alesi's attempt to set up a mixed government in collaboration with the Viceroy and the rest of the old establishment proved a complete failure.

By September the revolution was over. The city gave the Spanish troops an enthusiastic welcome on their return. The Archbishop of Monreale absolved the people from the sin of revolution and publicly exorcised in the central *piazza* the demons and witches who had caused the townsmen to rebel. To economise on food, everyone without a job or who had lived for less than ten years in Palermo had to depart at once on pain of death; all wheat stocks had to be declared, and half the proceeds was promised to anyone who gave information about concealed supplies. In puritanical reaction against the general laxness associated with the revolution, all gaming was prohibited *sub poena triremium*, and masks were forbidden lest they should become a cover for further misbehaviour; but agricultural labourers were given special permission to work in the fields on Sundays and feast days until food supplies had been replenished.

The new Viceroy, Cardinal Trivulzio, was a man of firm authority and apparently this was welcomed. He forbade people even to discuss the revolution. All vagabonds were turned out of Palermo, and a large area round the palace was cleared so that artillery could operate unhindered in any future emergency. Cannon were trained on the city in readiness. A rigorous curfew was imposed, and all arms had to be surrendered—with specially severe penalties for short-barrelled guns which were already the favourite weapon of the Sicilian underworld. Captains at Arms in the provinces were ordered not to wait for a trial before executing thieves. Nevertheless the Cardinal charitably visited the prisons and galleys and released many prisoners who apparently had been left by indolent or corrupt judges long after their sentences had been served. One guilty nobleman, despite his privilege of decapitation, was hanged just as though he were an ordinary Sicilian, and his naked body was exposed as a spectacle. When the clergy and the Inquisition tried to push their tax immunity too far, they too were overruled. Since one cause of the riots was that the aristocracy refused to pay tradesmen, Trivulzio made a special point that debts must be settled, and he tried to insist that the nobles should at once return to Palermo and so create more jobs. In 1648–9, further obscure plots were discovered, some apparently against the nobility, some against this unfamiliar assertion of forceful government; but there was a strong feeling of loyalty which usually kept the government secretly informed and it was thus able to put them down.

Evidently the inertia and submissiveness of Sicilian society had allowed the old-established order to be restored as if nothing had happened. Since the revolt had been against the Sicilian rich rather than against Spain, the nobility had much cause for gratitude that the King had won and that any promises of constitutional and economic reform had not been seriously intended. Trivulzio agreed to let the nobles bring their hired bands into Palermo to garrison the bastions, for it was important to end the existing dependence on the artisan guilds. The so-called popular representatives in the city senates of Palermo and Catania—one ecclesiastic said "the Greeks call this democracy but I call it government by demons"—did not last long, for it was felt that they demeaned the glorious title of senator.

The tax system was also readjusted in favour of the patrician classes. Even the *maestranze* joined in requesting the restoration of the excise duties on food, because the suspension of interest payments on civic loans was causing unemployment. All that the Cardinal could do here was to try to insist that these *octrois* should be more moderate than before and should be subject to fewer privileged exemptions. At the same time the rate of these interest payments was again reduced, this time to 4 per cent for Palermitans and 3 per cent for foreigners; but, in compensation for their loss of income, the restored *octrois* were to be supervised by nobles and clerics chosen from among the loan-holders, and once again the earnest hope was expressed that this particular kind of income would be given a top priority in the field of public finance.

Chapter 22

THE REBELLION OF MESSINA, 1674-8

Ten Viceroys ruled Sicily in the twenty-five years after 1648, during which time constitutional and social issues receded and government again reduced itself to little more than the basic questions of finding food and revenue. Taxes were needed first of all to keep the Spanish garrison paid and fed, otherwise mutiny might have resulted in enormous damage. Twenty thousand *scudi* had to be found for the Empress's dowry, fourteen thousand in another emergency were sent to Germany, four thousand to the Spanish ambassador in Vienna, fifteen thousand to Milan, and another fifteen thousand to the Duke of Mantua for garrison expenses. Some of these payments were recurrent, and periodic subsidies were sent to the Duke of Savoy who was regularly in the pay of Spain. Sicily was also required to help put down unrest in Spain and Sardinia.

To meet these demands, at least one Viceroy was again tempted to abrogate some tax exemptions of the privileged classes. Generally, however, it was agreed that selling titles and privileges was a safer form of revenue. When the royal town of Patti was sold to Duke Ansalone, the outraged citizens closed the city gates against this mercenary intruder; but in a world where each city and class fought for itself alone, this could be no more than an isolated act of rebellion. "Sell everything which can be sold and even which cannot be sold", was one peremptory order from Madrid, and usually the moneyed classes were only too happy to impoverish the royal patrimony at the same time as they enriched their own.

The problem of food supply now had a quite outstanding importance, for experience had shown that a sudden food shortage might precipitate another revolt which the small Spanish garrison could not contain. D'Alesi had asked for the *latifondi* to be ploughed up, and parliament agreed that landowners ought to cultivate at least one-sixth of their land; but coercion was impossible, and the government had no financial inducements to offer. On the contrary, wheat growing was, if anything, still discouraged by taxation, quite apart from the restrictive effect of price controls and compulsory quotas.

The events of 1647 showed that Palermo needed the most careful attention. Here was the largest mob, the greatest number of skilled and organised artisans, and here was a fluctuating population which was particularly difficult to provide for. When the Viceroy's court left for Messina, Palermo could seem almost deserted, and tradesmen suffered at once. At other moments the town would suddenly expand as outsiders flocked in to obtain subsidised bread. This created even worse difficulties. It was said that the population rose by a quarter during the famine of 1647, and in that of 1671 the town paid nearly a million *scudi* in bread subsidies. The city bank was forced to carry this deficit, to the loss of private depositors and of the town's credit and financial stability.

A great variety of regulations indicates the extent of this problem. During a serious scare, citizens of Palermo had to carry identity cards in order to exclude aliens from the bread queues. Those who had lawsuits at Palermo received special permission to enter the town, but only if they brought their own food; everyone else was liable to be excluded by a rigid watch and ward at the city gate. The making of sweet pastries was sometimes forbidden altogether, or only stale bread was sold so as to diminish consumption. Special police used to ferret out stocks of wheat concealed in the countryside, and Spaniards were preferred for this office since Sicilians had too many friends to favour and enemies to injure. Spanish marines also defended the Palermo food ships lest other Sicilian ports should try to seize them. No one could afford to be unselfish. When nobles were caught smuggling large quantities of bread out of Palermo in their carriages, the penalties were less severe than for petty theft; other rich people, when barley was lacking, gave their horses bread to eat, though this carried the condign penalty of excommunication.

Messina had been glad to help Spain put down revolutions at Palermo and Naples in 1647, but her loyalty was conditional on being treated almost as an independent city state. Messina was on occasion still seen to be in some ways closer to Calabria than to the rest of Sicily; her port was a main outlet for Calabrian produce, her dialect would have been more easily understood in Reggio than in Girgenti, and many Messinese owned property on the far side of the straits. Messina was often inaccessible by road from other parts of Sicily, and even by boat it was sometimes two or three days away from Palermo; hence there were strong geographical reasons for Messina's feeling of independence. Her port installations had expanded fast in the sixteenth century, and new suburbs had grown up outside the city walls. Together with these suburbs, her population probably grew to about 120,000 by 1620, and then remained stationary. Unlike those of Palermo, her nobles were for the most part a mercantile aristocracy who did not disdain commerce. Many foreign banking and trading houses chose Messina as the location of their Sicilian agencies, and an English church existed here as well as an English consul. Messina herself sometimes kept a resident agent in Alexandria, and her export of raw and manufactured silk was very important in the Sicilian economy. At one point the customs revenue from this one port was said to be half that of the whole country.

Messina was now administered by senators elected on a very narrow franchise; they were allowed equality in rank to the peers of Spain and hence could wear their hats in the Viceroy's presence. The King's powers were exercised by the *strategoto*, often a Spanish nobleman, who as a rule did not interfere too much; he knew that the senators had large sums of money to spend in buying his favour or in appealing against him to Madrid. Nevertheless, though the King was glad of the money, he also liked counter bribes from Palermo. Moreover he must have known that the efficient organisation of Sicily would sooner or later demand that Messina's pretensions to independent power should be curbed, and the realisation of this fact sharpened the sense of rivalry between Messina and other Sicilian towns. She was ready to dispute with Palermo the right to have St. Rosalia as an exclusive patroness, just as both these towns wrangled with Catania over St. Agatha. Messina started publishing tracts in Spain to prove the fantastic claim that she had been recognised as the Sicilian capital as early as 270 B.C. For a brief moment in 1639–40 she made a treaty of friendship with Palermo, sealed with an exchange of ambassadors; but soon the Messinese were protesting once again that Palermo was undermining their preferential rights to silk export, that she was interfering with their food supply, and was insisting that payments of interest to Palermo debt-holders should be made a prior claim on government funds.

One perennial disagreement was over whether the Viceroy should spend half his time living in Messina. Here was a privilege which had been purchased and repurchased a dozen times from the King, and in pursuance of her claim the town had spent millions putting up buildings for government offices. This was a vital matter if Messina were to hold her own against Palermo, where the territorial aristocracy was concentrated. The everyday expenditure of the viceregal court was worth at least 100,000 *scudi* a year, and moreover in a world governed by patronage and influence it was essential to have quick access to the main fount of power. The trouble was that most Viceroys preferred to live at Palermo and needed a good deal of persuasion to move, especially as the administration was notoriously corrupt in their absence. Messina resented this, and on one occasion reacted by torturing a royal tax collector and throwing the Viceroy's German guard into the sea.

Under the surface there were signs of economic malaise even in this seemingly prosperous town. Exports from Messina started to decline and so did her civic revenue, while the silk workers began to emigrate and by the 1660s her population was falling. The development of a government-sponsored silk trade in France was partly responsible for this. Another reason was that the landed aristocracy was ceasing to invest so much in agriculture. One scheme put up to the government in 1622 was to make regular replantation of mulberries compulsory; but this was out of the question, and in fact it looks as though government and local taxes were effectively taking much of the profit out of silk cultivation.

Equally important, however, was the fact that the governing oligarchy of Messina became more exclusive, and there was always a temptation for this narrow vested interest to use the city finances to bolster their supremacy. There had for a long time been evidence of a strong conflict of interest between the nobles and the plebs, as also between Messina and its surrounding villages. The real privileges of full citizenship were confined to those families inscribed in a book kept in the archives. The number of electors to the Messina senate had been reduced in 1611, and again in 1622, after which there were only five hundred people who enjoyed this privilege. One immediate result of this restriction was that more money was spent on strengthening the silk monopoly. Yet this monopoly not only antagonised the rest of Sicily; it harmed the Sicilian silk interest as a whole; it was very expensive for the Messinese to buy, and the money had to come from local silk taxes which further damaged trade; and in any case it was impossible to enforce. In 1644, for example, the silk industry of Catania bought independence from the monopoly of jurisdiction of Messina. Frequently, and for years at a time, Messina had ambassadors in Spain fighting to confirm her monopoly rights; but Palermo and parliament sent counter ambassadors to point out that other equally entrenched privileges were thus being violated by Messina's selfishness, and it was claimed that the jobs of thirty thousand silk workers and merchants in western Sicily would be threatened if Messina won her case.

Sometimes the Messinese were able to use their influence at Madrid to have a favourable Viceroy appointed, but sooner or later one was bound to be chosen who would actively support Palermo in restoring freer trade in silk. Messina was therefore in a dangerously exposed situation, especially after 1659 when parliament again began trying to override the city's claims to tax immunity. Her position as an *entrepôt* made her sensitive to any fluctuation in European prices, and yet her richer citizens could not fall back as much as those of Palermo on the produce of their country farms. Worse still, they had come to rely on an artificial prosperity which required frequent and massive bribes to Spain; and this, incidentally, meant borrowing, which in turn led to fierce taxation of the poor and hence provoked a build-up of class hatred. The money borrowed from the Genoese in 1591 for the benefit of the mercantile aristocracy thus remained a permanent burden on the poorer citizens and the peasants of the surrounding villages. So did the money spent on frequent embassies to Spain. To avert social disorder in the crisis year, 1647, the suffrage was temporarily enlarged, but the money needed for helping Spain to put down revolution at Palermo in that year meant another increase in the civic debt.

What finally drove the poor to rebel was several bad harvests after 1671. Strict food rationing had to be imposed and foreigners were forbidden to eat wheaten flour. Most of Messina's food had to come by sea, but supply ships were exposed to attack by Augusta and Milazzo. Messina therefore set up guns to command the straits, and five armed privateers intercepted cargoes of grain going to Naples; but this merely brought commerce to a stop. The *strategoto*, del Hoyo, had to inform the Viceroy of deaths from starvation. The municipal bakeries were assaulted. Some of the nobility had their houses sacked because rumour said that they were taking too much flour to make fancy cakes.

Del Hoyo criticised the rich burghers for the speculative profiteering and miscalculation of stocks which had created this terrible situation, and tried to restore social peace by enlarging the franchise again and giving the civic nobility only half the seats on the city council. They replied by attacking him for class prejudice; he was even said to have been partisan enough to invite members of the artisan guilds to dine at his palace; and, as if this were not enough, he was then said to have deliberately provoked the riots as an excuse for diminishing the city's privileges. The Viceroy, the Prince de Ligne, was a Flemish general who after the Turkish capture of Crete had been sent to build emergency fortifications in Sicily. To tide over the crisis he suspended del Hoyo, but also asked the city to surrender some of her more extravagant pretensions; yet it was sometimes four months before his reports to Spain received a reply, and so it was not easy to concert a remedial policy.

The revolution which broke out at Messina in 1674 was no hunger rebellion by the poor: prices seem to have been steady, wages almost twice as high as in other nearby areas, and the food shortage had become less acute. Unlike the Palermo movement of 1647, this was rather a revolution of rich people who were clinging to privileges which they thought necessary for their well-being. They feared any liberalisation of the constitution as an encouragement to lower-class unrest; they feared the growing centralisation of Spanish rule, as they feared the hostility of Palermo and the challenge to their rights over silk export. In 1671 another parliament at Palermo had requested that Messina and its dependent villages should lose their immunities over taxation and the census. Simultaneously there was alarm over the fortifications which de Ligne was erecting at Messina. Taxes required for the war against the Turks were equally disliked. So was the order to disarm the town's privateering ships. Spain, moreover, had shown an unwelcome readiness to accept democratic reforms and obviously lacked confidence in the capacity of the merchant aristocracy, so much so that the new *strategoto* was given greater powers to overrule the senate.

In July 1674, therefore, the revolutionary decision was taken at Messina to refuse entrance to the Spanish troops and to execute some of the democratic leaders in the town. The rebels immediately sought help from France, ironically the country which had the strongest interest in curtailing the Sicilian silk industry. An appeal was also sent to Turkey, and a tentative offer of the Sicilian throne was even made to an illegitimate son of the King of England. France was at war with Spain, a war in which Holland sided with Spain, and England more or less with France. Louis XIV of France, the strongest monarch in Europe, was aware of Sicily's strategic importance in such a war: according to intelligence which reached Spain in 1671, he had already sent a military engineer secretly to reconnoitre the ground. When Messina appealed to him, he named the Duke of Vivonne, brother of his current mistress, to be Governor of Sicily, and French troops reached the town early in 1675.

Once again the internal divisions of Sicily were provoking a destructive invasion and civil war. The Spanish Viceroy called up the militia, but some units failed to appear, others soon deserted, and others had to be sent home because of their complete unruliness. The Captains at Arms freely took bribes to exempt people from service. The nobility were summoned as usual to perform their duties of military service, but the results were equally unimpressive. There were complaints that no one could be found fit to command even a company of infantry, and after a year of war not a single regiment of Sicilians had been recruited. The government had to fall back on five regiments of Spanish troops and three of German, together with various units from Milan, Naples, Sardinia, Corsica and Albania. Bandits were also recruited, but this kind of soldier may simultaneously have been paid by the French. The most efficient fighting force on the Spanish side was the Dutch fleet under De Ruyter; but Sicilians were affronted by the religion of the Dutch, by their

drunkenness and libertinism. In return the Dutch were outraged by the feebleness of Sicilian military support, which was
a main cause of De Ruyter's death in a naval engagement off
Augusta.

The Viceroy was alarmed to discover that some of the nobles,
as soon as they started to think that France was likely to win,
showed signs of changing their allegiance; and they for their
part accused him of stirring up a peasants' revolt against landowners whose loyalty was in doubt. On the whole, however, although some Palermitans and even some Spanish
commanders negotiated secretly with Vivonne, this was probably
no more than an insurance, and in fact there were few active
attempts to take advantage of the Viceroy's difficulties. Messina
was perhaps surprised that no new Sicilian Vespers broke out
against foreign rule. Palermo could easily have risen in June
1676 when the main Spanish and Sicilian fleet was destroyed
by the French in full sight of the town: the Archbishop carefully
trained the castle artillery against the city instead of on the
enemy ships, but in fact there was no sign of rebellion. Perhaps
the loyalty of Palermo was assured by the disloyalty of Messina.
After three centuries, Spanish rule was accepted passively.
On the other hand, war on Sicilian soil was an unqualified
disaster and must have been blamed on Messina and the
French.

The Spanish had reason to be grateful for this attitude of
benevolent neutrality, and repeated orders came from Madrid
that undue demands should not be made on the population.
Loyalty was rather to be repaid by even more tax immunities,
honours and titles. Revenue dwindled to almost nothing, and
subsidies already granted by parliament were not collected.
Money had to be brought from Spain to pay for the war, yet
many soldiers and naval crews received no pay at all for more
than two years; and some of the subsidies which arrived,
instead of being used for the troops, were improperly diverted
to his own use by the new Viceroy, the Cardinal Luis Fernandez.

France retained her foothold in and around Messina, but
little more than that. Louis at one time tried to attract auto-
nomist sentiment by promising Sicily genuine independence
under a separate King. His secret intelligence assured him that
the Palermo aristocracy was waiting only for a decisive sign of

French strength before they deserted Spain. But Messina quickly tried to frustrate this possible development by sending ambassadors to Paris to win recognition of her own supremacy over Palermo. She asked to have a free port with no customs duties, and to have her monopoly of silk export confirmed; but above all she now wanted Messina to be recognised as the capital city and the normal residence of the court and administration. Louis was hardly accustomed to this kind of request from a subject city. He was beginning to lose interest in the whole venture, for he had evidently overstretched his resources, and his expeditionary force received little of the local help which Messina had promised.

Louis's ally England, furthermore, who had at first helped him ship supplies into beleaguered Messina, was changing sides after a more realistic appraisal of what was at stake. Mr. Pepys at the Admiralty had a memorandum drawn up which said that Messina was a better port than Toulon or Marseilles, and its possession would allow France to occupy Naples, Malta and North Africa. She might then even "set a tax upon all navigation [in the Mediterranean] as Denmark doth in the Sound". England could "thereby be debarr'd of at least one-third of the rent of our English manufactures of cloth, tin, lead", at the same time as losing the raw silk from Messina which kept so many London artisans at work. "Sicily is of more moment to us than Flanders", was the conclusion of this remarkable document.

Throughout 1677, the citizens of Messina were becoming disenchanted with the French. For three years commerce had been interrupted, and the rise in prices was provoking lower-class unrest. Villages had been sacked in the fighting, and many of the mills destroyed on which Messina depended for food. Olive and mulberry trees had been cut down by both sides as part of a deliberate scorched-earth policy which made it hard to feed man or beast. The citizens resented the billeting of French soldiery upon them, partly because it was often unpaid, but even more because it was a threat to their honour to have strange men living in their houses. The French commander for his part resented the "infinite" cases of venereal disease which he blamed rather on the Messinese. Examples were reported of wives being poisoned by fathers and husbands in order to avoid family disgrace. Respectable citizens were further scandalised to find heretical books in circulation, and one French colonel even turned out to have been a protestant pastor at London in Cromwell's day. This was a sudden confrontation with a new and challenging world from which Sicilians had been protected by the benevolent solicitude of the Inquisition.

Another problem was that the Messinese could not speak French; and although Vivonne held state balls for the nobility, neither he nor his officers showed much regard for ordinary citizens. There was only resentment when the French tried to restrain the burghers from overtaxing the poor and bullying the peasants. Even more annoyance was created when unpaid troops began deserting in large numbers and creating serious damage. Furthermore, local privileges were respected as little by France as by Spain: the city's ambassadors to Paris, when they called on Louis, were given only two horses for their carriage instead of the six which protocol required, and were not received as 'ambassadors' but were even placed behind the representatives of Malta. Suddenly the citizens began to suspect that Louis had never intended more than a minor diversionary campaign in his war against Spain. Such a suspicion was enough to paralyse the most fervent rebels, and some of them secretly opened negotiations with the other side and offered to expel the French if Spain would now pardon them.

Meanwhile the French had learnt not to be unduly pre-occupied with the interests of Messina. Vivonne did not deceive himself that his initial welcome betokened a general love of France. He had little esteem for the local aristocracy with their evident lack of all the civic virtues and their insular conviction "que Messine est la capitale du monde". The Messinese expected France to provide everything while doing nothing themselves. They demanded shipments of wheat but would not pay for them. They clamoured for salaried sinecures. They refused to give up their old protective restrictions on trade or to allow free import of wheat even when the city was starving. In four centuries, said Vivonne, Spain had never discovered where they secretly stored their wheat underground and had never succeeded in making them pay the correct taxes. They were as idle as they were ignorant, and in every way contrived to make government difficult. False French money was freely coined in the town. Daily assassination went unpunished 'à la mode de ce pays', and the city's privileges interfered with his attempts to bring criminals to justice.

While the ambassadors of Messina were still at Paris receiving assurances of help, already a withdrawal was being secretly prepared. 'The interests of Europe' were Louis's excuse for not negotiating a peace guaranteeing Messina against the revenge of Spain and Palermo. Suddenly realising the fate in store for them, the leading burghers of Messina fled. Louis at first guiltily gave them asylum and a little money, but soon decided that this was "incompatible with the royal dignity". They were told to depart from France at once; and, teased by the *gamins* of Marseilles, they left to find help elsewhere, even going to live in Tunis and Constantinople.

Messina was thus deserted by most of the senatorial families who for so long had tried to monopolise the city government, and they took with them all the money and stocks of silk they could. A sudden fear spread among those who were left that the peasants and unemployed artisans would use this opportunity to sack the town in revenge against the ruin brought upon them by the nobility. A civic guard was therefore urgently formed. As looting began to spread, many citizens welcomed the return of Spanish troops and shed "tears of joy at being freed from the tyranny of France".

Chapter 23

THE LAST YEARS OF SPANISH ADMINISTRATION

The new Spanish Viceroy in 1678, General Gonzaga, was astonished to find the Messinese still asking for confirmation of their privileges. They had put Spain to immense expense, and tax revenue in Sicily had virtually ceased for three years; Gonzaga's troops were unpaid; many of them had no boots, even no trousers; in their eyes Messina was a conquered city which had caused infinite suffering and could expect no favours. Sack was prevented, and for this Spain deserved more gratitude than she received. Gonzaga abolished the elective city council and deprived Messina of authority over the villages outside the walls. He debated whether to sell the town—apparently he thought that there were some people rich enough to put in a bid—but in the end simply reduced it to the same level as other unprivileged royal cities.

Many people in Spain and Palermo wanted more punitive action than this, and so Gonzaga was replaced in 1679 by Count Santisteban, who pulled down the town hall and as a symbolic gesture ploughed up the site and sowed it with salt. The cathedral bell which had summoned the citizens of Messina to rebellion was melted down, and the Palermitan sculptor Serpotta—the same who later became famous for his versatile technique of stucco—used the metal to portray the Spanish King trampling the hydra of rebellion. The famous letter from the Virgin Mary could not be found, but other documents were taken away by sackloads, and many fraudulent and genuine testimonies to a glorious past disappeared for ever. *Strategoto* and senate were both abolished. City councillors were no longer to be 'most illustrious', no longer to wear toga and bonnet, no longer to carry their official umbrellas and be heralded by trumpeters; a third of them were henceforward to be Spaniards, and the nobles were now placed in a clear minority.

Santisteban also abolished Messina university and spent the money instead on an immensely formidable castle which commanded the town. Firearms were confiscated. The royal mint was transferred to Palermo. Property belonging to rebel families was sold off, including fiefs, jurisdictions and some-times whole villages. The citizens of Palermo, delighted to exploit the difficulties of their defeated rival, helped to rig the auction sales, so much so that the Council of State complained that the King was being defrauded. The Messinese, though they did not give up hope of a possible Turkish invasion, lacked the power to resist. They encountered little sympathy elsewhere in Sicily; instead, dozens of adulatory poems in Latin, Sicilian, Spanish and Italian praised the good fortune which brought about this restoration of Spanish rule.

The desire for revenge against Messina was understandable, but no practical purpose was served by ruining a city which, however selfish, had been the main centre of Sicilian commerce. The most enterprising Messinese had by now fled abroad and set up their silk factories elsewhere, while growing unemploy-ment soon resulted in still further emigration. Foreign buyers were not coming to Messina, foreign agencies there were closed, and the customs and excise revenue greatly reduced. Her tax exemptions disappeared even though interest was still payable on the money she had borrowed to buy these exemptions. The Viceroy's establishment, the court of appeal and the commercial courts were henceforward firmly established at Palermo—Syracuse vainly put in a plea to be considered as an alterna-tive—and any seekers after public office and government contracts had for preference to leave the town and live in western Sicily. The population of Messina therefore declined by more than half in a single decade.

By the 1690s it was possible to count some of the damage and try to repair it. A new Viceroy allowed Messina some privileges of a free port where goods could be kept in bond without paying duty. Special regulations prohibited the import of manufactured silk, and an attempt was made to bring Jews, Greeks and even Moslem merchants to live there. The Inquisition, however, raised the objection that these foreign traders would open the way to heretical books and opinions. The silk weavers of Palermo also objected to restoring Messina's prosperity, opti-mistically hoping to capture the market in fine silks which had hitherto eluded them. In any case it would have needed more than legislation to repair the fortunes of this defeated town. At the end of the seventeenth century, outsiders were still surprised to find that most of Sicily's foreign trade was in the hands of the Genoese. The population of Messina was only 33,000 in 1714 and apparently went on declining until the 1720s.

War and revolution had shattered Sicily and not just in economic terms; the ordinary bonds of society had been dissolved, and only martial law and foreign troops kept the country together. Anyone had been able to obtain weapons in the war, and disorders were reported everywhere. No one trusted his neighbour in anything. It was even said that each village now gave employment to three or four lawyers just because the smallest agreement had to be notarised. Sicilians were always talking about their honour, commented a north-Italian observer, yet they would never keep their word; they were concerned only with private objectives and not the public good. With so little sign of mutual confidence or political liveliness, firm Spanish rule was all the more needed. Since in Catania and other cities there had been popular riots in the crisis years of 1678–9, Santisteban abolished what remained of civic elections: until now there had been some element either of voting or of selection by drawing lots, but experience showed that this often opened the way to dangerous social conflict, and sometimes merely played into the hands of boss rule or the local aristocracy. Not much could be done for security outside the city walls, but a few armed posts were established on some more frequented routes, for example in the hills above Palermo where assassination had been particularly frequent. When an exceptionally zealous policeman arrested a Spanish soldier for theft, the Viceroy tried to secure the latter's release but was overruled by Madrid: evidently the rights of subject peoples were not a matter of complete indifference to Spain.

The Duke de Uceda, who became Viceroy in 1687, arrived to find a reign of violence everywhere, with bandits protected by the aristocracy and by the judiciary. Commerce was almost at a standstill. The refusal to pay debts was worse than ever. Not only were labourers often too frightened to leave the safety of their villages, but Palermo itself was again almost out of control. Uceda tried to forbid all weapons, without exception, especially the deadly 'Messina knife'; a regulation was even made against soldiers using real weapons when they drilled, which suggests that many of the arms in circulation had come from government arsenals; nor were the army and admiralty courts to be allowed to protect servicemen from the law. Likewise if the Knights of Malta continued to be an element of disorder, the Viceroy was encouraged by Madrid to use force or to stop their food supplies.

At best this was only a holding operation, for Spain still had no intention of intruding further into Sicilian affairs than was necessary for certain limited strategic and economic aims. There were only about four thousand Spanish soldiers in the island, apart from a few Germans or 'Burgundians' who acted as the Viceroy's guard. Three more naval ships were laid down to make nine altogether, but defence costs had if possible to be held at just over half a million *scudi* a year; and yet this was still far the biggest item of government expenditure, for the wars against France seemed to be never-ending.

Demands for taxation went on being dutifully met. The Viceroy had orders if possible to avoid the bother of calling parliament, and, instead of parliaments being held every three years, in fact only four met in the last thirty years of the century; yet the spirit was lacking to protest at the 'illegal' practice whereby the *donativi* went on being collected in the intervals. One parliament in 1680, after being formally thanked by the Viceroy for continuing to pay taxes so obediently during the previous ten years, agreed among other things to set up a new government tobacco monopoly. In 1684 another had to be called because of war with France, and it imposed a duty on imported sugar. More money in fact was granted on these occasions than ever before, and the submissiveness of the three Houses was especially stressed in the Viceroy's reports to Madrid.

The general allocation of the extraordinary *donativi* had by now been somewhat changed. The ecclesiastics still paid usually a sixth, but steps were taken to spread their contribution more widely over the whole body of clergy. A special grant was demanded from the merchants as a class, and foreigners who had goods in Sicily could be included as the parliamentary Deputation thought fit. Feudatories, too, came into the net and were expected to pay first a tenth and later a sixth. The

Deputation, in other words the higher aristocracy, still had wide powers of choice in the more detailed allocation of the *donativi* between members of each class, and no doubt this remained an important reason why these taxes were so easily accepted: for example, they now placed a fairly heavy tax on non-titled feudatories and others with titles who were not represented in the baronial House. At the other extreme, the very poor and all day labourers were specifically free from this tax, at least in theory, though in practice most of the revenue continued to be raised through *octrois* on food which fell most heavily on these very people. Each town was told to appoint one 'popular' representative on the statutory committee of nine which chose how precisely the money should be raised to meet their quota, but this small concession to the middle class was as far as the authorities would go.

The Viceroy was warned that parliament might create "much embarrassment and inconvenience" if he did not take care to supervise the choice of representatives. In practice, however, the management of parliament proved relatively simple. The Viceroy just had to distribute a few minor favours to the members of the parliamentary Deputation, and his chief problem was how to avoid unduly favouring one family over its rivals. Some of the richer aristocrats, for example the Marquis of Geraci, were already in receipt of a government salary, and other leading nobles received 'rewards' for voting correctly. From a protest by Archbishop Palafox of Palermo, in 1683, we know that it was now an accepted practice for the Viceroy to begin by summoning representatives of all three Houses to private meetings when presumably business was pre-arranged: the Prince of Butera generally represented the barons on this procedural committee, and as his family controlled about forty votes in parliament, the outcome was hardly in much doubt. The Archbishop on this one occasion stood down, but the Bishop of Syracuse deputised for him and ensured that the ecclesiastical House accepted the taxes proposed; and the rich reward was held out to him of an even fatter bishopric in Spain. The domanial House needed less attention, though the prince who presided over it was for good measure accorded an honorary Key of the Bedchamber.

Although many taxes had been granted in 1684 for only

three years ahead, parliament did not meet again until 1690, and not after that until 1698, but this bothered nobody. The Viceroy could again supplement the *donativi* by selling fiefs and towns. He created sixteen new princes in the 1670s, and fourteen new dukes in the 1680s. An official list handed down by each Viceroy to his successor shows that large numbers of official posts were regularly sold: some of them carried no duties but were simply bought as a source of income. A profit was also made from another recoinage, even though people once again lost half the value of the coins they were obliged to exchange. The confiscation of property at Messina produced further non-parliamentary revenue. One way and another the Sicilian exchequer was thus able to make contributions each year to help Spanish policy in north Italy and Catalonia, and to pay Spanish troops as far away as Flanders and North Africa. Meanwhile the nation's representatives in parliament had virtually given up seeking a share in legislation: to judge by their petitions, they were more interested in asking that the King should intervene with the Pope to confirm their veneration for St. Rosalia and to request that more Sicilians should be beatified. Once the ambitions of Messina had been tamed, the dominant classes in society showed no sign of wanting to use this moment of Spain's weakness to win even a minor degree of political initiative or autonomy.

Most Sicilians were infinitely less concerned with problems of government than with economic difficulties and natural disasters. No man-made events had quite the impact of the eruption of Mount Etna in 1669 and the terrible earthquake of 1693. Minor eruptions of Etna were fairly frequent, and there had been two memorably disastrous ones in 1329 and 1537, when villages had been destroyed, forests burnt, and hundreds of square miles of agricultural land devastated. That of 1669 was one of the worst of all. A tongue of lava two kilometres wide flowed for over twenty-five kilometres from the central crater, crumbling the walls of Catania and filling up part of its port. Vast areas of the countryside were sterilised. The Viceroy sent what help he could, though some Catanians feared that this concealed an attempt by Palermo to steal the sacred veil of St. Agatha which was their most prized defence against the destructiveness of nature.

The earthquake of 1693 did even more damage, almost entirely destroying Noto and Modica, leaving Syracuse and Ragusa largely in ruins, and reducing Catania to rubble. Horrified observers told how the earth opened up and swallowed people, how rivers disappeared and enormous waves swamped the coastal villages. The terror of this nocturnal destruction made tens of thousands of town dwellers flee into the country-side. It is possible that 5 per cent of the island's population died on this occasion, especially as infections spread and made the damage even worse. Over a large area the normal workings of society came to a halt. The only university in Sicily ceased to exist.

The inglorious reign of Charles II (1665–1700) ended the direct Habsburg line in Spain and Sicily, for he had no son. Louis XIV of France, having failed to conquer Sicily in the 1670s, was waiting only for Charles's death to seize what he could of the Spanish empire on behalf of the Bourbons, and French agents in Sicily again reported that the local inhabitants would welcome a change. When the news of the King's death reached Palermo, the Viceroy summoned the nobility and the consuls of the guilds and asked them to wait until he knew what Charles had decided for their future. The Viceroy was a Portuguese, the Duke of Veraguas, a man who had aroused much dislike by defying the proprieties and dabbling in com-merce: what was worse, he and his son managed to corner the local market in oil, bricks and charcoal. Personal opposition, however, did not become political. When the late King's testament was finally published, Spain and Sicily found them-selves simply bequeathed like so much personal property, bequeathed moreover out of the Habsburg family to a grandson of King Louis; and yet Palermo was unmoved. Apparently there was no need for ratification of this bequest by the Sicilian parliament. Veraguas simply proclaimed three days of festivity in honour of Philip V, and the nobles and populace were said to have joyfully participated in a spectacle more lavish than had ever been seen there before.

Sicily had for years been involved by the Habsburgs in a wearisome war against the Bourbons; and now, at the whim of the latter, she was condemned merely to change sides, and hence to go on fighting in the same seemingly irrelevant contest. Louis

XIV's plans for Sicily were ultimately foiled, but not because of local opposition against him. For twelve years a Grand Alliance of England, Holland and Germany fought the War of the Spanish Succession to prevent the union of France and Spain, or in other words to restore a balance of power. These allies wanted the Archduke Charles, an Austrian Habsburg, to be King of Sicily, and had good reason for wishing to prevent the island from becoming a forward base for a French Mediterranean empire.

One sign of French influence in Sicilian politics after 1700 was that King Philip, without consulting officials at Palermo, restored to favour that one-time French ally, Messina. The largest baronial 'state' in Sicily, the County of Modica, was also confiscated from the Spanish family of Cabrera which had held it for three centuries; so were the large estates of the non-resident Terranova and Montalto families, who decided to back the Austrian claimant. The Sicilian parliament was then called, to make a large grant towards fighting against the Habsburgs. Consignments of food were requisitioned, and the military quartermasters took a census of all the horses in Sicily. The barons were also called up for military service. As the Viceroy reported to Paris, the nobles "are thoroughly resigned and obedient to the crown"; so long as they were indulged in minor ways, they would support the new dynasty, and their support was almost the only thing worth bothering about as far as the government was concerned.

Nevertheless, when Austrian forces reached Calabria and prepared to invade Sicily in 1707, suddenly the prospect changed. There were now only three thousand troops defending Sicily, and some of these were Germans and suspected of remaining loyal to the Habsburgs. There was also a revolt among the galley-slaves. As an emergency step, it was decided to use French and Irish soldiers to garrison Palermo, a proposal which was apparently accepted by the urban aristocracy; but the town guildsmen reacted strongly the other way, for it would deprive them of their right to man the city bastions. The Irish regiment of Colonel Mahony had had a bad reputation when in Spain. There was also a suspicion that the Viceroy was trying to make them a charge on the town. Worse still, billeting them on private citizens was a matter which touched on delicate questions of sexual taboo and family pride. This was enough to spark off one more in the long series of Palermo riots, when once again for a short while the *maestranze* and the town proletariat were at one. The bi-monthly interest on the city debt was two years in arrears, and this inevitably meant that many craftsmen and labourers could not find work. Moreover the city bank had illegally lent money for these interest payments without having sufficient reserves of cash; the result was that people had become more reluctant to deposit in the bank, and the consequent crisis of credit was something which the government did not know how to deal with.

Again it was the fishermen who took the lead. After capturing the arsenal, cannon were trained down the main streets; some of the foreigners who lived in Palermo were killed and their heads impaled on sticks in the traditional manner; the excuse was also taken to sack a number of houses. For a month the Viceroy could not leave the palace, and the French ships standing off the coast were afraid to act. Some of the nobles tried to counter the insurrection by employing armed gangs recruited in the countryside, but this only enraged the guildsmen, and soon many of the leading citizens thought it best to flee to their country estates. Again, just as in 1647, the artisan guilds were left in a position where they could set up their own kind of civic administration and police force: and incidentally it was claimed that they were able to find and return considerable amounts of stolen goods. Each of the *maestranze* had its own men under arms. This included not only the main groups of tradesmen, but also the accountants, the customs officers, the lawyers, the admiralty clerks and even the staff of the Inquisition; for in Palermo, just as in the countryside, Sicilians instinctively reacted to lack of governance by turning to self help, and public law was often replaced by individual initiative and individual codes of law.

For a short time this improvised administration was remarkably successful. The consuls of the guilds used to meet to discuss policy, and they persuaded the Viceroy to send the French and Irish troops away to Messina. To diminish unemployment he ordered the nobles to return to Palermo, but they mostly preferred to wait until he was more obviously in charge of events. When some guildsmen made a deal with him and proceeded to dismantle the cannon on the barricades, the fishermen rose against their own leaders and put the guns back. Nevertheless internal divisions and inexperience exposed the *maestranze* to corruption and weakening of purpose; eventually the government was able to regain control and deal out torture and execution to many participants in this minor revolution. One of these was a friar who had used the occasion to advocate republicanism. Others were found guilty of being secretly in touch with English ships off the coast. Obviously there existed certain elements of disaffection which were ready to take advantage of a French defeat.

The Viceroy at this point decided to brave unpopularity and go to live permanently in the more loyal town of Messina. He wrote desperately to Philip that the small Sicilian garrison was not nearly enough to ward off invasion, and he asked for money from Spain to make up for the fact that the local taxes produced little revenue in wartime. There were isolated enemy landings on the coast, and English ships once bombarded Mazara, while, as the war came closer, the German and Spanish troops stationed in Sicily became more restless. In 1711 the Viceroy had to execute a number of officers, after which he had their heads marinated in brine and exposed publicly at Messina as a warning. But before any invasion or revolution took place, an international congress at Utrecht confiscated Sicily from the Bourbon Philip V and gave it to his father-in-law, Victor Amadeus, the Duke of Savoy. The long years of Spanish rule had suddenly come to an end.

DATE DUE